Cooking with Love and Butter

Dedicated to Mary C. Crowley

Home Interiors & Gifts, Inc.
4550 Spring Valley Road
Dallas, Texas 75244-3705

Sprinkled with love,
Garnished with care,
Prepared with my heart
For generations to share...

I saw these precious words in a *"Grandmother Remembers"* family recipe book, and thought, what a beautiful way to prepare family recipes for the generations following. This is not just for my own family, but for all the families of Home Interiors including our Hostesses, who are really our larger family.

This book is dedicated to the Hostesses of Home Interiors & Gifts who, for more than 30 years, have invited us into their homes and given us hospitality. They have invited their friends to enjoy our accessories, our ideas, and our service. We want to continue to serve, in an even greater way through the coming years, all of the Hostesses and Guests across this wonderful United States of ours.

In our family, and in our Home Interiors Family, we give thanks before each meal — so let us give thanks...

> *For the providence of our loving Heavenly Father who has given us the resources to grow bountiful harvests of food, and the creative imagination to prepare and serve it beautifully and colorfully.*
>
> *For the satisfaction and fellowship of "breaking bread together".*
>
> *For the home. Love has a locale on earth — it's called home. Here love most deeply expresses itself, most surely receives its nourishment, and most purely radiates its power.*

Every one of us, whether we are single or married, are in some stage of building a home. Houses are made of wood and stone — only love can make a home.

So our book, **Cooking with Love and Butter,** is dedicated to the showing of love for family and friends by Happy Cooking. We thank our very important Home Interiors & Gifts Hostesses who have contributed so much to our success as a company, and who have contributed their favorite recipes for this book.

May God fill your cup of love full and overflowing.

Mary C. Crowley

Founder of Home Interiors & Gifts, Inc.
April 1, 1915 — June 18, 1986

3

Food photographs furnished by The Image Bank.
Copyrights reserved.

Table of Contents

DINNER AT MARYS'

DINNER AT MARY'S . . .

Mary Crowley loved to cook for and to entertain friends and family. Each December it was her custom to invite Home Interiors Team leaders and their spouses to her home. . .

Here is her story of a delightfully delicious holiday dinner. . .with her menu and the very special recipes for creating it!

First of all I want to welcome you to my home. I love having small groups in for dinner and love cooking for them. Mostly, it's our family and our associates.

Special greetings to all of you who **love** to cook, or **have** to cook, or would **like** to be a good cook, or who just plain **read** cookbooks for recreation.

I'm going to share one of my favorite menus with you, and the recipes for each part of the menu. One of my very favorite things I love to serve is Tenderloin Roast. But first, let me give you the menu. I don't use the same menu every time, but this is typical.

Mary's Holiday Dinner

Tenderloin Roast

Italian-Style Green Beans — à la Mary C.

Cheese Grits   Broccoli Souffle

Very Special Jello Salad
(unceremoniously called "Mary's Green Goop"

Orange Rolls

Coffee   Tea

Mary's Trifle

9

DINNER AT MARY'S...

In cold weather when guests arrive, I like to serve Hot Spiced Tomato Juice; but in Texas we don't have a whole lot of cold weather.

I usually served iced tea, as in Texas it is served year-round and everyone likes it.

For dessert, I make a very special "Texas Rendition" of English trifle.

The recipes for all these delightful goodies are included on the following pages.

TENDERLOIN ROAST

Good quality tenderloin roast	Dill weed
2 pkgs. Roast Seasoning (I use Schilling's or McCormick's)	Fresh ground black pepper

Use a good quality tenderloin roast. Take several large pieces of aluminum foil, placing roast in center of wrap. Rub it carefully with dill weed and roast seasoning. (On a large roast I use two packages — one on the front side, turn it over and use the other on the back side.) Rub it in thoroughly with lots of dill weed and fresh ground black pepper.

Roll very tightly in the foil. Wrap several times, usually three times, and fold edges over very tightly. Place in a large baking pan and bake at 350° for 1½ hours. Then raise temperature to 400° for about 30 minutes. (If you are short for time, you can increase temperature and decrease time.)

When you take it out, peel off foil and carefully drain off the excellent gravy, slice and serve. The flavor is superior!

ITALIAN-STYLE GREEN BEANS — À LA MARY C.

3 strips bacon	Dill weed
1 large onion, chopped	Fresh ground black pepper
Canned Italian-style green beans (1 can per person*)	

Chop bacon into small pieces and cook in a large kettle until partially done. Add the chopped onion and braise. Add entire contents of canned green beans (liquid and beans) to onions and bacon. Add lots of dill weed (please understand LOTS of dill weed) and fresh ground black pepper. Bring to a good rolling boil, then turn down to simmer for about 3 hours. Stir occasionally and taste for additional seasoning.

When they are finished they taste exactly like fresh picked green beans, and people think they *are* fresh. They are that good!

* I use the formula of one can per person to be served — believe me — they will eat them!

11

CHEESE GRITS

7 cups water	2 cups grits
2 tsp. salt	

Cook according to directions on box. I use Quick Grits — do NOT use Instant Grits, they do not work.

Into hot grits stir:

⅓ cup grated onion	1 tsp. garlic salt
1 small jar Cheese Whiz	Dash of red pepper
½ pound grated cheddar cheese	1 small can of diced green chilies (These are green
2 eggs, slightly beaten	chili peppers and add
1 stick butter	ZEST. They are optional)
1 tsp. Accent	

Sprinkle with paprika and bake at 350° for 30 to 40 minutes. Serves about 15 people.

BROCCOLI SOUFFLE

1 large package frozen broccoli	1½ cups milk
¼ cup flour	1 8-oz. carton sour cream
1 tsp. salt	8-10 slices American cheese
¼ cup butter or margarine	1 cup cornflake crumbs
	¼ cup melted butter

Cook broccoli according to directions on package. Drain and set aside. Melt butter in saucepan, stir in flour and salt. Cook until bubbly. Add milk and cook until thick, then stir in carton of sour cream, and a few onion flakes if you want. Put a layer of broccoli in a buttered casserole dish, then a layer of cheese slices, and half of white sauce. Add another layer of broccoli, cheese slices, and white sauce. Combine cornflake crumbs with the melted butter and use this as final layer. Bake at 350° until heated through — 20 to 25 minutes. (Longer if casserole has been in refrigerator before cooking.)

This is a very easy recipe and can be added to very easily. If you want more, just cook more broccoli, increase flour and butter to ½ cup each and use about 2 cups of milk.

VERY SPECIAL JELLO SALAD

Otherwise known as

MARY'S GREEN GOOP

I won "Best Cook Award" on this 25 years ago. Unfortunately this name got hung on it by my adorable brother-in-law and it has stuck through the years. This is the size recipe that I always make for either family or guests because everybody loves it.

Please make exactly as instructed. Do NOT substitute.

40 large marshmallows (approximately)
2 large packages lime Jello
1 large and 1 small size Philadelphia cream cheese

1 large and 1 small size can crushed pineapple, drained, reserving juice
½ pint whipping cream
1 cup chopped pecans

Melt marshmallows and lime Jello in 7 cups boiling water. Stir until completely dissolved. Set aside to congeal.

Next day, or later, at least one hour before ready to serve, whip congealed Jello with mixer and add softened cream cheese. Work cream cheese with a fork to soften it, adding a little pineapple juice to make it soft enough to whip with Jello. Fold in drained pineapple, pecans, and whipped cream. Decorate top with pecan halves if you wish. ENJOY!!

ORANGE ROLLS

Grated peel of 1 orange	**Add 1½ cups sugar to the peel and**
Juice of 1 orange	**juices (not soupy — have a little bit of**
	consistency. Perhaps add additional
	sugar)

Use this orange mixture with rolls that have been split open and brushed with melted butter. Put about 1 teaspoon of the orange mixture in each roll, close it up, and bake on a well-buttered cookie sheet.

Several variety of rolls can be used. I use Kroger Country Oven Country rolls, whole wheat or white. Parker house rolls, brown & serve rolls also work well.

An interesting variation is to use small pop-over rolls. Dip them in melted butter, then the orange mixture, and heat on well-greased cookie sheet.

You can use Pillsbury crescent rolls. Roll out dough, brush with melted butter, add orange mixture, roll up and bake. (You must be sure cookie sheet is well-greased if you do this.)

Once you've done these rolls you will see how you can vary the recipe. The main thing to remember on these is the orange mixture should not be too thin and runny — and don't put too much in each roll.

MARY'S TRIFLE

This serves 40 people — or 20 people twice! Use large crystal or "see through" bowl, preferably with fairly straight sides.

Sliced angel food cake
Thawed frozen strawberries
Small package of strawberry Jello
3 Tbls. lemon juice
Sliced bananas
Vanilla instant Jello pudding
3½ pints whipping cream

Layer: Sliced angel food cake
      Thawed frozen strawberries
Repeat Layer.

Take small package of strawberry Jello and dissolve with only one cup water. Add 3 tablespoons lemon juice. Let cool a little. Pour over layers in bowl. Set aside for several hours or overnight in refrigerator. When mixture is set, add a large layer of sliced bananas.

Fix vanilla custard (I use several packages of instant Jello pudding) and cover layers about 1 inch at least. Cover all layers with whipped cream (I use 3½ pints whipping cream). Let set up about an hour in refrigerator.

This is absolutely, beautifully delicious.

*I firmly believe that **"God never takes time to make a nobody"** — we're all created in God's image, with great potential and ingenuity. And as our inner knowledge that God has His hand in every single minute of our lives grows, we can stop thinking "lack" and start thinking in terms of a glowing inner self-image. A self-image of esteem and pride that can be transferred into our homes and into the lives of those we love.*

—Mary C. Crowley,
from *Decorate Your Home with Love*

Make Your World More Beautiful

Make your world more beautiful for everyone,
Let your light shine brighter every day —
For you're someone, especially to those you love,
And love will always find a way. . .

To make your life a lovely place for all to share;
Make your heart a shelter of God's love,
Make your home a refuge for your family —
A place of happiness for everyone!

APPETIZERS

NUTS AND BOLTS

3 sticks butter or oleo
1 large Tbls. onion salt
1 large Tbls. celery salt
1 large Tbls. garlic powder
¼ cup (or more) Worcestershire sauce

1 40-oz. can peanuts
Stick pretzels, broken into
small pieces
Small box Cheerios
Small box Rice Chex

Combine first 5 ingredients together and melt in saucepan. Combine remaining ingredients in a large roasting pan and stir in the melted mixture. Mix well and bake in oven at 225°, covered, for 45 minutes. Stir about every 15 minutes. Bake 30 minutes longer without lid. Cool. Put into container to store.

—Linda Abel

CHEESE BALL

2 8-oz. packages Philadelphia
cream cheese
1 jar Old English cheese
2 Tbls. mayonnaise

2 Tbls. lemon juice
2 Tbls. Parmesan cheese
1 Tbls. grated onion
Crushed pecans

Combine all ingredients and roll ball in crushed pecans.

—Billie Ramsey

CHEESE ROLLS OR BALL

1 pound Velveeta cheese
½ pound cheddar cheese
1 small pkg. cream cheese

¼ cup chopped pecans
½ tsp. garlic powder
Paprika

Mix all the above ingredients except paprika together after cheeses have softened. Roll into 3 rolls, about the size of a quarter in diameter. After these rolls have been formed, roll each one in paprika. Wrap each roll in waxed paper and chill until ready to serve. Slice; serve with assorted crackers. This is better made 24 hours before serving.

—Gail Gowar

CHEESE BALL

2 8-oz. packages cream cheese
1 8-oz. can crushed pineapple, drained

½ cup bell pepper, finely chopped
½ cup onion, finely chopped
2 cups chopped pecans

Mix all ingredients. Shape into a large ball. Roll in pecans that have been chopped very fine. Serve with chips or crackers.

—Kathy High

SAUERKRAUT BALL

1 large can sauerkraut, drained and chopped
2 cups grated cheddar cheese
2 Tbls. chopped pimento
2 Tbls. chopped onion
2 Tbls. chopped green pepper

1 hard-boiled egg, chopped
½ cup dry, very fine, bread crumbs
¼ cup mayonnnaise
½ tsp. salt
1 Tbls. sugar

Combine all ingredients and form into a ball.

FROSTING

1 8-oz. pkg. Philadelphia cream cheese

2 Tbls. milk
olives and parsley for garnish

Frosting: Mix all ingredients. Ice ball with cheese mixture, garnish, and let stand overnight in refrigerator.

—Chris McKinley

POPCORN BALLS

3 cups miniature marshmallows
2 tsp. butter

¼ tsp. salt
food coloring
7-8 cups popped popcorn

Melt marshmallows, butter and salt in top of double boiler. Add food coloring. Pour into popped corn. Stir. With well-buttered hands, shape into approximately 12 balls.

—Carol Martin

WARM CHIP BEEF DIP

2 8-oz. packages Philadelphia
  cream cheese
4 Tbls. milk
1 cup sour cream
4 Tbls. minced onions

4 Tbls. chopped green pepper
¼ tsp. pepper
½ 3-oz. package chipped beef,
  chopped

Put in pan, bake at 350° for 15 minutes. Keep warm in chafing dish. Serve with chips.

—Dona Balciar

CRAB DIP

1 small can crab
1 small can water chestnuts

1 tsp. soya sauce
1 skimpy cup mayonnaise

Mix and chill overnight.

—Christine Content

LIME PICKLES

Cucumbers
1 cup lime
1 qt. vinegar
5½ cups sugar

1½ Tbls. salt
1 tsp. whole celery seed
1 tsp. mixed pickling spices
Green food coloring

Peel large cucumbers, cut in half and hollow out soft seeded part, and cut into strips. Place strips in roaster and cover with one gallon of water. Add one cup of lime and let stand overnight. Next day, drain the lime water off and soak in tap water for three hours. While soaking, mix other ingredients together in another pan and bring to a boil, stirring constantly. Add green food coloring to boiling mixture. Drain off tap water from cucumbers, pour boiled solution over them, place on stove and simmer for 30 minutes. Fill fruit jars while cucumbers are warm so they will seal well.

—Marvis Johnson

SHRIMP DIP MOLD

1 can cream of tomato soup
8 oz. pkg. cream cheese
½ cup minced onions
½ cup minced celery
½ cup minced green pepper

2 Tbls. Knox unflavored
  gelatin
½ cup water
2 cups chopped boiled shrimp
1 cup mayonnaise

Heat soup over low heat. Add cream cheese, melt and let cool. Dissolve gelatin in water, stir remaining ingredients into soup and cream cheese. Pour into mold and refrigerate overnight.

—Linda Jody

CHILI CON QUESO DIP

2-3 fresh tomatoes, chopped
1 medium onion, chopped
1 small can green (El Paso)
  chili peppers

1 small can red chili peppers
1 lb. Velveeta cheese, similar
  to American cheese

Saute chopped onions and tomatoes. Add chopped chilies. Melt Velveeta, add. Should set 2-4 hours before serving. Can be refrigerated. Serve with Doritos Tortilla Chips or Doritos Taco Chips. Can also be served warm in fondue dish.

—Doris Stark

RUBY RED JAM

5 cups cut up rhubarb
3 cups sugar

1 3-oz. pkg. raspberry gelatin
1 pkg. raspberry Kool-Aid

Cook rhubarb and sugar over low heat until slightly thickened. Remove from heat. Add gelatin and Kool-Aid. Pour in hot jars and seal with paraffin.

—Dodie Carpenter

RHUBARB STRAWBERRY JAM

6 cups sugar
6 cups rhubarb

1 10-oz. pkg. frozen
strawberries

Chop rhubarb. Start cooking without water on low heat. Add sugar after rhubarb is juicy. Cook and skim until clear. Add strawberries and bring to boil. Do not cook after adding strawberries as they will dissolve. Put in pint jars and seal.

—Mary McKinney

SQUASH PICKLES

8 cups sliced squash
4 medium onions, chopped
2 sweet peppers, red or green,
   chopped
½ cup salt

3 cups sugar
3 cups vinegar
1 tsp. celery seed
1 tsp. mustard seed

Combine first 4 ingredients and cover with water and ice for 3 hours. Drain. Bring to a boil and add remaining ingredients. Boil for 3 minutes and put into jars.

—Barbara McDonald

COLD PIZZA

Cream cheese, softened
Pizza or taco sauce
Green pepper
Onions
Mushrooms

Sausage
Olives
Pepperoni
Cheese
Taco or Dorito chips

Cover pizza pan with softened cream cheese; add pizza or taco sauce to cover. Then add any of the remaining ingredients you wish using the chips to scoop up onto to eat. This is an absolutely terrific snack!

—Linda Hollinshead

DILL DIP

1 cup mayonnaise
1 cup sour cream
1 tsp. beau monde seasoning
1 tsp. parsley

1 tsp. onion flakes
1 tsp. dill weed
Pinch of salt

Mix together, and store overnight in refrigerator. Use as a dip for raw fresh vegetables.

—Chris McNair

TAPPONAIDE

2 cups mayonnaise
1 6-oz. can tuna
2 anchovy fillets, optional
3 Tbls. black olives
1 small onion

2 garlic cloves
½ cup chopped celery
1 can cream of potato soup
½ tsp. Worcestershire sauce
Dash of Tabasco, optional

Combine all ingredients at once in blender. Blend until smooth. Serve with cucumbers, peppers, celery, carrots, etc. Also good as a chip dip.

—Connie Anne Hanna

FRUIT DIP

8 oz. cream cheese
7 oz. marshmallow fluff

4 Tbls. frozen concentrate
(orange juice or 5-Alive)

Whip together and serve with apple slices, orange sections, pear, peach, banana, strawberries . . .

Time was — is past; thou canst not it recall;
Time is — thou hast; employ the portion small.
Time future is not and may never be;
Time present is the only time for thee.

SHRIMP DIP

1 cup Minute Rice, cooked
1 cup raw cauliflower, small
    buds
1 cup tiny shrimp, canned

1 cup Hellmann's mayonnaise
Chopped green onions
Salt and pepper to taste

Mix all ingredients together and chill. Serve with crackers.

—Bonnie Kelley

CRISPY FRIED MUSHROOMS

8 oz. whole fresh mushrooms
½ cup all-purpose flour
½ tsp. salt
¼ tsp. dry mustard

¼ tsp. paprika
Dash pepper
½ cup buttermilk
Oil for frying

Mix flour, salt, mustard, paprika, and pepper in large plastic food storage bag. Set aside. Place buttermilk in small bowl. Dip a few mushrooms at a time in buttermilk. Place in bag with flour mixture. Shake to coat.

Heat 2 to 3 inches oil in deep-fryer or heavy saucepan to 375°F. Fry a few mushrooms at a time, 2 to 3 minutes, or until deep golden brown, turning over several times. Drain on paper towels. Serve hot with catsup, if desired. 4 to 6 servings

CHEESE LOG SUPREME

3 8-oz. pkgs. cream cheese
2 pkgs. corned beef
2 bunches spring onions

2 Tbls. Accent
3 Tbls. Worcestershire sauce
1 pkg. chopped pecans

Have cream cheese at room temperature. Chop corned beef and onions including green tops. Mix first 5 ingredients well — form into log — roll in chopped pecans. Wrap in foil and refrigerate or freeze. Serve with Town House crackers.

KNAPIK BRANCH'S FAVORITE CHEESE SOUP

⅓ cup carrots, finely chopped
⅓ cup celery, finely chopped
1 cup green onions, finely
   chopped
2 cups water
1 medium white onion, finely
   chopped
½ cup butter or margarine

1 cup flour
4 cups milk
4 cups chicken broth
2 lg. jars Cheese Whiz
¼ tsp. cayenne pepper
1 Tbls. dry mustard
Salt and pepper to taste

Combine carrots, celery and green onions with water and boil for about 5 minutes. Saute onion in butter or margarine. Add flour and whip until smooth. Blend onion and flour mixture with milk and add to first ingredients. Add the broth, Cheese Whiz and seasonings. Cook over low heat. Special hints: If you like spicy dishes, use 1 jar of Cheese Whiz with jalapeños. I blend the flour/onion mixture with the milk in small quantities in the food processor for a better texture.

TORTILLA SOUP

1 medium onion
2 garlic cloves, minced
1 Tbls. oil
2 lbs. ground chuck
1 14½ oz. can tomatoes
1 can Rotel tomatoes
1 can beef bouillon
1 can chicken broth
2 cups water

½ tsp. ground cumin
1 tsp. chili powder
½ tsp. seasoned pepper
2 tsp. Worcestershire sauce
1 Tbls. Tabasco sauce
1 can tomato soup
1½ cups cheddar cheese,
   grated
Large pkg. Tostados or Doritos

In a large, heavy pot, saute onion, garlic and ground chuck in oil. Drain off excess grease. Add remaining ingredients, except chips and cheese. (Tomatoes may be put through a blender or chopped.) Simmer for one hour. Place broken chips and cheese in separate bowls. Place chips in bottom of serving bowls. Pour in soup and top with cheese. M-M-M-M-M GOOD!!!!

—Trish Baird

ARTICHOKE HORS D'OEUVRES

1 bunch green onions,
 chopped
1 bunch parsley, chopped
9 eggs, beaten
3 sm. jars marinated
 artichokes with marinade

1 lb. sharp cheese, grated
14 soda crackers, crushed
Salt and pepper to taste
Couple dashes Tabasco sauce

Mix all ingredients together, folding in eggs. Pour into greased 9"x13" pan. Bake 40 minutes at 325°. Cool and cut into bite-size pieces and serve with toothpicks. Freezes well. Also great to use at a brunch...just cut into larger pieces.

—Betty Goertzen

APPETIZER

1 3-oz. pkg. cream cheese,
 softened
2 Tbls. milk
1 tsp. chopped onion flakes

1 tsp. prepared horseradish
⅛ tsp. hot pepper sauce
12 thin slices Lebanon
 bologna (½ lb.)

Early in the day, in a small bowl, mix all ingredients except bologna with a fork. To make a bologna stack, spread half of mixture on 5 bologna slices, stack these and top with an unspread bologna slice. Wrap and refrigerate. Repeat. To serve, cut each stack into 8 wedges. Makes 16 appetizers.

VEGETABLE DIP

8 oz. mozzarella cheese,
 shredded
2 Tbls. Parmesan cheese
2 cups real mayonnaise
1 cup sour cream
1 Tbls. parsley flakes

1 tsp. pepper
1 tsp. Accent
1 tsp. onion salt
1 tsp. sugar
1 Tbls. onion flakes

Mix ingredients well. Chill and enjoy!

—Donna Viebrock

27

FRESH FRUIT DIP

1 jar marshmallow cream   1 pkg. cream cheese

Mix ingredients together and beat until consistency is smooth. Serve with fresh fruit!

—Linda Hollinshead

MEX-TEX DIP

3 medium ripe avocados
2 Tbls. lemon juice
½ tsp. salt
1 cup sour cream
½ cup mayonnaise
1 pkg. taco seasoning mix
1 bunch green onions, chopped

3 ripe tomatoes, chopped
1 lg. can black olives, drained
   and chopped
2 cans bean or enchilada dip
8 oz. cheddar cheese,
   shredded

In a bowl peel and mash avocados, add lemon juice and salt and mix. In another bowl, combine sour cream, mayonnaise and taco seasoning mix. Assemble on a large round dish, first the dip, then avocado mixture, then sour cream mixture. Top with onions, tomatoes, cheddar cheese and black olives. Serve with lots of your favorite chips. Makes enough for a large crowd. Teenagers love this.

—Sue Cornelius

HOT APPLE CIDER

2 qts. apple cider
1 pt. cranberry juice
¾ cup sugar (some like less)
1 tsp. whole allspice

1 small orange, studded with
   cloves
2 cinnamon sticks

Combine all ingredients and boil on high heat for 1 hour, then turn to low and simmer for 4 to 8 hours.

—Sue Cornelius

HOT BUTTERED LEMONADE

9 cups hot water
1¾ cups sugar
2 Tbls. shredded lemon peel

1½ cups lemon juice
Butter

In a large saucepan, combine hot water, sugar, lemon peel and lemon juice. Bring to a boil, stirring to dissolve sugar. Pour into mugs, add about 1 teaspoon butter to each. Makes 12 servings. This can be made in a crockpot. Allow 4 to 6 hours for heating.

—Sue Cornelius

ICED GREEN TOMATO PICKLES

7 lbs. green tomatoes, sliced
2 gal. water
3 cups lime
5 lbs. sugar
3 pts. vinegar
1 tsp. cloves

1 tsp. ginger
1 tsp. allspice
1 tsp. mace
1 tsp. celery seed
1 tsp. cinnamon
1 cup raisins, optional

Dissolve lime in water. Add tomatoes and soak for 24 hours. Drain and soak in fresh water for 4 hours, changing water every hour. Drain. In a kettle, combine remaining ingredients except raisins. Bring this syrup to boiling and pour over tomatoes. Let stand overnight. In the morning, boil for an hour and seal in glass jars. Raisins may be added 10 minutes before canning if desired.

We search the world for truth,
We cull the good — the true — the beautiful
From graven stone and written scroll,
And all old flower-fields of the soul,
And, weary seekers of the best,
We come back laden from our quest,
To find that all the sages said
Is in the Book our Mothers read...

—John Greenleaf Whittier

MEATBALLS

4 lbs. ground beef	1 Tbls. onion powder
4 tsp. cumin	1 small onion, chopped
1 tsp. garlic powder	1 lg. can pineapple chunks
2 Tbls. Worcestershire sauce	Salt and pepper to taste

Combine all ingredients except pineapple chunks and chopped onion. Shape into one-inch balls. Brown chopped onion and meatballs together in a large skillet. Drain off fat. Drain pineapple, reserving syrup; set pineapple aside. Pour syrup over meatballs. Bring to a boil. Cover and simmer 10 minutes. Serve on toothpicks with one chunk of pineapple and one meat ball on each toothpick. May be served cold or hot.

—Pearl Edmondson

COCKTAIL MEATBALLS

½ cup cornflakes, crushed	1 bottle chili sauce
1 small onion, grated	1 6-oz. jar grape jelly
1 garlic clove, crushed	Juice of 1 lemon
2 eggs, beaten	Salt and pepper to taste
2 lbs. ground beef	

Combine first five ingredients and salt and pepper. Shape into half-inch balls and place on a baking sheet. Bake at 500° until browned. In a saucepan combine chili sauce, jelly and lemon juice. Mix until well blended over low heat. Add meatballs to mixture. Pour into fondue dish (must be kept warm for better flavor) and serve.

—Diana M. Herrera

HAM ROLL-UPS

2 pkgs. pressed ham	Horseradish to taste
6 oz. Philadelphia cream cheese	Salt and pepper
1 tsp. mayonnaise	Dash garlic salt

Put ham slices between paper towels to dry. Mix other ingredients together to spreadable consistency. Spread mixture on ham slices, roll, and stick with 5 toothpicks. Refrigerate overnight and slice between toothpicks. Serve attractively.

30

—Marge Moore

SALADS

SALADS...

Salads are ideal accompaniments for rich dishes. They provide a welcome astringency of flavor and their brilliant colors enliven any menu. In all salads, texture is important — cooked vegetables should be firm, not mushy, and crisp vegetables should be really crisp. Wash and chill vegetables in the refrigerator or if necessary soak them in ice water for a short time.

Remember to taste a salad for seasoning when it is complete — often a dressing that is perfectly seasoned on its own will taste bland when mixed with vegetables. Many of the following salads are also suitable as appetizers.

GRACE'S SPECIALTY SALAD DRESSING

½ cup vinegar
¾ cup oil
1 cup sugar
1 tsp. dry mustard

1 tsp. celery seed
2-3 tsp. dry onion flakes
Dash of salt

Mix vinegar, oil and sugar in saucepan and heat until sugar is melted. Then add mustard, celery seed and salt. Put in blender and blend until thickened. Then add onion flakes. Chill at least two hours before serving over your favorite salad greens.

—Grace Manley

ITALIAN SALAD DRESSING

1 cup oil
1 cup vinegar
1 cup sugar
2 tsp. salt

1 tsp. pepper
2 tsp. garlic powder
1 tsp. celery seed
1 tsp. oregano

Mix in blender.

—Connie Ramsey

FIVE CUP SALAD

1 cup sour cream
1 cup pineapple tidbits
1 cup orange tidbits

1 cup coconut
1 cup miniature marshmallows

Mix all together and let set 24 hours. Then serve.

—June Flye

PARTY PRETTY & EASY COMPANY SALAD

(Double and triple as needed for large crowd.)

1 can artichokes (packed in
  water)
1 can early June peas, drained
1 can ripe pitted olives, drained

2 fresh tomatoes
1 bottle Wishbone Italian
  dressing

Drain and quarter artichokes; cut tomatoes in wedges. Combine all and chill overnight.

—Maxine Root

SHRIMP SALAD

1 box curly noodles
1 bag frozen cooked small
  shrimp
1 bottle Catalina salad
  dressing

Onions, celery, green peppers
  and mayonnaise
Salt and pepper to taste

Cook noodles and add shrimp and dressing. Serve on a bed of lettuce leaves with a hot roll. Great for luncheons.

—Corinne Kasten

FROZEN FRUIT SALAD

2 3-oz. pkgs. Philadelphia
  cream cheese
2 Tbls. salad dressing
½ cup drained crushed
  pineapple
2 cups diced ripe bananas

½ cup chopped maraschino
  cherries
½ cup chopped pecans
½ cup diced marshmallows
1 cup whipping cream
½ tsp. salt
1 Tbls. lemon juice

Mash cheese with fork, add salt, salad dressing, lemon juice and mix well. Fold in pineapple, cherries, nuts, bananas, and marshmallows. Whip cream until thick and add to cheese and fruit mixture, turn into freezer tray and freeze until firm.

—Nona Balke

FROZEN SALAD DESSERT

1 #1 can (14-oz.) Thank You
    cherry pie filling
1 #1 can (12-oz.) can crushed
    pineapple, drained

1 can Eagle Brand Milk
    (sweetened)
10 oz. container Cool Whip

Fold pie filling and pineapple together. Gently stir in milk, then fold in Cool Whip until well blended. Put in 9"x13" pan. Sprinkle with chopped nuts. Cover with foil, then freeze. Keeps forever in freezer. Also good with peaches or blueberries.

— Julia Mrvan

LEMON LIME SALAD

¼ lb. miniature marshmallows
1 pkg. lemon gelatin
1 pkg. lime gelatin
1 cup hot water
1 cup pineapple juice
1 #2 can crushed pineapple,
    drained, use juice

1 3-oz. pkg. cream cheese,
    crumbled or cut into small
    pieces
½ pt. cream whipped, or 1 can
    evaporated milk, chilled
    and whipped

Dissolve gelatin in hot water and pineapple juice and stir until dissolved. Cool until slightly thickened. Fold in pineapple, cheese and whipping cream. Pour into 8" x 8" x 2" (or larger) pan. Chill until firm. Serve in lettuce or cut into squares in serving dish. Makes 12 servings.

— Marie Green

ORANGE SALAD

1 3-oz. pkg. orange gelatin
1 small can crushed pineapple
1 cup cheese

½ cup nuts
1 small size Cool Whip

Mix hot water with gelatin. Add pineapple, let thicken. Add other ingredients. Chill until ready to serve.

— Marie Keel

DREAMY BANANA SALAD

1 can crushed pineapple	1 box vanilla wafers
1 pint heavy whipped cream	3-4 bananas

Whip cream. Put layer of vanilla wafers in bottom of rather large shallow dish. Add layer of crushed pineapple with juice, layer of sliced bananas, layer of whipped cream. Start again with layer of vanilla wafers, pineapple, bananas, and cream. Approximately 3 layers. I top the cream off with some design made with vanilla wafers. Refrigerate, and serve.

—*Kathi Batson*

CREAM CHEESE SALAD

1 pkg. gelatin, lime, lemon or pineapple	1 cup cream, whipped
	½ cup celery, cut fine
1 cup boiling water	1 3-oz. pkg. cream cheese
1 small can crushed pineapple and juice	1 cup miniature marshmallows
	Grated American cheese
½ cup nutmeats, chopped fine	

Disolve gelatin in water. When syrupy, add pineapple, nutmeats, celery, marshmallows, and grated cheese. Mix thoroughly. Whip the cream and cream cheese together and add to other ingredients. Pour in mold and chill till firm.

—*Mary Weir*

COOL WHIP SALAD

1 lg. pkg. Cool Whip	1 cup pecans
1 pkg. peach Jello	1 cup pineapple
1 cup cottage cheese	

Mix Cool Whip and Jello together. Add other ingredients. Chill one hour.

—*Linda Wallingsford*

FRUIT SALAD

2 11-oz. cans Mandarin
   oranges, drained
1 lg. can crushed pineapple
   (packed in its own juice),
   drained

1 12-oz. carton cottage cheese
1 6-oz. pkg. orange Jello, dry
1 9-oz. carton Cool Whip

Mix well-drained oranges and pineapple together. Add remaining ingredients one at a time, mixing well after each. Good with ham.

—Martha Lowery

LEMON JELLO SALAD

1 family size pkg. lemon Jello
2½ cans crushed pineapple
   (drained, but reserve juice)
3 bananas
4 Tbls. flour
1 cup sugar

2 beaten eggs
2 cups pineapple juice (may
   add water to make 2 cups)
1 med. size Cool Whip
Chopped walnuts for garnish

Mix Jello, bananas and pineapple and pour into a cake pan. Cover with marshmallows. Mix flour with sugar, add eggs and pineapple juice, boil until thick. Cool. Mix Cool Whip into flour mixture, pour over set Jello mixture. Sprinkle chopped walnuts on top. Refrigerate.

—Linda Napier

PISTACHIO SALAD

1 pkg. instant pistachio
   pudding
1 lg. tub Cool Whip
1 can crushed pineapple, do
   not drain

1 cup miniature marshmallows
1 small jar maraschino
   cherries

Mix together and refrigerate.

—Beverly Kuck

DESSERT SALAD

1 lg. box Jello, any flavor, but raspberry is good	1 8-oz. pkg. cream cheese, softened
1 lg. can crushed pineapple, well drained	1 cup pineapple juice
½ cup finely chopped nuts	1 tsp. lemon juice
1 pkg. Dream Whip, prepared as directed	¾ cup sugar
	2 Tbls. flour
	2 eggs, well beaten

Prepare Jello as directed on box and mix together with pineapple and nuts. Chill. Whip cream cheese and Dream Whip together and pour over Jello mixture. Combine juices, sugar, flour and eggs and cook over moderate heat until it thickens. Cool and spread over Dream Whip mixture.

Garnish several ways: Sprinkle top with nuts, or add more Dream Whip to top. Serve with fancy cookies. Excellent for pot lucks in a large casserole dish. Serve in individual dishes. Will keep in refrigerator for several days.

—Betty Moore

HEAVENLY ORANGE FLUFF SALAD

2 small pkgs. orange gelatin	1 large can crushed pineapple
2 cups hot water	2 cans Mandarin oranges
1 small can undiluted frozen orange juice	

TOPPING

1 cup cold milk	1 4½-oz. Cool Whip (fold into pudding)
1 small pkg. lemon instant pudding	

Mix gelatin and water in cake pan, size 11¾"x7½"x1¾". Add frozen orange juice and mix in. Drain pineapple and oranges. Add to the gelatin mixture. Put in refrigerator until set. Make topping and pour on top. Cut into squares and serve.

—Barbara Murphy

JELLO SURPRISE

1 lg. pkg. Jello
2 pkgs. Dream Whip

1-2 cups miniature
marshmallows
Fruit (drained if in juice)

Prepare Jello according to directions. Let set overnight. Just before serving prepare Dream Whip. Stir into Jello along with your favorite fruit and the marshmallows. My favorite is bananas.

—Shirley Borses

BLUEBERRY SALAD OR DESSERT

1 can blueberries, drained
1 sm. can crushed pineapple, drained
2 pkgs. blueberry Jello (may use blackberry Jello)

2 cups boiling water
1 cup juice drained from pineapple and blueberries

TOPPING

1 cup sour cream
1 8-oz. pkg. cream cheese
½ cup sugar

1½ tsp. vanilla
½ cup chopped nuts for topping

Dissolve Jello in hot water. Add fruit and cup of juice. Let congeal. Blend together topping ingredients and spread on top of Jello a few hours before serving. Sprinkle chopped nuts on top. Serves 10-12.

—Rosalie Rumph

WATERGATE SALAD

1 lg. can crushed pineapple
1 sm. box instant pistachio pudding
1 cup miniature marshmallows

1 cup chopped nuts
1 lg. size Cool Whip
Coconut — optional

Combine and chill.

—Vercie Cole

CUCUMBER AND PINEAPPLE SALAD

1 Tbls. gelatin	⅔ cup cold water
4 Tbls. cold water	6 Tbls. lemon juice
¾ cup boiling water	¾ cup sugar
½ cup mayonnaise	Pineapple
½ cup whipped cream	Cucumbers

Mix gelatin with 4 tablespoons cold water and let soften. Add softened gelatin to boiling water. Add cold water, lemon juice, sugar and stir until sugar dissolves. Add equal parts of diced cucumber and pineapple. When partially set, fold in ½ cup each of mayonnaise and whipped cream. Chill. Cut into squares for serving.

—Barbara McDonald

CRANBERRY SALAD

1 pkg. (1 lb.) ground cranberries	1 cup sugar
2 cups crushed pineapple	2 pkgs. raspberry Jello
	1 cup chopped nuts

Combine sugar, cranberries and pineapple and let stand. Make Jello, let partially set and then add cranberry/pineapple mixture and nuts. Mix well and let set.

—Ethel Anderson

WHITE SALAD

1 lb. lg. marshmallows	1 8-oz. pkg. cream cheese
½ cup milk	1 can crushed pineapple,
1 cup cottage cheese	drained
1 cup sour cream	1 medium container Cool Whip

Combine marshmallows and milk in top of double boiler and melt. Cream together cottage cheese, sour cream and cream cheese. Fold in pineapple. Fold in cooled marshmallows. Fold in Cool Whip. Refrigerate overnight.

TORTILLA CHIP SALAD

1 16-oz. can red kidney beans, drained	4 small tomatoes, cut into wedges
1 head of cut lettuce	1 avocado, sliced
1 cup diced onions	1 lb. hamburger meat
1 lb. cheddar cheese	1 pkg. taco seasoning mix
1 cup Thousand Island dressing	1 16-oz. pkg. tortilla chips

Break up hamburger meat into small pieces and brown in skillet. Drain off excess fat and add taco seasoning mix. Let stand. Shred the lettuce, wash and drain. Grate the cheese, place all ingredients in a large bowl and toss with the Thousand Island dressing.

Note: Save some tomatoes and avocado slices and chips for a garnish. Serves 8-12.

—Trudy DeJung

STRAWBERRY BAVARIAN

1 3-oz. pkg. wild strawberry flavor gelatin	¾ cup cold water
¼ cup sugar	1 box of whipped topping
1 cup boiling water	1 cup fresh strawberries, sliced

Dissolve gelatin and sugar in boiling water. Add cold water. Chill until slightly thickened. Blend in 1½ cups of the whipped topping, chill until very thick. Fold in strawberries. Push into 4-cup mold or individual molds. Chill firm, unmold in about 4 hours. Garnish with remaining whipped topping and fresh strawberries if desired. Makes about 4 cups or 8 servings.

—Anna Marie Galvan

Give for the joy of giving. . .
If you only give to get. . .
You are not giving. . .
You are trading.

—From *"Be Somebody"* by Mary Crowley

41

HAWAIIAN CHICKEN SALAD

4 chicken breasts, cooked,
  boned and cubed
2 cups celery, chopped fine
2 tsp. salt
2 small cans pineapple tidbits,
  drained

1 cup mayonnaise
1 cup sour cream
2 cups green grapes, chopped
  in half
1 cup coconut
Pecans

Add all together and mix. Add some toasted coconut and pecans.
Top with toasted coconut and pecans.

—Fern Mears

BLUEBERRY SALAD

2 3-oz. pkgs. red raspberry
  Jello
3 cups boiling water
1 pkg. plain Knox gelatin
1 cup half and half

1 cup sugar
1 tsp. vanilla
1 8-oz. pkg. cream cheese
½ cup walnuts
1 can blueberries in juice

FIRST LAYER: Dissolve one package Jello in 2 cups boiling water.
Pour into ring mold and let set really good.

SECOND LAYER: Dissolve Knox gelatin in ½ cup cold water.
Heat half and half until just before boiling. Stir in sugar and Knox
gelatin. Add vanilla and blend in cream cheese and nuts. Chill
till partly set and pour on first layer.

THIRD LAYER: Dissolve one package raspberry Jello in 1 cup
boiling water. Add blueberries and juices. Chill and pour on second
layer. Refrigerate.

—Lee Obermeyer

*What you are is God's gift to you . . . What
you make of yourself is your gift to God.*

BROCCOLI SALAD

1 head broccoli	1 medium onion
½ lb. bacon	8 oz. shredded longhorn cheese

TOPPING

½ cup mayonnaise	1 Tbls. vinegar
¼ cup sugar	

Cut broccoli into bite-size pieces. Fry bacon and break into bite-size pieces. Toss all ingredients together. Combine all topping ingredients and mix well. Add to salad.

—Janice Brodbeck

WATERGATE SALAD

1 9-oz. size Cool Whip	½ to ¾ cup chopped nuts
1 can (15¼-oz.) crushed	1 box dry instant pistachio
pineapple, don't drain	pudding mix

Fold each of the ingredients into the Cool Whip. Cool to enhance the flavor. Maraschino cherries placed on the top add a festive touch at Christmas.

—Dixie Thorne

JANIE'S "AIN'T THIS SUMPIN'" SALAD

1 pkg. strawberry Jello	1 small jar stuffed olives, cut
Tomato soup diluted to make	up
2 cups	1 tsp. lemon juice
½ cup chopped celery	

Heat soup and add to Jello. Stir well and add remaining ingredients. Place in mold, chill until set.

—Janie Pollock

SALADS...

SYLVIA'S FAVORITE SALAD

1 can condensed milk
1 9-oz. container Cool Whip
1 small can crushed
   pineapple, drained

1 can coconut
⅓ cup lemon juice
½ cup chopped pecans
½ cup marachino cherries

Mix all ingredients very thoroughly and chill.

— Sylvia Kerr

GRANDMA REASONER'S WHITE GRAPE SALAD

(This recipe won 1st place at the World's Fair in New York City some-where around the 1930's.)

2 lbs. white seedless grapes
   (can de-seed white grapes
   if you can't find seedless)
1 8-oz. pkg. Philadelphia
   cream cheese

1 med. can crushed pineapple
   (drained, but save juice)
1 cup miniature marshmallows
½ cup pecan pieces

Wash grapes and cut in half. Add about 1 oz. (more if needed) of the pineapple juice to the Philadelphia cream cheese to reach a consistency of thick soup, then pour on top of the grapes. Add pineapple, marshmallows, pecans and mix all ingredients until they are completely coated with the cream cheese mixture. Refrigerate until chilled. Serve — and receive "yum-yum" compliments!!

— Jim Morrow

STRAWBERRY FLUFF

1 small box strawberry Jello
1 small carton cottage cheese

1 #2 can pineapple, drained
1 large container Cool Whip

Sprinkle Jello over cottage cheese to dissolve. Fold drained pineapple and Cool Whip into cottage cheese mixture. Refrigerate. Serve as salad or dessert.

— Jayle Riecken

COBB SALAD

3-4 cups finely chopped
   iceberg and Romaine lettuce (about ½ lb.)
½ (to ¾ cup) finely chopped,
   skinned and boned cooked
   chicken breast
3 green onions, minced
1 hard-cooked egg, finely
   chopped
1 medium tomato, peeled,
   seeded and minced

4 slices bacon, fried crisp and
   crumbled
1 1¼-oz. pkg. blue cheese,
   crumbled
1 small ripe avocado, peeled,
   seeded and minced
⅓ cup oil & vinegar dressing
1 tsp. lemon juice, if necessary
Freshly ground black pepper
   to taste
Lettuce leaves

Spread chopped lettuce evenly over bottom of a shallow, medium-large salad bowl. Arrange ingredients in rows over lettuce with minced chicken in a narrow strip down center, tomato, blue cheese and avocado on one side, and green onion, hard-cooked egg and bacon on other side. To delay serving, toss minced avocado in lemon juice to prevent darkening. Cover salad with a damp paper towel and refrigerate. Before serving, add oil and vinegar dressing and pepper to taste. Toss at table. Serve on chilled lettuce-lined plates. Makes 2 servings.

Variation: Cobb Salad à la Mer: Substitute a 3½-oz. can solid white tuna, drained and flaked, for chicken breast. Substitute lemon juice for vinegar in oil and vinegar dressing.

PISTACHIO DESSERT-SALAD

1 lb. can crushed pineapple
   and juice
1 pkg. pistachio instant
   pudding

1 med. size Cool Whip
1 cup miniature marshmallows
1 cup chopped nuts

Stir dry ingredients into pineapple and juice. Mix in other ingredients. Pour into mold and chill. Can be used either for light dessert or a salad. Serves 10.

—Bonnie Dunn

PRETZEL SALAD

1½ cups crushed pretzels   ¾ cup sugar
½ cup melted butter

TOPPING

1 8-oz. pkg. cream cheese   1 cup sugar
1 tsp. vanilla   1 3-oz. pkg. lemon Jello
1 13-oz. can evaporated *cold*   ½ cup boiling water
     milk in large bowl

Mix pretzels, butter and sugar together and put in 9" x 13" pan (save enough to sprinkle on top). Dissolve Jello in boiling water and cool. Cream sugar, vanilla and cream cheese. Whip canned milk (make sure this is *cold*) and fold in Jello mixture. Add sugar, vanilla and cream cheese mixture and fold into whipped cream. Pour over pretzel mixture and sprinkle the rest of pretzels on top. Refrigerate 2 hours and let set.

—*Joyce Candelario*

PARTY DESSERT SALAD

1 3-oz. pkg. cherry gelatin   ½ cup whipping cream,
1 cup hot water   whipped
½ cup pineapple juice   ½ cup chopped maraschino
1⅓ cups drained crushed   cherries
     pineapple   ½ cup chopped almonds
½ cup cottage cheese

Dissolve gelatin in hot water. Add pineapple juice and chill until slightly thickened. Fold in crushed pineapple, cottage cheese, and blend well. Fold cherries, almonds and whipped cream into the gelatin mixture. Chill until firm.

—*Erlene Hauser*

The best things in life must come by efforts from within . . . and not by gifts from without.

A MULTITUDE OF SINS

1 lg. pkg. lime Jello
2 cups miniature
   marshmallows
1 cup grated cheese
1½ cups diced celery

1 #2 can crushed pineapple
½ cup chopped walnuts
2 Tbls. lemon juice
½ pt. whipping cream
⅓ cup mayonnaise

Dissolve gelatin and marshmallows in 2 cups boiling water. Chill until it thickens. Add cheese, celery, pineapple, nuts and lemon juice. Combine whipped cream and mayonnaise and fold into first mixture. Chill for 12 hours before serving.

—Rosie Blackford

SHRIMP-TOMATO ASPIC MOLDED SALAD

1 box lemon gelatin
2 cups tomato juice
2 Tbls. Worcestershire sauce
2 Tbls. vinegar

1 avocado, chopped
5 green onions, chopped
¾ cup celery, chopped
1 can shrimp

Dissolve gelatin in 1 cup boiling tomato juice. Add 1 cup cold tomato juice and stir well. Add remaining ingredients and pour into a mold. Chill until set. Unmold. Serves 6 to 8.

—Carol Penner

FESTIVE TACO SALAD

1 lb. ground beef
1 pkg. taco seasoning mix
1 head lettuce
1 lg. tomato
1 pkg. Doritos

8 oz. Viva Italian dressing
½ cup onion, chopped
2 cups cheese (Colby or
   cheddar), grated
Mild hot sauce

Brown and drain ground beef. Mix taco seasoning mix with meat. Add lettuce, torn up. Cup up tomato, add dressing, pour in mild hot sauce to top of bottle (use as needed for salad). Add Doritos.

FLYING FARMER CHICKEN SALAD

5 cups cooked chicken, cut in
    chunks
2 Tbls. salad oil
2 Tbls. orange juice
2 Tbls. vinegar
1 tsp. salt
3 cups cooked rice
1½ cups seedless green
    grapes

1½ cups celery, finely sliced
1 13-oz. can pineapple tidbits,
    drained
1 11-oz. can Mandarin
    oranges, drained
1 cup toasted almonds,
    slivered
1½ cups mayonnaise

Combine chicken, oil, orange juice, vinegar and salt and let stand while preparing remaining ingredients. Gently toss all ingredients. Absolutely delicious! 8 to 10 servings.

—Althea Darling

ORANGE-PINEAPPLE SALAD

1 3 oz. pkg. orange Jello
1 sm. can crushed pineapple,
    drained (reserve juice)

2 bananas
1 cup miniature marshmallows

TOPPING

Juice from pineapple
⅔ cup sugar
1 egg

1 3-oz. pkg. cream cheese
1 cup nuts
1 sm. container Cool Whip

Make Jello according to directions and combine with pineapple, bananas and marshmallows. Refrigerate until firm. To make the topping, combine the reserved pineapple juice, sugar and egg. Mix and cook until thick. While still warm mix with softened cream cheese. Cool mixture completely. Add the nuts and Cool Whip. Spread this mixture on Jello mixture. Pour into 9" glass casserole dish. Chill.

—Jackie Ragland

Every person is important — to God there is no such thing as an "unwanted child."

From *"Be Somebody"* by Mary Crowley

48

CAULIFLOWER-BROCCOLI MEDLEY

1 head cauliflower
1 bunch broccoli
2 small onions, sliced, and
    separated into rings
½ cup mayonnaise

⅓ cup vegetable oil
⅓ cup vinegar
¼ cup sugar
½ tsp. salt
¼ tsp. pepper

Wash cauliflower and remove green leaves. Cut into bite-sized pieces. Remove leaves and tough ends from broccoli. Cut into bite-sized pieces. Combine vegetables in a large bowl. Mix remaining ingredients and pour over vegetables. Toss lightly. Chill several hours or overnight. Can garnish with bacon bits when served.

—Jackie Ragland

ARTICHOKE RICE SALAD

1 6-oz. pkg. cheddar flavored
    Uncle Ben's rice mix (do
    not use instant)
4 green onions, chopped
½ green pepper, chopped

12 pimento-stuffed olives, sliced
2 6-oz. jars marinated
    artichoke hearts
¾ tsp. curry powder
⅓ cup mayonnaise

Cook rice as directed except add no butter. Cool in a large bowl. Add onions, green pepper and olives. Drain artichokes, reserving marinade liquid. Cut artichokes lengthwise into quarters. Combine marinade, curry and mayonnaise and whip together. Add all ingredients to large bowl and chill. You may add cubed chicken if you like a heartier salad. This makes a nice summer salad. Serves six.

—Sandie Bergstrom

There are two ways of attaining an important end — force and perseverance. Force falls to the lot of only a few, but austere and sustained perseverance can be practiced by the most insignificant. Its silent power grows irresistible with time.

LAYERED PEA SALAD

1 sm. head lettuce, cut up
1 pkg. frozen peas, cooked
   and cooled
½ cup celery, cut up
1 sm. onion, chopped

2 Tbls. sugar
½ lb. bacon, broiled
Miracle Whip
Parmesan cheese

Layer in 9"x13" pan in this order, the lettuce, peas, celery and onion. Sprinkle the sugar. Ice completely with Miracle Whip. Crumble the broiled bacon and place on top of Miracle Whip. Sprinkle Parmesan cheese generously over bacon. Cover and chill overnight.

CAULIFLOWER SALAD

Combine raw cauliflower with any or all of the following diced vegetables — radishes, onions, tomatoes, celery, peppers, cucumbers, and carrots. Combine the following dressing and add to salad — mayonnaise, lemon juice and powdered sugar (enough to give it a sweet taste).

MOTHER TO SON

Do you know that your soul is of my soul such part
That you seem to be fiber and core of my heart?
None other can pain me as you, dear, can do;
None other can please me, or praise me, as you.

Remember, the world is quick with its blame,
If shadows or stain ever darken your name.
"Like mother, like son," is a saying so true —
The world will judge largely of mother by you.

Be yours then, the task — if task it shall be —
To force the proud world to do homage to me,
Be sure it will say, when its verdict you've won:
"She reaped as she sowed; lo, this is her son."

—Author and source unknown

STORING FRESH FRUITS AND VEGETABLES

COLDEST PART OF REFRIGERATOR
35° to 40°F (2° to 5°C)

Less Than One Week	One Week or More
Strawberries	Romaine Lettuce
Raspberries	Parsley
Sweet Corn	Beets
Soft Leafy Lettuce	Radishes
Spinach	Leeks
Asparagus	Cabbage
Mushrooms	Carrots
Watercress	Celery
Brussels Sprouts	Celery Root
Iceberg Lettuce	Artichokes
Cauliflower	Turnips
Broccoli	Apples
Green Onions	Blueberries
Summer Fruits, ripe	

WARMEST PART OF REFRIGERATOR
45° to 55°F (5° to 15°C)

Less Than One Week	One Week or More
Tomatoes, ripe	Cucumbers
Green Beans	Zucchini
Avocados, ripe	Summer Squash
	Green Peppers
	Melons, ripe
	Oranges

COOL ROOM TEMPERATURE
50° to 60°F (10° to 15°C)

One Week or More
Grapefruit
Lemons
Limes
Potatoes
Sweet Potatoes
Winter Squash, uncut

ROOM TEMPERATURE
65° to 70°F (20° C)

Less Than One Week	One Week or More
Bananas	Dry Onions
	Garlic

ENTREES

SWEET AND SOUR MEAT LOAF

1 15-oz. can tomato sauce	2 eggs, slightly beaten
1/2 cup brown sugar	1/2 cup onion, minced
1/4 cup vinegar	1/2 cup bread crumbs, dry
1 tsp. mustard	1 Tbls. salt
2 lbs. lean ground beef	1/4 tsp. pepper
1/2 lb. ground pork	

Preheat oven to 350°. Combine tomato sauce, sugar, vinegar, and mustard in a bowl. Mix well, set aside. Combine remaining ingredients with 1 cup sauce mixture in a bowl. Mix well. Place in lightly greased 1½-quart casserole dish. Pour remaining sauce evenly over loaf. Bake 1 hour or until done.

—*Norma Jackson and Cheryl Burke*

BAKED CHOP SUEY

1½ lbs. hamburger meat, browned	1/2 cup uncooked rice (do not use Minute rice)
2 medium onions, chopped	2 tsp. soy sauce
2 cups celery, chopped	2 tsp. Worcestershire sauce
1 can mushroom soup	2 cups water
1 can cream of chicken soup	Chow mein noodles for top

Mix together and bake in greased casserole dish at 350° for 1½ hours. Top with 1/2 can of chow mein noodles and bake 15 minutes more.

—*Bonnie Eisentrout*

If your purpose is worthwhile enough, and your belief in it is strong enough, the strength of the purpose will take over and keep you keeping on even when you are physically exhausted.

From *"Be Somebody"* by Mary Crowley

ENTREES...

BEEF STROGANOFF

1½ lbs. round steak	1 6-oz. can tomato paste
1 lb. fresh mushrooms, sliced	1 tsp. salt
1 cup butter	⅛ tsp. soy sauce
2 lbs. onions, finely chopped	1 cup sour cream
1 can tomato soup	Minced parsley

Cut meat in very thin strips, trim off excess fat. Brown meat and mushrooms in butter. Add onions. Combine soup, tomato paste and seasonings. Add to meat mixture. Cover, simmer for 1 hour. Just before serving, stir in sour cream. Thicken gravy if desired. Serve in rings of fluffy hot rice. Garnish with parsley.

—Jan McLaughlin

QUICKIE BEEF STEW

1 1-lb. can sliced carrots	1 envelope (about 1½ ozs.) dry
1 8-oz. can whole potatoes	onion soup mix
1 8-oz. can cut green beans	3 cups cut-up cooked beef
¼ cup all purpose flour	

Drain vegetables, reserving liquid. Combine flour and soup mix in large skillet. Add water to reserved liquid to measure 3 cups. Stir into mixture in skillet. Heat to boiling, stirring constantly. Boil and stir 1 minute. Stir in vegetables and beef. Cover and cook over low heat about 10 minutes or until heated through. 4 servings, about 1½ cups each.

—Eunice Armstrong

About Closed Hands

A closed hand can't receive. Even God Himself cannot give you or me any more than we are mentally, emotionally, and spiritually conditioned to receive. If our hands are already full of ourselves then God can't fill them.

From "Be Somebody" by Mary Crowley

ENCHILADAS

1 lb. ground beef	1 cup water
2 tsp. salt	Dash of pepper
1 Tbls. vinegar	Flour
1 tsp. chili powder	Cheddar cheese
1 Tbls. tequila	Lettuce
1 can kidney beans	Tortillas
3 Tbls. oil	

Brown ground beef. Add salt, vinegar, chili powder, tequila, salad oil, pepper, and, if desired, hot sauce. Mix well. Add kidney beans and water. Keep over medium heat. Then slowly add flour until mixture thickens. Shred cheese and mix with cut lettuce. Put tortillas in salad oil in drying pan, but do not let fry. Just leave until soft. Put mixture in tortilla, add cheese and lettuce mixture over top. Roll. Spread remaining ingredients over top of rolled tortillas. Heat in oven until cheese on top is melted.

—Kathy Kaufman

CHILI VERDE WITH MEAT

Round steak, cut in small cubes	Salt
Garlic powder	½ can hot chilies (Ortega)
Onion powder	2 fresh tomatoes, chopped
Cominos	1 small can tomato sauce
	1½ cups water

Cook steak, flavored with garlic powder, onion powder, cominos and salt in an uncovered pan with water approximately 20 minutes. Add remaining ingredients and let come to a boil. Serve with rice on the side and crisp fresh lettuce salad.

CHILI VERDE SAUCE

1 can chilies (Ortega)	Garlic powder
2 fresh tomatoes	Onion powder
1 can tomato sauce	Salt

Chop up the chilies with the tomatoes, add the garlic and onion powder and a dash of salt. Mix in bowl with the tomato sauce and a little bit of water. No cooking, ready to serve over rice, noodles, refried beans, etc.

—*Blanca Arias*

CHILI

4 lbs. chili meat	1 tsp. sugar
8 Tbls. chili powder	½ cup flour
4 Tbls. Spanish paprika	2-3 onions, chopped
2 tsp. ground cominos	6-7 garlic buttons
2 tsp. ground oregano	Salt to taste

Use very coursely ground chili meat or cut meat in small cubes (it makes prettier chili). Use Spanish paprika; it's richer and darker than Italian paprika. Saute meat. If meat does not have enough fat, add enough oil to lightly cover bottom of pan. Add onions and garlic and cook until onions are clear, but not brown. Mix dry ingredients and add just enough water to make a paste. Add to meat mixture and simmer ten minutes. Add water and cook about 3 hours. Thicken before serving. This is super chili, and makes great enchiladas. The recipe can be increased many times without loss of flavor.

—*Mary Jewett*

School is a building that has four walls — with tomorrow inside.

—Lon Waters

58

SPANISH ENCHILADAS

1 15-oz. can Hunts tomato
   sauce
1 doz. corn tortillas
1 can Hormel chili without
   beans

1½ lbs. hamburger meat,
   browned
1 garlic clove
1 small onion, chopped
2 cups shredded cheddar cheese

Have all ingredients chopped and in individual containers. Combine tomato sauce, chili and garlic, and any other seasonings you might like. Brown corn tortillas in hot oil, 10 seconds on each side. Dip tortillas in tomato and chili sauce, add handful of meat, onion, and cheese. Roll tortilla shells closed and place closed ends on the bottom. Place in a 9" x 13" baking dish. Place leftover hamburger meat, onion, sauce and cheese on top. Bake at 400° for 15 minutes. Serves 6.

—Debbie Potts

LASAGNA

2 boxes lasagna noodles
1 lb. ground beef
¼ cup onion
1 6-oz. can tomato paste
1 8-oz. can tomato sauce
1 garlic clove, crushed
2 tsp. Italian seasoning
1 tsp. salt

¼ tsp. pepper
1½ cups water
1 carton creamed cottage
   cheese
2 eggs
2 lg. bags Mozzarella cheese
Parmesan cheese

Cook lasagna noodles as directed on package. Brown beef with onion in skillet. Add tomato paste, sauce, salt, pepper, Italian seasoning and water. Simmer 1 hour. Combine cottage cheese, eggs and mozzarella cheese. In baking pan, alternate layers, starting with noodles, then meat mixture and lastly cheese mixture. Sprinkle top with Parmesan cheese. Bake at 350° for 30 minutes. Remove from oven and let stand for 15 minutes before serving. Serves 10.

—Roberta Mullis and Linda Gordon

LASAGNA

FIRST MIXTURE

2 lbs. ground meat
1 garlic clove, minced
1½-2 Tbls. parsley
½ tsp. basil
1 tsp. oregano

2 tsp. salt
1 1-lb. can tomatoes
1 12-oz. can tomato paste
2 12-oz. cans tomato sauce
10-12 oz. lasagna noodles

SECOND MIXTURE

3 cups creamed cottage
    cheese
2 eggs, beaten
2 tsp. salt

½ tsp. pepper
2 tsp. parsley flakes
1 3-oz. can Parmesan cheese
1 lb. mozzarella cheese, grated

Slowly brown meat, drain off excess fat. Add next eight ingredients. Simmer uncovered for 30 minutes. Stir occasionally. Cook noodles in boiling, salted water until tender. Drain noodles then rinse in cold water. Meanwhile, combine cottage cheese and eggs, seasoning and Parmesan cheese in a medium-sized bowl. Place ½ cup noodles in a 13"x9"x2" buttered dish. Spread ½ of cottage cheese mixture over noodles, then ½ of meat sauce, then ½ of mozzarella. Repeat layers. Bake at 375° for 30 minutes. Let stand 10 minutes. Serve with salad and French bread. Serves 12.

—Gayla Moates

LASAGNA

1 lb. ground beef
1 onion, chopped
1 lg. can tomato sauce
1 lb. cottage cheese

1 lb. Mozzarella cheese
1 lb. lasagna noodles
Salt and pepper to taste

Brown ground beef and onions together. Add tomato sauce and simmer. Add cottage cheese and set aside. Cook noodles in boiling water. Drain; then layer in baking dish sauce, lasagna noodles, Mozzarella cheese. Continue in this order until all ingredients are used. Bake uncovered in 375° oven about 25 minutes or until thoroughly heated.

—Darlene Elerick

ENTREES...

ITALIAN SPAGHETTI AND MEATBALLS

1 small onion
4 cans tomato sauce
4 cans water
⅛ tsp. cloves, ground
¼ (to ½) tsp. oregano
½ tsp. celery salt (or 2 stalks celery)
¼ tsp. pure garlic juice (or ½ tsp. garlic salt)

2 Tbls. Parmesan cheese
2 Tbls. Italian seasoning
1 egg
3 lbs. ground beef
1 Tbls. Parmesan cheese
Cracker crumbs
Small amount olive oil
Salt and pepper

Prepare sauce in Dutch oven or large heavy pan. Chop onion very fine and cook to transparency in olive oil. Add tomato sauce, cloves, oregano, celery salt, garlic juice, Parmesan cheese. Wrap Italian seasoning in small piece of cheese cloth or other clean soft rag and drop into sauce. Cook on simmer for 30-40 minutes while sauce thickens and you are preparing meat balls. Make paste of cracker crumbs and egg and add to ground beef. Season with salt, pepper and Parmesan cheese. Shape into balls and drop into hot fat. Allow to brown on all sides. Drain and drop into sauce to simmer 4-6 hours. After sauce has thickened you may put it and meat balls into crock-pot and cook on low all day or all night.

—Jean Landrum

BREAKFAST OR BRUNCH

1 lb. bulk pork sausage
1 can crescent dinner rolls
2 cups mozzarella cheese, shredded

¾ cup milk
¼ tsp. salt
⅛ tsp. pepper
4 eggs, beaten

Crumble sausage in a medium skillet; cook over medium heat until brown, stirring occasionally. Drain well. Line bottom of a buttered 13"x9" baking dish with crescent rolls, firmly pressing perforations to seal. Sprinkle with sausage and cheese. Combine remaining ingredients; beat well and pour over sausage. Bake in 425° oven for 15 minutes or until set. Let stand 5 minutes, cut into squares and serve immediately. Yield 6 to 8 servings.

MEATBALLS IN ONION SOUP

1 lb. ground beef
¾ cup rolled oats, quick or
   regular
1 egg
½ cup milk
1 tsp. salt
½ tsp. tarragon, optional

⅓ cup flour
2 Tbls. fat
1 envelope dry onion soup mix
2¼ cups water
½ cup dry wine, optional
Shredded Parmesan cheese

Combine beef, rolled oats, eggs, milk, and seasonings. Blend thoroughly. Shape into 18 medium-sized balls, and roll lightly in flour. Save excess flour. Melt fat in frying pan and brown the meatballs at moderate heat. Dissolve onion soup in 2 cups water and add to meatballs. Cover, cook over low heat until done, 20-25 minutes. Mix remaining flour and water to a smooth paste and stir into onion soup. Cook until thick and smooth. If desired, five minutes before serving, sprinkle with cheese.

—Dorothy Eckert

VELVET HOTCAKES

3 eggs, separated
½ cup flour
2 tsp. baking powder
½ cup milk

3 Tbls. sugar
2 Tbls. cornstarch
¼ tsp. salt
½ cup yogurt

Cream together egg yolks and sugar. Sift flour, measure, and sift again with cornstarch, baking powder and salt. Combine with creamed mixture, milk and yogurt. Mix well. Beat egg whites until stiff, and fold into mixture. Bake on a medium-hot griddle. Serve with butter and granulated sugar. Serves 4 to 6.

These are the best pancakes I've ever eaten! Don't be afraid of the yogurt...you'll never taste it and your family will not know the difference. These are so light that they almost float from your plate. The original recipe called for sour cream but by using the yogurt, the calories will be greatly reduced. You may also omit the sugar or use a sugar substitute as I have done in the past. Try 'em...you'll love 'em!

—Barbara McMullen

HAWAIIAN MEATBALLS

1 lb. ground round	½ cup wine vinegar
½ lb. pork sausage	¼ cup white sugar
¾ cup bread crumbs	3 Tbls. brown sugar
¾ cup milk	1 tsp. soy sauce
½ cup chopped onion	¾ tsp. cornstarch
1 egg, slightly beaten	1 tsp. water
¾ tsp. salt and pepper	2 Tbls. green pepper
2 Tbls. salad oil, heated	1 garlic clove
½ cup pineapple juice	

Combine meat, sausage, bread crumbs, milk, onion, egg, salt and pepper. Make small meatballs and brown a few at a time in the oil. Put pineapple juice, wine vinegar, sugars and soy sauce in saucepan, bring to boil. Blend cornstarch and water until smooth. Add to boiling juices. After all meatballs are brown, add green pepper and garlic and cook for five minutes. Remove garlic and add this mixture to the juices and pour over meatballs. Bake at 325° for 45 minutes in a covered casserole dish.

—Joyce Kissler

CHILI MARVEL

2 lbs. ground beef	2 lg. cans tomatoes
2 medium onions	1 lg. can tomato juice
2 medium cans kidney beans	Salt and pepper to taste

Brown slowly together the ground beef and onions. Add salt and pepper to taste, then add the remaining ingredients. Simmer 1½ to 2 hours.

—Marge Anderson

Blessings are not to hoard, but to share. As Christians we are blessed to share our blessings with others.

From *"Be Somebody"* by Mary Crowley

63

HAMBURGER MEDLEY SOUP

1½ lbs. ground chuck
6 onions, sliced
4 stalks celery
4 carrots
4 potatoes

3 Tbls. margarine
6 cups water
1 lg. can tomatoes
Salt and pepper to taste

Simmer meat, pour off excess grease. Add margarine, sliced onions and water and cook 1½ hours. Add tomatoes, cut-up vegetables, and seasonings. Cook until done, about one hour.

—Trin Jones

CHEESEBURGER PIE

2½ lbs. ground beef
½ cup onions, chopped
¾ cup cream of mushroom soup

1 pie crust
Cheese slices

Mix beef, onions and soup together and put into a 9"x13" pan. Cover mixture with a layer of cheese slices. Then cover with your favorite pie crust. Bake in 325° oven for one hour.

—Bernie Kolbo

PORCUPINES

½ cup uncooked rice
1½ lb. ground beef
½ cup chopped onion
½ cup green peppers, chopped
½ cup celery, chopped

1 egg, beaten
2 tsp. prepared mustard
1 tsp. salt
2 cans tomato soup
2 soup cans water

Mix all ingredients except soup and water. Make balls at least 2" in diameter. Place in baking dish. Pour soup and water over balls, cover and bake in 350° oven for 1½ hours. Makes 6 servings.

—Susan Ewald

STUFFED BURGER BUNDLES

1 cup herbed seasoned stuffing mix	1 10½-oz. can condensed cream of mushroom soup
⅓ cup evaporated milk	2 tsp. Worcestershire sauce
1 lb. ground beef	1 Tbls. ketchup

Prepare stuffing according to package directions. Combine evaporated milk and meat. Divide into 5 patties. On wax paper pat each patty into a 6" circle. Put ¼ cup of stuffing in center of each patty. Bring sides of patty up and seal over stuffing. Place in 1½-quart casserole dish. Combine remaining ingredients. Heat and pour over meat. Bake uncovered for 45 minutes in 350° oven.

—*Sandra Welch*

SHORT RIBS WITH LIMA BEANS

2 cups large dry lima beans	½ cup celery and tops, chopped
5 cups water	1 garlic clove, minced, or 1 tsp. garlic salt
3 lbs. short ribs	
½ cup catsup	3 tsp. salt
½ cup chopped onions	Pepper to taste

Rinse beans and add the 5 cups of water. Boil 2 minutes, remove from heat and let stand 1 hour. Brown ribs in skillet, remove excess fat. Bury ribs in beans and add remaining ingredients. Cover and cook gently until meat and beans are tender. If needed, add more water, season with salt and pepper to taste in the last ½ hour.

—*Paula Barton*

When the Lord created the world, He looked at it and said, "That's good." Then He created man, looked at him and said, "That's good, but I believe I can do better."

So — He created woman.

From *"Be Somebody"* by Mary Crowley

ENTREES...

DINNER BEEF PATTIES

1 large Bermuda onion
2 Tbls. butter or margarine
¼ cup water
3 Tbls. brown sugar

2 lbs. ground beef
2 tsp. salt
Paprika

CHILI GLAZE

½ cup chili sauce
½ cup water

1 Tbls. corn syrup
1 Tbls. Worcestershire sauce

Peel onion and cut crosswise into 4 thick slices. Saute in butter or margarine until lightly browned on bottom. Turn carefully. Add water and brown sugar. Cover and simmer 10 minutes or until tender. Sprinkle with paprika. Keep hot while preparing and cooking meat. Mix ground beef lightly with salt, shape into 4 large and 4 medium size patties about 1 inch thick. Pan fry over medium heat 8 minutes, turn, cook 5 minutes longer. Spoon chili glaze (see directions below) over patties and continue cooking, basting the glaze in pan, 3 minutes longer for medium, or until meat is done as you like it. Put one each large and medium size pattie together with onion slice between on a plate. Top with any sauce left in pan.

Chili Glaze: Combine glaze ingredients in a 2-cup container. Makes 1 cup.

—Bonnie Broadhurst

GOOD, GOOD SANDWICH

Roman Meal bread, or any
  whole grain bread
Monterey Jack cheese
Alfalfa sprouts

Tomatoes
Bacon
Durkee's dressing

Grill bread in butter with cheese, but do not melt cheese too soft. Pull bread apart and add other ingredients. (Alfalfa sprouts are less expensive if bought in a health food store.) If desired add salt and a little garlic powder.

—Rossie Harwell

66

FLEMISH CARBONNADES (Crock Pot Recipe)

2 lbs. round steak, 1" thick
1/4 cup flour
1 tsp. sugar
1/8 tsp. pepper

6-8 small new potatoes, peeled
1 envelope or 1 1/2 oz. dry
   onion soup mix
3/4 cup beer

Trim round steak. Cut into serving portions. Combine flour, sugar and pepper. Toss with steak to coat thoroughly. Place potatoes in crock pot and cover with steak pieces. Thoroughly combine soup mix and beer. Pour over steak, moistening well. Cover and cook on low setting 8 to 12 hours. Thicken gravy before serving if desired. 4-6 servings.

—Cindy Halsey

BAKED ZUCCHINI

Ground beef or sausage,
   browned
Onion
Poultry seasoning
Garlic powder

Salt
Pepper, as desired for all
   spices
Package seasoned stuffing mix
Parmesan cheese

Cut zucchini in half lengthwise and spoon out center; put it in frying pan with ground beef or sausage, onion and seasonings. Simmer until about half-done. Put package seasoned stuffing mix in large bowl, add mixture from frying pan, add Parmesan cheese (as much as desired), mix well. If dry, add small amounts of hot water until moist. Now sprinkle cheese into zucchini shells and stuff. Sprinkle cheese on top, if desired, and wrap each half in foil separately. Place on cookie sheet and bake at 375° until tender. Pierce bottom of zucchini with large fork to check for tenderness. Large zucchinis take about 1 hour, smaller ones about 1/2 hour.

—Mary Schwarm

BEEF STEW BURGUNDY

2 lbs. beef stew meat
2 Tbls. cooking oil
3 Tbls. flour
1 medium onion
1 garlic clove
1 cup red wine, Burgundy or
   other dry red wine
1 cup water
½ tsp. thyme
1 bay leaf
1 bouillon cube

1 lb. mushrooms or 1 large
   can and liquid
6 carrots
4 large potatoes
15 small white onions, peeled
   or 1 can onions
1 bell pepper, cut in ½"
   squares, about ½ cup
Parsley and celery leaves
Salt and pepper

Shake meat cubes in bag with flour, salt and pepper until meat is well coated. Brown in hot oil or shortening in skillet. When the chunks are a rich brown on all sides, remove with tongs to a Dutch oven. In the remaining fat in skillet cook the onions and garlic over low heat just until tender, not brown, stirring constantly. With slotted spoon transfer them to the Dutch oven along with the meat, and add the water, bouillon, wine, mushrooms, dry herbs, parsley and celery leaves and simmer over low heat for about 2 hours. The last 45 minutes add the carrots, potatoes, onions, and bell pepper. Continue simmering until meat and vegetables are tender. Season to taste. Serve hot with a tossed salad and French bread. If there are any leftovers, serve them the next day on steamed rice. *Variations:* add green beans, peas, or cut-up stalk of celery.

—Deidre Meyers

CHICKEN AND DUMPLINGS

1½ cups flour
¼ cup Crisco
½ tsp. salt

¼ cup milk
1 egg
1 chicken, boiled and deboned

Cut flour, Crisco and salt in mixing bowl until it resembles corn-meal. Add milk and egg. Roll out on floured board and cut into strips. Let dry for 30 minutes before placing over your boiled and deboned chicken. Cook for 20 minutes without taking the lid off the pan.

—Cynthia Waters

NOODLE CASSEROLE

2 cans onion soup
2 cans beef consomme
½ lb. oleo
8 oz. very small noodles

2 Tbls. soy sauce
2 cans water chestnuts or
mushrooms

Place *uncooked* noodles in butter and brown, using any skillet large enough to stir this mixture easily. After brown, put in casserole dish. Add onion soup and consomme, then soy sauce. Stir sliced water chestnuts or mushrooms into this mixture. Bake 45 minutes in 350° oven. This serves 10-12 people and can be divided into 5 or 6 servings so easily.

—*Mary Ann Mansker*

BEEF ZUCCHINI CASSEROLE

1½ lbs. ground round
½ cup onion, chopped
¼ tsp. garlic powder
½ tsp. salt
⅛ tsp. pepper
⅛ tsp. oregano
½ cup bread crumbs

¼ cup flour
¼ cup butter
¼ tsp. salt
¼ tsp. pepper
2 cups milk
1 cup grated cheddar cheese
6-8 medium zucchini squash

Grease two-quart casserole dish. Wash and cut ends off squash and boil in lightly salted water just till tender. Slice ½ inch or larger. Cook onions, ground round and pour off excess drippings. Stir in bread crumbs and spices. Consistency will be dry. Remove from heat. In saucepan, melt butter; add flour, salt, pepper and milk. Then add cheese, and cook till thickened. Begin to layer, placing squash on bottom, then a layer of meat, then a layer of cheese sauce and repeat layers. Grate an extra amount of cheese, sprinkle on top. Paprika may also be added. Bake in 350° oven for ½ hour. Serves 6 to 8.

—*Marietta Mullenaux*

SHARON'S CHEROKEE CASSEROLE

1 lb. ground beef	Dash of pepper
1 can cream of mushroom soup	⅛ tsp. garlic
1 lb. can whole tomatoes	⅛ tsp. oregano
¼ cup onion, chopped	1 cup Minute rice
1½ tsp. salt	3 slices American cheese

Brown ground beef and onion, drain. Stir in seasonings. Add tomatoes, mushroom soup and rice. Mix well. Simmer 5 minutes, stirring occasionally. Top with cheese. Replace lid and simmer 2-3 minutes. Serves 4-6, takes 15-20 minutes.

—Sharon Adcock

HAMBURGER CASSEROLE

1 lb. ground beef	1 tsp. salt
2 Tbls. butter	1 cup tomato soup
4 medium size potatoes	Dash pepper
2 onions	

Brown the beef in skillet with butter. Cut potatoes in ½" cubes and spread in a baking dish. Cover with half the meat. Add half the soup and a sliced onion. Season with salt and pepper. Repeat layers using remaining ingredients. Bake 1½ hours in 350° oven. More soup may be added during baking if needed.

—Barbara McDonald

Advice to a wife about her husband: You have to lean on him on one side . . . and prop him up on the other.

From "Be Somebody" by Mary Crowley

ENTREES...

HAMBURGER POTATO PIE

1 lb. ground beef
1 medium onion
1 cup cooked peas
2 cups tomatoes
½ cup catsup
2 Tbls. butter
½ tsp. salt
½ tsp. pepper
5 potatoes, cooked and
    mashed
1 egg

Brown the chopped onion in butter. Remove onion and brown ground beef with salt and pepper. Place ground beef and onions, peas, tomatoes and catsup in a casserole dish to combine. Mash potatoes, beat in egg and spoon potatoes on top of other mixture. Brown in 375° oven till peaks are golden.

—Barbara McDonald

HAMBURGER NOODLE STROGANOFF

1 lb. ground beef
½ cup onion, chopped (can
    also use onion flakes)
1 can cream of mushroom
    soup
½ cup sour cream
½ cup water
½ tsp. salt
⅛ tsp. pepper
½ tsp. paprika, optional
2 cups noodles, cooked
Tomato slices
Buttered bread crumbs

Brown beef and cook onion in skillet until tender. Stir to separate meat and pour off fat. Add remaining ingredients. Pour into 1½-quart greased shallow baking dish. Bake in 400° oven for 25 minutes. Remove from oven and stir. Garnish with tomato slices and buttered bread crumbs. Place in oven for 5 more minutes of baking. Makes 4½ cups.

—Doris Carey

If you are doing more for others, they will be drawn to you. If you help other people get what they want out of life, you will get what you want out of life.

From *"Be Somebody"* by Mary Crowley

MORE BEEF CASSEROLE

1 8-oz. pkg. noodles
1 lb. lean ground beef
1/4 cup chopped onion
1 Tbls. cooking oil
1 cup tomato sauce or tomato
   catsup

1 8½-oz. can cream style corn
½ cup chopped green pepper
1 Tbls. chili powder
½ cup shredded cheese

Cook noodles according to package directions. Cook beef and onions in cooking oil until meat turns white. Add tomato sauce or catsup, corn, green pepper and chili powder to meat mixture, and cook about 10 minutes. Put a layer of noodles in a 2-quart casserole dish, then a layer of meat mixture. Bake for 20 minutes in 325° oven. Add shredded cheese and continue cooking until cheese melts. Makes 6-8 servings.

—*Barbara McDonald*

RICE CASSEROLE

1 lb. ground meat
1½ cups rice
1/4 cup onion, chopped
1/4 cup bell pepper
1/4 cup celery
1 tsp. celery salt

1 tsp. garlic salt
1½ tsp. black pepper
½ jalapeño pepper
1 slice cheese
1/4 cup parsley
1½ tsp. salt

Cook rice until done and set aside. Saute the onion, bell pepper and celery. Brown meat and add onion, pepper, celery, seasonings and rice. Mix well and add cheese. Cook on top of stove.

—*Brenda Gipson*

One person with a belief is equal to ninety-nine with only interest.
From *"Be Somebody"* by Mary Crowley

CHICKEN AND VEGETABLES

1 onion, diced
½ head cabbage, chopped
1 cup celery, sliced
1 cup carrots, sliced

1 tsp. tumeric
2 chicken boullion cubes
1 chicken, cut in pieces
Salt and pepper to taste

Place all ingredients in large soup pot, cover, simmer slowly for 1 hour, and add ½ cup water or chicken broth.

—*Maylene Flagg*

GROUND CHUCK AND PASTA IN A POT

2 lbs. lean ground chuck
1 garlic clove crushed
1 14-oz. jar Ragu spaghetti
   sauce
1 lb. can stewed tomatoes

1 3 or 4-oz. can sliced
   mushrooms
½ pt dairy sour cream
½ lb. sliced Provolone cheese
½ lb. sliced Mozzarella
8 oz. small shell macaroni

Cook beef in large skillet in small amount of vegetable oil. Drain off fat. Add onions, garlic, spaghetti sauce and mushrooms. Mix well. Simmer till onions are soft. Meanwhile cook 8 oz. small shell macaroni. Drain and rinse in cold water. Layer ½ macaroni, cover with ½ of meat, spread ½ sour cream, top with Provolone cheese. Repeat. Bake until cheese is melted.

—*Fern Mears*

CRUNCHY CORN DOGS

1 cup pancake mix
1 cup milk
½ cup corn meal
2 tsp. chili powder
¼ tsp. salt

⅛ tsp. pepper
12 skewers
12 frankfurters
Vegetable oil

Combine pancake mix, milk, corn meal, chili powder, salt and pepper; mix until batter is fairly smooth. Insert wooden skewers into franks. Dip into batter; drain off excess. Fry in deep hot oil (375°) 1-2 minutes, until golden brown. Drain on absorbent paper. Serve with mustard.

—*Mariam Sumner*

CALICO BEANS

¼ lb. bacon
1 lb. ground beef
½ cup onion, chopped
½ cup brown sugar
½ cup catsup

2 Tbls. vinegar
1 Tbls. prepared mustard
1 lb. can butter beans
1 lb. can pinto beans
1 lb. can pork and beans

Cut bacon in bite-size pieces and brown with ground beef and onion. Do not drain. Mix beans together (do not drain) and add to the meat mixture. Bake uncovered 1½ hours in 300° oven.

—Wanda Copeland

MACARONI AND CHEESE CASSEROLE

12 oz. elbow macaroni
9 cups water
4½ Tbls. butter, 1 block
4½ Tbls. flour
⅜ tsp. salt

1½ cups milk
1 lg. can evaporated milk
1 16-oz. block Kraft American
  cheese
Dash of pepper

Cook macaroni in water until tender. Do not add salt. Drain. Melt butter in small pan; stir in flour, salt and pepper. Add milk slowly. Cook, stirring constantly, until blended. Grate cheese and put 1 cup of cheese aside for topping of casserole. Add remaining grated cheese to milk, cooking and stirring until melted. Blend together cheese sauce and macaroni and place in casserole dish. Sprinkle 1 cup grated cheese over macaroni casserole. Bake in 325° oven until cheese on top is browned.

—Patricia R. Lormand

Resolve to be tender with the young, compassionate with the aged, sympathetic with the striving, and tolerant with the weak and the wrong. Sometime in life you will have been all of these.

"Dandy Lion," quoted by Bob Goddard
in The St. Louis Globe-Democrat

PIZZA

Bridge Port Bread (store
    freezer type)
5 tsp. oregano leaves
2½ 6-oz. cans tomato paste
1½ cups onion, diced
1½ Victor brand salami

1½ pkgs. Monterrey Jack
    cheese, grated
1½ pkgs. Mozzarella cheese,
    grated
Garlic powder
Parmesan grated cheese
Mushrooms, canned or fresh

Section bread into five balls. In each ball sprinkle oregano leaves, then roll out dough. Spread tomato paste, sprinkle garlic powder and then onions. After the onions place the salami, the Jack cheese, and Mozzarella cheese, then the Parmesan cheese. Spread mushrooms on top. Sprinkle a few oregano leaves on top of mushrooms. Make sure your oven is at 450°. Bake 15 minutes. Each pizza serves 6-8. Recipe makes 5 medium pizzas.

—Pat Dillard

PRESIDENT'S FAVORITE MACARONI AND CHEESE

½ lb. macaroni
1 tsp. butter
1 egg, beaten
1 tsp. salt

1 tsp. dry mustard
3 cups grated cheese, sharp
1 cup milk

Boil macaroni in water until tender and drain thoroughly. Stir in butter and egg. Mix mustard and salt with 1 tablespoon hot water and add to milk. Add cheese leaving enough to sprinkle on top. Pour into buttered casserole, add milk, sprinkle with cheese. Bake at 350° for about 45 minutes or until custard is set and top is crusty.

—Nancy Reagan

Judge not another from your high and lofty seat. Step down into the arena, where he and his problems meet.

From *"Be Somebody"* by Mary Crowley

OVEN-FRIED CHICKEN

3 lb. young frying chicken, cut up as for frying	Salt and pepper
	Flour
½ cup melted butter	Homogenized seet milk

Salt and roll chicken in flour, put melted butter in baking pan. Place chicken in pan and cover with milk, sprinkle with pepper. Bake until tender, turning so it will brown on all sides. You'll find this is a change and delicious. Makes its own gravy. Bake at 400° for 1 to 1½ hours.

—Carla J. Gragus

BARBECUED CHICKEN

1 large frying chicken, cut up	Garlic
2 bottles hickory-smoked Open Pit barbecue sauce	Onion salt
	Regular salt

Put chicken in roaster or deep pan. Pour sauce over chicken. Rinse out bottle with a little water and add also. Sprinkle garlic and onion salt and regular salt to taste over sauce. Bake at 325° to 350° at least 1 hour or until done. Can be covered. Also for country style ribs instead of chicken.

—Oneth Lovetinsky

HOT BEEF SANDWICHES
(Makes six dozen)

15 lbs. lean beef, cubed	2 oz. flavored croutons
2 lbs. onions	2 6-oz. cans mushrooms
2 oz. McCormick beef flavor	12 oz. white wine

Mix all ingredients and cover with water. Cook 1½ days in crock pot on high during the day and on low overnight (36 hours). Stir with fork after 6 hours. It will thicken by end of cooking time. May also be cooked in oven at 450° for 10½ hours. ½ of this recipe makes three dozen sandwiches.

—Jean Hoffman

CHILI

5 lbs. meat	1 tsp. black pepper
1 large onion	5 tsp. salt
2 cans tomato paste	2/3 cup flour
2½ tsp. comino seed	¾ tsp. garlic powder
5 Tbls. chili powder	

Brown meat, onion and comino seed with salt, pepper and garlic powder. Then add chili powder and mix thoroughly. Add tomato paste and equal amount of water. Simmer about 2 hours, adding water as needed. About 20 minutes before chili is done, mix flour in a glass of water and add to mixture. Stir to thicken.

—Mrs. Juan Gonzales

CHICKEN ENCHILADAS

2 whole chickens	1 lb. cheddar cheese
2 4-oz. cans Ortega diced green chilies	3 Tbls. flour
	3 Tbls. shortening
2 4½-oz. cans chopped olives	3 cups water
1 small onion, chopped	1 19-oz. Las Palmas enchilada sauce
2½-3 dozen corn tortillas	
1 cup oil	3 8-oz. cans tomato sauce

Melt shortening, add flour and brown. Add water and enchilada sauce, simmer 10 minutes. Set aside. Boil chicken until done, cool, bone. Add chilies, olives and onion. Mix well with hands. Put aside. Heat oil, dip each tortilla quickly to soften. Set aside. Put filling in tortilla, roll up, add sauce and sprinkle cheese on top. Bake 15 minutes at 350°. Makes servings for 12.

—Debbie Delgado

If righteousness is in the heart, there will be beauty in the character;
If beauty is in the character, there will be harmony in the home;
If harmony is in the home, there will be order in the nation;
If order is in the nation, there will be PEACE IN THE WORLD.

From *"Be Somebody"* by Mary Crowley

CHIPPED BEEF CASSEROLE

1 cup dry (uncooked) shell macaroni	1 cup sharp cheddar cheese, shredded
1 can cream of mushroom soup	¼ onion, minced
1 cup milk	1 4-oz. pkg. chipped beef, snipped fine

Place macaroni in buttered baking dish. Pour the other ingredients over macaroni. Do not stir. Cover and place in refrigerator 6 to 8 hours or overnight. When ready to bake, take a spoon and go to the bottom of the casserole in several places without stirring. Bake 1 hour at 350°.

BAKED SPAGHETTI

1 onion	1 cup water
1 lb. ground beef	½ lb. uncooked spaghetti
1 tsp. salt	1 cup grated cheese
1 envelope spaghetti seasoning	Garlic
1 large jar Ragu	Pepper to taste

Brown meat, adding onion, garlic, salt and pepper. Stir in seasoning, sauce and water. Cover and simmer 25 minutes. Break half spaghetti (raw) into lightly greased casserole, cover with half the sauce and half the cheese. Repeat layers. Cover and bake at 350° for 30 minutes covered and 15 minutes uncovered.

—Susan Bahner

PEPSI CHICKEN

1 stick oleo	1 chicken, cut up
1 can Pepsi	Salt and pepper to taste
1 20-oz. bottle ketchup	

Melt oleo in electric skillet. Place chicken in skillet and pour Pepsi and ketchup over chicken. Cook at 250° for 2 hours. Serves 4.

—Cheryl Cape

ITALIAN SPAGHETTI

1 medium onion, chopped	1 tsp. chili powder
1 lb. ground beef	½ tsp. salt
1 15-oz. can tomato sauce or tomato juice	½ tsp. parsley flakes
	1 tsp. white sugar
1 6-oz. can tomato paste	1-3 bay leaves
Salt and pepper to taste	Garlic salt if desired

Brown ground beef and onion in skillet. Add the tomato sauce (or juice), tomato paste, salt and pepper to taste. Add remaining ingredients and simmer for 1 hour. Served on cooked spaghetti. Serves 6.

—Gayle Gieselman

GREEN BEAN CASSEROLE

2 lbs. ground beef	6 potatoes
1 can green beans, drained	2 eggs
1 onion, chopped	Butter
2 cans tomato soup, no water	

Cook potatoes and whip with butter and eggs. Brown meat and onion. Add green beans and soup. Put in casserole dish Spoon potato mixture on top. Bake at 350° until bubbly. About 20 minutes.

—Becky Clubb

GOOD 'N' EASY CROCKPOT DINNER

Sirloin steak or round steak	4-5 cubes beef bouillon
Mushrooms	1 lg. onion
3-4 pkgs. brown gravy mix	

Put the meat in the crockpot either overnight or all day for about 12 hours with the onion and bouillon cubes. Approximately one hour before serving, add mushrooms and gravy mix. That's it! Serve over baked potatoes. Recommended for a dinner when you have a group in and can't spend a lot of time fussing over the meal.

—Cathy Brown

EVERYDAY MEAT LOAF

⅔ cup dried bread crumbs
1 cup tomato juice or milk
1½-2 lbs. ground beef
2 eggs, beaten

¼ cup onion
½ tsp. sage
1 tsp. salt
Dash of pepper

PIQUANTE SAUCE

3 Tsp. brown sugar
¼ cup catsup

¼ tsp. nutmeg
1 tsp. dried mustard, optional

Soak crumbs in juice or milk. Add ground beef and other ingredients. Mix well and form into individual loaves and cover with piquante sauce. Bake at 350° degrees for 45 minutes.

—Gloria Crenshaw

GRANDMA ROY'S MEAT PIE

2 lbs. ground pork
1 lb. ground beef
½ tsp. cloves
½ tsp. cinnamon
½ tsp. poultry seasoning

2 cups onion, diced
3 large potatoes, cooked and
   mashed
2 Pastry shells

Cook pork and beef with water. Saute onions in butter. Combine all ingredients, pour into pastry shell, top with pastry shell and bake until golden brown in 350° oven.

—Karen Orr

ITALIAN BEEF

5 lbs. roast beef
Onion
½ tsp. onion salt
½ tsp. garlic salt
½ tsp. oregano

¼ tsp. basil
½ tsp. Italian seasoning
½ tsp. seasoned salt
1 tsp. Accent

Bake roast with onion until done. Cool then add remaining ingredients. Let stand overnight. Next day, slice beef thinly, bring to boil then bake at 350° for 30 to 40 minutes. Serve over French bread.

—Linda Hollinshead

80

BEEF STROGANOFF

2 lbs. beef — ¼" thick, sirloin
or top round
1 med. onion, chopped fine
2 cups meat broth (2 bouillon
cubes)
½ lbs. fresh or 1 can
mushrooms

3 Tbls. tomato paste
1 cup sour cream
1 tsp. Worcestershire sauce
⅓ cup butter
Sliced beets, 1 per person

Strip and cut meat to bite size. Melt butter and brown meat and onions. When brown, add broth and beets. Simmer for 25 minutes or until meat is tender. In another skillet slowly brown mushrooms. Blend together sour cream, tomato paste and Worcestershire sauce. When meat is tender, remove from heat and add mushrooms. Then in small amounts, stirring constantly, add mixture. Return to heat and stir constantly until hot. Serve over rice or noodles.

—Donna Mauricio

IMPOSSIBLE TACO PIE

1 lb. ground beef
½ cup onion, chopped
1 envelope taco seasoning mix
1 4-oz. can chopped green
chilies, drained
1¼ cups milk

¾ cup Bisquick baking mix
3 eggs
2 tomatoes, sliced
1 cup Monterrey Jack or
cheddar cheese, shredded

Heat oven to 400°. Grease a 10" to 11½" pie plate. Cook and stir beef and onion until brown; drain. Stir in seasoning mix. Spread in plate; top with chilies. Beat milk, baking mix and eggs until smooth (15 seconds in blender on high or 1 minute with hand beater). Pour into plate. Bake 25 minutes. Top with tomatoes and cheese. Bake until knife inserted into center comes out clean, 8 to 10 minutes longer. Cool 5 minutes. Serve with sour cream, chopped tomatoes, shredded lettuce and shredded cheese if desired. 6 to 8 servings.

—Pat Gamble

JUST DUMP AND MIX MEAT LOAF

4 lbs. ground beef	1 48-oz. jar spaghetti sauce
4 eggs	1 tsp. salt, or to taste
2 cups Contadina seasoned	1 tsp. pepper
bread crumbs	2 Tbls. parsley flakes, dried
1 cup Parmesan cheese, grated	

Microwave: Crumble beef in large mixing bowl. Add all ingredients, but only one-half jar of sauce. Divide into two casserole dishes and mold into shape. Cover with plastic wrap and microwave on high for 15-20 minutes. Drain. Add remaining sauce and microwave on high for 5 minutes. Let stand covered for 5 minutes and serve.

Conventional Oven: Cover with aluminum foil and bake for 1 hour at 350°. Drain. Add remaining sauce and bake for 15 minutes. Serve. This is not an ordinary meat loaf. It's so good it just melts in your mouth. All ages love it. Never have any leftovers with this recipe.

Makes two meat loaves. Just make the mess once and freeze one. An easy and quick dinner — just heat and serve in individual slices or all at once.

—Diane Hayden

MEATBALLS AND SAUCE

1½ lbs. ground beef	1 Tbls. parsley
¾ cup dry bread crumbs	1 tsp. salt
⅓ cup onion, minced	⅛ tsp. pepper
¼ cup milk	½ tsp. Worcestershire sauce
1 egg	

SAUCE

1 12-oz. container chili sauce	1 10-oz. container grape jelly

Mix together all of the dry ingredients, then add the non-dry ingredients. Make into balls and brown. Combine chili sauce and jelly and add the balls to mixture. Makes 5 dozen.

—Linda Hollinshead

HAM LOAF

2½ lbs. smoked ham, ground
½ lb. fresh ham, ground

2 eggs
1 cup cracker crumbs, rolled

GLAZE

½ cup brown sugar
½ cup vinegar, scant
½ cup water

¾ tsp. dry mustard
⅓ cup pineapple juice

Combine loaf ingredients and mix well. Make loaf in 9"x13" pan. Bake at 350° for 1¼ hours. Remove from oven, drain drippings and add glaze. Return to oven for 30 minutes, basting every 5 minutes.

—Helen Taylor

BREAKFAST PIZZA

1 lb. bulk pork sausage
1 8-oz. pkg. refrigerated
   crescent rolls
1 cup frozen loose pack hash
   brown potatoes, thawed
1 cup (4 oz.) sharp cheddar
   cheese, shredded
5 eggs, beaten

¼ cup milk
½ tsp. salt
⅛ tsp. pepper
2 Tbls. Parmesan cheese,
   grated
Whole pimentos, optional
Fresh oregano, optional

Cook sausage in a medium skillet until browned; drain and set aside. Separate crescent dough into 8 triangles; place triangles with elongated points toward center in a greased 12 inch pizza pan. Press bottom and sides to form a crust; seal perforations. Spoon sausage over dough; sprinkle with hash brown potatoes and cheddar cheese. Combine eggs, milk, salt and pepper; pour over sausage mixture. Sprinkle top with Parmesan cheese. Bake at 375° for 25 minutes. Garnish with pimentos and oregano, if desired. Yields 6 to 8 servings.

—Dixie Haworth

BARBECUED PORK

6 pork steaks, cubed	3 cups catsup
2 onions, diced	6 Tbls. tarragon vinegar
3 garlic cloves, sliced	3 Tbls. Worcestershire sauce
3 stalks celery, diced	3 tsp. salt
2 small green peppers, diced	¾ tsp. pepper

Rub a small amount of fat from meat over bottom of frying pan, add meat and brown well. Combine all other ingredients and pour mixture over the meat. Cover, reduce heat to simmer and cook for 45 minutes or until meat is tender. Turn occasionally during cooking. Serve over rice. Serves about 7.

—Marilyn Smith

BAKED BEANS

2 lbs. lean ground beef	3 16-oz. cans pork and beans
1 medium onion, chopped	2 Tbls. prepared mustard
2 small green peppers, seeded and chopped	Dash of hot sauce
	Dash of Worcestershire sauce
½ cup firmly packed brown sugar	

Combine meat, onion and peppers in a skillet and cook until meat is browned and onion is tender. Drain. Combine meat mixture with remaining ingredients in a bowl; stir well. Pour into a lightly greased 4-quart baking dish. Bake in 350° oven for 1 hour. Yields 20 to 25 servings.

—Sue Cornelius

I never go out to meet a new day
Without first asking God as I kneel down to pray
To give me the strength and courage to be
As tolerant of others as He is to me.

—Ned Nichols

ENTREES . . .

JAMBALAYA

2 lbs. smoked pork sausage,
   cut in small pieces
8 pork chops, cut in 1" pieces
Chicken pieces (use meaty
   pieces such as thighs and
   drumsticks)
3 large onions, chopped
1 bunch celery, chopped
2 Tbls. parsley

3 beef boullion cubes
3 chicken boullion cubes
1 tsp. Kitchen Bouquet
4 cups long grain rice
3 Tbls. lemon juice
Salt and pepper to taste
   (about 1 Tbls. salt, ½ tsp.
   cayenne pepper)

Brown all the meat separately and remove from the pot, preferably an iron one. Brown seasonings in the same pot as the meat. Dissolve boullion cubes in water and add Kitchen Bouquet to the mixture. Add other seasonings to taste. Measure rice and place in a large roasting pan. Pour 8 cups liquid over this. Use the boullion water and plain water to make 8 cups. Layer the meat and the sauteed seasonings over the rice. Add lemon juice and stir. Cook in 350° oven until all the liquid is absorbed by rice. Lift the cover of the pan only to check the absorption. This is a large recipe, but it freezes extremely well. Just freeze in casserole dishes, then reheat in a preheated 350° oven until hot. It is sometimes a good idea to have the casserole partially thawed before you heat it.

—Dorothy Cutrer

QUICK PORK AND POTATO BAKE

6 pork chops
1 can cream of mushroom soup
Salt and pepper

Medium sharp cheese, grated
Chopped onion
Tater-Tots, frozen

Place pork chops in an oblong cake pan. Salt and pepper lightly. Spoon soup over top of chops, grate cheese all over lightly. Sprinkly with a little chopped onion. Place frozen Tater-Tots all over the top of this so meat is completely covered. Sprinkle more cheese over this. Bake 1 hour at 350°. Turn heat down to 200° and bake an additional 15 minutes. Serve with cottage cheese or tossed salad for a complete meal.

—Nell Herrington

85

ENTREES...

GREEN CHILI SAUSAGE SWIRLS

PASTRY

4 cups Bisquick
½ cup margarine, softened
1 cup milk

FILLING

1 lb. roll pork sausage, hot
    (Owens is good)
1 lb. roll pork sausage, mild
1 4-oz. can diced green chilies
½ medium onion, chopped
    fine

Mix pastry ingredients thoroughly and chill for one-half hour. Mix filling ingredients and let stand at room temperature. Divide dough in half. Roll out each to a large rectangle of about one-fourth inch thickness. Spread one-half sausage mixture completely over each piece of dough. Roll up as for jelly roll. Wrap in plastic wrap and freeze for **only** 1 hour. Remove from freezer and slice one-third inch thick. Freeze until ready to use. (Freeze on wax paper on cookie sheet, then pop them in a plastic bag for storage in freezer.) Bake in preheated 400° oven for 20 minutes (cover cookie sheets with foil for easier clean-up). Makes 60 to 70.

DELIGHTFUL PAN-FRIED FILLETS

1½ lb. fish (flounder, sea
    trout, or any good, thin
    white fillet of fish)
1 egg
2 Tbls. mayonnaise
1 Tbls. cream or milk
½ cup flour

½ cup seasoned bread crumbs
1 stick margarine or butter
2 Tbls. onion, grated
2 Tbls. cooking sherry
Lemon Pepper seasoning
Grated Parmesan cheese

Mix egg, mayonnaise and cream; dip fillets, then coat with flour and crumbs. Fry until lightly browned in skillet with butter, onion and sherry. Sprinkle with Lemon Pepper seasoning and cheese.

— *Rosemarie Celozzi*

To ease another's heartache is to forget one's own.
—Abraham Lincoln

86

CHOPSTICK TUNA

1 can condensed cream of
   mushroom soup
¼ cup water
2 cups chow mein noodles
1 6½ or 7-oz. can tuna,
   drained and flaked

1 cup celery, sliced
¼ cup chopped onion
Dash pepper

In mixing bowl, combine the soup and water. Add 1 cup of the noodles, the tuna, celery, onion and pepper. Toss lightly. Turn into 10"x6"x2" baking dish. Sprinkle remaining noodles on top and bake in 375° oven for 30 minutes or until casserole is heated through. Makes 4 servings.

—*Audrey Jean Warner*

TUNA CHEESE SANDWICHES

2 6½-oz. cans tuna, drained
3 eggs, hard-boiled and
   chopped
¼ cup onion, finely chopped
1 cup cheese, cheddar or other
   favorite, cubed

¼ tsp. celery salt
Salt and pepper to taste
Mayonnaise
12 slices bread or 6 ham-
   burger buns, halved

Mix tuna, eggs, onion, cheese, celery salt, salt and pepper. Add mayonnaise until desired consistency is reached. Spread on top of bread or buns. Place in oven and broil 4-5 inches from heat 3-5 minutes or until cheese bubbles. Serve immediately.

—*Lynn Letarski*

Every morning lean your arm awhile upon the window sill of Heaven and gaze upon your God. Then with that vision in your heart, turn strong to meet the day.

From *"Be Somebody"* by Mary Crowley

SHRIMP CREOLE

1½ cups onion, chopped
1 cup celery, finely chopped
2 medium green peppers,
    finely chopped
2 garlic cloves, minced
¼ cup butter or margarine
1 15-oz. can tomato sauce
1 cup water

2 tsp. snipped parsley
1 tsp. salt
⅛ tsp. cayenne red pepper
2 bay leaves, crushed
14-16 oz. fresh or frozen
    cleaned raw shrimp
3 cups hot cooked rice

Cook and stir onion, celery, green pepper and garlic in butter until onion is tender. Remove from heat; stir in tomato sauce, water and seasonings. Simmer uncovered 10 minutes. Add water if needed. If using frozen shrimp, rinse under running cold water to remove ice glaze. Add shrimp and heat to boiling. Cover and cook on medium heat 10-20 minutes or until shrimp are pink and tender. Serve over rice. Makes 6 servings.

—Helen Whitaker

SHRIMP MOLD

1 can tomato soup
1 8-oz. pkg. Philadelphia
    cream cheese
1½ Tbls. Knox unflavored
    gelatin (1 pkg.)

2 cans medium shrimp
    (or 1 lb.)
½ cup mayonnaise
¾ cup celery, chopped
¼ cup onions, chopped

Dissolve gelatin in ½ cup cold water. Heat tomato soup to boiling and dissolve cream cheese in soup. Add gelatin and let cool. Grind celery and onions together. Add mayonnaise, celery and onions to soup, then season to taste. Grind shrimp, and when mixture begins to thicken, add shrimp. Pour in mold and cool in refrigerator. Serve as a dip with crackers, or serve as a sandwich spread.

—Patricia Lormand

GREEK BAKED FISH WITH VEGETABLES

2 lbs. whole fish (turbot is
   inexpensive)
¼ cup Crisco oil
1½ cups onion, chopped
2 garlic cloves, minced
1½ cups canned tomatoes
½ cup parsley, snipped
½ tsp. salt
¼ tsp. pepper
2 Tbls. lemon juice
1 lb. fresh spinach
½ cup dry white wine,
   optional
¼ cup fresh dill, snipped (or 1
   Tbls. dry dill weed)

Heat oven to 350°. In skillet sauté onions in oil until soft. Add garlic, tomatoes, parsley, dill, salt and pepper; cook 10 minutes (simmer). Sprinkle fish lightly with salt to taste. Sprinkle with lemon juice. Arrange tomato mixture in 9"x12" baking dish. Lay fish on top. Arrange spinach on top of fish. Pour wine over all. Cover with foil and bake for 50 minutes. Uncover and bake another 15 minutes. Serve with cornbread. Serves 4-6

—Betty Cantrell

CRAB-RICE MIXTURE ON TOMATOES

1 pkg. (6-8 oz.) frozen crab
   meat or 7½ oz. (1 can)
   crab or chicken
1¼ cups rice, cooked and
   chilled
⅓ cup celery, chopped
2 green onions, chopped
1 Tbls. lemon juice
½ tsp. soy sauce
¼ tsp. salt
⅛ tsp. pepper
½ cup mayonnaise
6 medium tomatoes
Crisp lettuce

Drain crab. Break into pieces. Combine crab with rice, celery and onions. Mix lemon juice and seasonings with mayonnaise. Add to crab mixture and toss to coat lightly. Chill well. Fill tomato rosettes with crab mixture. Serve on bed of crisp lettuce.

—Ann Kottmier

Kindness is a language which the deaf can hear and the blind can read.
—Mark Twain

SALMON CASSEROLE

¼ cup onion	1 can mushroom soup
¼ cup celery	½ cup cheese, shredded
1 Tbls. butter	2 cups rice, cooked
2 #303 cans salmon	Cornflake or bread crumbs

Combine salmon, soup, cheese and rice. Saute onion and celery in butter. Add celery and onions to salmon mixture. Pour in casserole dish. Top with cornflake crumbs or bread crumbs. Bake 30 minutes in 350° oven.

—Julie Jones

GREAT CLAM CHOWDER SOUP

1 stick margarine	2 cans Campbell's New England clam chowder
1 lg. onion, chopped	
1 qt. half and half	3 cans Campbell's potato soup
1 stalk celery	1 can minced clams, undrained

Saute onions and celery in margarine. Mix with all other ingredients in a Dutch oven. Bake at 200° for 4 hours. Stir hourly.

—Linda Hollinshead

TUNA IN SPAGHETTI SAUCE

1 28-oz. can Hunt's tomato sauce	1 medium onion, finely chopped
	Salt and pepper
1 lb. spaghetti	¼ tsp. oregano
1 can tuna (6½-oz.) packed in oil	Garlic powder

Squeeze oil out of tuna can into medium sauce pan. When oil is hot add onion. Fry onion about 5 minutes. Add sauce with salt and pepper to taste, ¼ teaspoon oregano, a little garlic powder, and the tuna. Stir, partially cover and simmer. Now proceed to cook spaghetti. When spaghetti is done, sauce will be also. This takes a total of 1 hour and your family will love it. You can substitute salmon for tuna.

—Annette Patterson

CHICKEN PAPRIKA

1 chicken, cut up
2 Tbls. Crisco shortening
2 Tbls. oleo
1 onion, chopped
1 tsp. paprika

1 cup water
2 Tbls. cold water
1 Tbls. flour
½ cup sour cream
Salt and pepper

Melt oleo and Crisco. Brown chicken and remove from pan. Add more Crisco and oleo if needed. Brown chopped onion then add water and paprika. Put the chicken in and cook until done, about an hour. Make paste and pour over chicken. Cook about 10 minutes.

DUMPLINGS

2 eggs
½ cup milk
1 tsp. salt

1 cup flour
Salt and pepper

Mix to a firm batter. Drop by teaspoon into boiling water. Cook 10 minutes or until they are tender. Add to chicken and paprika.

—Karen Rieuitti

CHICKEN ALMONDINE

8 chicken breasts
8 oz. sour cream
1 can cream of chicken soup

1½-2 sticks margarine/butter
1 stack Ritz crackers
Slivered almonds

Remove skins from chicken, place in baking dish single layer. Mix sour cream and cream of chicken soup and pour over chicken undiluted. Melt margarine/butter and pour over chicken. Crush crackers and spread over top of chicken, put slivered almonds on top and bake uncovered at 350° about 30 minutes or until lightly brown.

—Fern Mears

Today is the only day I have for family tenderness — for graciousness — for kindness — for love. Say "I love you" to someone today.

CHICKEN FRICASSEE WITH DUMPLINGS

4½-5 lb. stewing chicken, cut up	2 tsp. paprika, if desired
1 cup all-purpose flour	1 cup water
2 tsp. salt	3 Tbls. flour
¼ tsp. pepper	Milk
	Shortening or salad oil

DUMPLINGS

1½ cups all-purpose flour	3 Tbls. shortening
2 tsp. baking powder	¾ cup milk
¾ tsp. salt	

Wash chicken pieces and pat dry. Mix 1 cup flour, salt, pepper, and paprika. Coat chicken with flour mixture. Heat thin layer of shortening in large skillet; brown chicken on all sides. Drain off fat and reserve. To skillet, add water, and if desired, chopped onion, lemon juice or herbs such as rosemary or thyme leaves. Cover tightly. Cook chicken slowly 2½ to 3½ hours or until fork tender, adding water if necessary. Remove chicken to warm platter; keep warm. Pour off liquid in skillet and reserve. To make gravy, heat 3 tablespoons reserved fat in skillet. Blend in 3 tablespoons flour. Cook over low heat, stirring until mixture is smooth and bubbly. Remove from heat. Add enough milk to reserved liquid to measure 3 cups; pour into skillet. Heat to boiling, stirring constantly. Boil and stir 1 minute. Return chicken to gravy.

To prepare dough for dumplings, measure flour, baking powder and salt into bowl. If desired, add 3 tablespoons snipped chives. Cut in shortening thoroughly until mixture looks like meal. Stir in milk. Drop by spoonful into hot chicken. Cook uncovered for 10 minutes. Cover and cook 20 minutes longer.

Note: To fricassee a broiler-fryer chicken, select 3-4 pound broiler-fryer chicken and cook slowly 45 minutes or until fork tender.

—*Sharon Pierson*

The smallest deed is better than the grandest intention.

—Larry Eisenberg

CHICKEN AND BROCCOLI CASSEROLE

2 10-oz. pkgs. frozen broccoli
  pieces
2 cups chicken breasts
  (about 3), cooked and diced
2 cans cream of chicken soup
1 cup mayonnaise

1 tsp. lemon juice
½ tsp. curry powder
½ cup bread crumbs
½ cup cheddar cheese,
  shredded

Cook broccoli, drain most liquid, place in casserole dish. Cut up cooked chicken and layer over broccoli in casserole dish. Combine soup, mayonnaise, lemon juice and curry powder. Mix well and pour over chicken and broccoli. Cover top with bread crumbs, sprinkle with cheddar cheese and bake in 350° oven for 30 minutes or until all is hot through. This can be prepared and refrigerated earlier in the day but must be baked a little longer if chilled.

—Kathy Herman

CHICKEN SUPREME SANDWICH

4 cooked chicken breasts (or
  approximately the same
  amount of any meat part
  of the chicken you may
  have left over)
1 can Franco American
  chicken gravy

1 can cream of mushroom
  soup
1 jar pimento, optional
1 can water chestnuts, sliced
2 Tbls. onions, chopped
1 loaf sandwich bread

COATING

1 twin pack potato chips
6 eggs

4 Tbls. milk

Mix filling ingredients together. Cut the crust from the bread and make sandwiches using two slices of bread with filling inside. Wrap in foil and freeze. To make the coating, mix beaten eggs and milk together. Crush potato chips. When ready to make sandwiches, dip frozen sandwiches in the egg batter and then into the crushed potato chips. Place on well-buttered cookie sheet and bake for one hour at 300°.

—Mary Whisenhunt

ENTREES . . .

CHICKEN WILD RICE CASSEROLE

2 cups chicken, cooked and
  diced
1 box long grain wild rice
1 can mushroom soup

1 can mushrooms
½ lb. cheddar cheese
2 Tbls. butter or margarine
2 Tbls. flour

Melt margarine in pan and add flour. Mix well and add mushroom soup and mushrooms. Set aside, but keep warm. Buy the cut of chicken you prefer. Boil, remove from bone, cut up and set aside. Take 2½ cups of the broth from the chicken and cook the rice by using directions on package, using broth instead of water. Use a casserole dish and layer the mushroom mixture, chicken and the wild rice. Alternate until all is used. Put slices of cheese on top. Put in oven long enough to melt cheese. Serves 4.

—Nancy Howard

TURKEY OR CHICKEN RICE CASSEROLE

4 Tbls. butter
2 cups boullion or mushroom
  juice
1 cup whipping cream or
  evaporated milk
5 Tbls. flour
1½-2 cups cooked rice

1 8-oz. can mushrooms,
  drained
1 10-oz. pkg. frozen peas
2-3 cups chicken or turkey,
  cooked
Paprika
Bread crumbs

Mix rice, mushrooms, peas, and chicken or turkey together in baking dish. Mix butter, boullion, milk and flour together and pour over chicken mixture. Sprinkle with bread crumbs and paprika. Bake in 325° oven for 30 minutes. Serves 6.

—Donna Parsley

Every evening I turn "worries" over to God. He's going to be up all night anyway.

From *"Be Somebody"* by Mary Crowley

CHICKEN AND SAFFRON RICE

1 2½ to 3 lb.broiler/fryer
   chicken, ready to cook, cut
   up and salted
1 garlic clove, minced
¼ cup salad oil
1 cup long grain rice,
   uncooked
1 12-oz. can vegetable juice
   cocktail (1½ cups)
¾ cup water
1 3-oz. can (⅔ cup)
   mushrooms, broiled,
   sliced, undrained

1 cup celery, chopped
1 cup onion, chopped
1 tsp. salt
¼ tsp. pepper
1 tsp. dried marjoram
   (crushed)
⅓ cup ripe olives, halved
½ 10-oz. pkg. frozen peas,
   (about 1 cup), thawed
1 tomato, cut in wedges
Pinch powdered saffron

Season chicken pieces with salt. Heat garlic in oil. Brown chicken slowly in hot oil; remove chicken. Add rice, brown slowly, stirring occasionally. Stir in vegetable juice, water, undrained mushrooms, celery, onion, salt, pepper, marjoram, saffron and olives. Bring to boiling. Turn mixture into a 13"x9"x2" baking dish. Top with the chicken pieces. Cover dish tightly with foil. Bake at 375° about 1 hour. Uncover and sprinkle thawed peas around chicken. Top with tomato wedges, season with salt and pepper. Cover dish again and bake 15 minutes longer. Makes 6 servings.

—Jan Brodl

CHICKEN AND RICE CASSEROLE

1½ cubes margarine (¾ cup)
4 beef boullion cubes
1 pkg. dry onion soup mix

2 cups regular long grain
   white rice
4 cups water
1 whole chicken, cut up

Melt margarine and boullion cubes, then add soup mix, rice and water. Mix well and pour into buttered casserole dish. Salt and pepper drained chicken and place on top of rice mixture. Bake in covered casserole dish at 350° for 1½ hours. Serves 8.

—Gail Scott

CHICKEN SUPREME

1 cup dry rice
6 pieces of chicken
1 cup cooking sherry

1 can mushroom soup
1 can celery soup
1 pkg. dry onion soup mix

Put rice in bottom of pan and lay chicken parts on top. Mix sherry, mushroom soup and celery soup. Pour over rice and chicken. Sprinkle dry onion soup on top and bake at 350° for two hours.

—Carol Mervan

CHICKEN CASSEROLE

1 chicken, boiled and deboned
1 can chicken soup
1 can celery soup
1 can chicken broth

1 small onion, diced
1 can chow mein noodles
2 cups potato chips
Salt and pepper to taste

Mix chicken, soups, broth, onion, salt and pepper. Add the noodles, in a buttered casserole dish. Top with crushed potato chips. Bake in 370° oven for 1 hour.

—Marge Christian

CHICKEN NOODLE CASSEROLE

1 4-lb. chicken
1 lg. pkg. noodles

1 can cream of mushroom soup
1 cup crushed cornflakes

Cook chicken until tender. Cook noodles in salted water until tender. Drain, add chicken and soup to noodles, make a gravy with broth, add to chicken, soup and noodles. Mix well, turn into pan and top with cornflakes. Bake at 350° for 30 minutes.

—Stella Sterling

You have freedom of choice, but not freedom from choice.
—Wendell Jones

EASY CHICKEN DIVAN

3 cans asparagus, long stalk,
   drained
4 chicken breasts, cooked and
   boned
2 cans condensed cream of
   chicken soup

¾ cup mayonnaise
1 tsp. lemon juice
½ cup sharp cheese, shredded
1 cup soft bread crumbs
1 Tbls. butter, melted

Arrange asparagus in greased 12"x7½"x2" baking dish. Layer chicken on top of asparagus. Combine soup, mayonnaise and lemon juice. Pour over chicken and asparagus. Sprinkle with cheese. Combine bread crumbs and butter, sprinkle over all. Bake in 350° oven for 35 minutes. 8-10 servings.

—Rita Angelo

CHICK AND CHIPS

1 can (1¼ cup) condensed
   cream of chicken soup
1 cup chicken, cooked and
   cubed (or 5 oz. can boned
   chicken)

½ cup milk
1¼ cups potato chips, crushed
1 cup green peas, cooked and
   drained

Preheat oven to 375°. Empty soup into a 1-quart casserole dish and add milk. Mix thoroughly. Stir in chicken (or you may use tuna) and 1 cup of potato chips and peas. Sprinkle top with remaining ¼ cup of chips. Bake for 25 minutes at 375°.

—Irma Holzworth

CHICKEN CASSEROLE

2 large fryers, boiled and
   boned, seasoned to taste
1 can cream of mushroom
   soup

1 can cream of chicken soup
2 cups chicken broth
Pepperidge Farm stuffing mix
Butter

Butter casserole dish, put in chicken that has been cut in small serving pieces. Add the soups, broth and stuffing mix. Dot with butter. Cook in 350° oven for 30 minutes. Serves 8-10 people.

—Irene Noblin

CHICKEN GUMBO

3½ lb. broiler-fryer chicken,
   cut up
2 cups water
1 garlic clove, finely chopped
2 tsp. salt
1 large bay leaf, crumbled
2 large celery stalks with
   leaves, cut diagonally
   making about ½ cup

½ cup onion, chopped
1 28-oz. can whole tomatoes
1 10-oz. pkg. frozen okra
1 7-oz. can whole kernel corn
⅓ cup regular rice, uncooked
½ tsp. red pepper sauce

Heat chicken pieces, water, salt, garlic and bay leaf to boiling in Dutch oven. Reduce heat, cover and simmer until chicken is done, about 45 minutes. Remove chicken from broth, strain broth., Refrigerate chicken and broth. When cool, remove chicken from bones (skin may be removed, if desired). Cut chicken in bite-size pieces. Skim excess fat from broth and place broth and chicken in Dutch oven. Stir in celery, onion and tomatoes with liquid. Break up tomatoes with fork. Heat to boiling. Reduce heat, cover and simmer until okra and rice are tender, 20-30 minutes. garnish with snipped parsley.

—Donna Borland

CHICKEN AND DRESSING CASSEROLE

1 3-lb. chicken
1 can cream of chicken soup
1 can cream of celery soup
1 small can Pet Milk

1 Tbls. sage
1 pkg. Pepperidge Farms
   cornbread mix
1 cup chicken broth

Cook chicken, skin and debone. Arrange in long cake pan or casserole dish. Add soups and milk. Mix and add the remaining ingredients so that cornbread will be on the top. Bake at 450° for 20 minutes

—Darla Givens

What sunshine is to flowers, smiles are to humanity.
—Joseph Addison

SPIFFY SPANISH CHICKEN

2 chickens, quartered
½ Tbls. Kitchen Bouquet
2 Tbls. tomato sauce
Garlic powder
Salt
Oregano
6 potatoes, cut in quarters
½ cup olive oil

1 small can tomato sauce
2 garlic cloves, chopped
1 large onion, chopped
1 large green pepper in rings
1 small bottle olives, pitted
1 Tbls. capers
1 cup water

Preheat oven to 325°. In large baking pan, arrange chicken pieces. Mix together Kitchen Bouquet and 2 tablespoons tomato sauce. Brush mixture over chicken, covering well. Sprinkle with garlic powder, oregano and salt. In sauce pan, heat olive oil and quickly brown potatoes, drain and place around chicken. Add garlic, onion and peppers to olive oil and sauté until golden brown. Add tomato sauce, olives and capers and cook slowly for 10 minutes. Add water; and salt to taste. Bring to boil and then pour over chicken. Cover tightly and cook 1 hour at 325°. Serve over rice with peas. Yields 8 servings.

—Dorothy Gonzales

SWEET AND SOUR CHICKEN

2½ lbs. chicken, cut into eight
   pieces
¼ cup all-purpose flour
1 tsp. salt
1 can (1 lb.) tomatoes, broken
   up (or 2 small cans of
   tomato sauce)

¼ cup oil
1 Tbls. brown sugar
1½ tsp. lemon juice
1 Tbls. Worcestershire sauce

Dredge chicken with flour and salt. Heat oil in skillet. Simmer covered 45 minutes.

—Barbara McDonald

Success does for living what sunshine does for stained glass.

—Bob Talbert

CURRY CHICKEN

1 whole chicken	½ tsp. poultry seasoning
¾ oz. curry	1 Tbls. tomato paste or
1 medium onion	ketchup
4 large garlic cloves	2 Tbls. vegetable oil or Crisco

Cut chicken into eight or ten pieces, removing as much fat as possible. Add salt, lemon juice or vinegar and rub in well about an hour before cooking. Wash thoroughly and squeeze all the water when ready to cook. Mix curry powder into smooth paste with water, adding part of onion finely chopped or grated with chopped or grated garlic, and poultry seasoning. Heat oil. When hot, add curry stirring well until slightly brown, then add chicken stirring very well. Cook until moisture is out. When chicken starts to fry, add water covering the chicken. Add tomato paste or ketchup and salt to taste. Boil chicken to whatever thickness of sauce you prefer, and chicken is properly cooked. It goes well with rice.

—Mrs. Dhanmatty Menzies

EXTRA SPECIAL CHICKEN

3 oz. sliced dried beef	6 slice bacon
3 large chicked breasts	1 can condensed cream of
(skinned, deboned and cut	mushroom soup
in half)	1 cup sour cream

Run cold water over dried beef and drain. Place in bottom of 12"x8"x2" dish. Place chicken over beef. Salt and pepper. Top each half of chicken breast with a slice of bacon. Bake uncovered in 350° oven for 30 minutes. Stir soup and sour cream together and spoon over chicken. Bake uncovered 25 minutes. Serve.

—Gail Gibbs

When one tugs at a single thing in nature, he finds it attached to the rest of the world.

—John Muir

MEXICAN RECIPE – FLAUTAS

1 lb. roast beef
12 corn tortillas
2 avocados
2 jalapeño peppers
¼ cup mayonnaise
¼ small onion

3 garlic cloves
¼ tsp. oregano
¼ tsp. salt
¼ tsp. lemon juice
Oil

Begin by cooking beef with 2 cloves of garlic and ¼ teaspoon oregano. Break beef into small stringy pieces. Put shredded beef on tortilla, roll and hold together with a toothpick. Pass rolled tortillas one at a time through hot oil, leaving them there until hard. Prepare guacamole topping. Roast jalapeño peppers, peeled and chopped. Mix together mashed avocados, jalapeño peppers, onion, garlic, salt, lemon juice and mayonnaise. Spread topping on prepared tortilla. Dish can be served with a side of Spanish rice and salsa.

—Dora Padilla

MEXICAN CHICKEN CASSEROLE

1 whole chicken
1 lg. pkg. crushed taco
   flavored Doritos

4 jalapeño peppers, chopped
1 can cream of chicken soup
1 can cheddar cheese soup

Boil chicken until done. Bone when cool. Crush Doritos. Dilute chicken soup with ½ cap of broth from boiled chicken. Layer crushed Doritos, chicken, peppers and chicken soup. On top of this, spread the can of cheddar cheese soup. Sprinkle with a few of the crushed Doritos. Bake in a 325° oven until casserole is bubbly. Serve with a salad and Doritos.

—Betty Whitehouse

Man — by himself is priced. For thirty pieces Judas sold himself, not Christ.

From *"Be Somebody"* by Mary Crowley

PAN-FRIED BARBECUED CHICKEN

1 frying chicken, cut up	3 tsp. garlic salt
1 can tomato soup, undiluted	3 Tbls. prepared mustard
½ cup brown sugar	3 Tbls. Worcestershire sauce
½ cup celery, chopped	Few drops Tabasco sauce

Brown unfloured chicken in frying pan. An electric frying pan is nice to use with this recipe. Add barbecue sauce which has previously been mixed in a bowl. Cook slowly until chicken and celery are well done. Delicious.

—Maxine Maycock

BARBECUED CHICKEN

2 lbs. chicken parts	2 Tbls. Worcestershire sauce
2 Tbls. shortening	2 Tbls. lemon juice
1 can tomato soup	2 tsp. prepared mustard
⅓ onion, celery	2-4 drops Tabasco sauce

In skillet brown chicken parts in shortening. Mix together and stir in remaining ingredients. Cover, simmer 45 minutes until chicken is tender, stirring now and then.

ELEGANT CHICKEN

4-5 chicken breasts, split	1 can cream of mushroom
1 4-oz. pkg. dried beef	soup
1 8-oz. ctn. sour cream	Paprika

Grease large baking dish and line bottom with dried beef. Place chicken on top of beef. Mix sour cream and mushroom soup together. Pour mixture over chicken and sprinkle with paprika. Do not add salt as the beef is salty. Bake uncovered at 275° for three hours. (This dish will "hold" nicely up to 45 minutes.)

—Ernestine Embrey

CHICKEN ELEGANTE

1 chicken breast per person,
  halved and deboned
½ pt. sour cream
1 can cream of mushroom
  soup

Loe's spicy or sliced beef
Garlic, salt and pepper to
  taste
Bacon

Line baking dish with spicy or sliced beef. Sprinkle chicken with garlic, salt and pepper. Wrap with one slice of bacon. Place in baking dish. Pour one can of cream of mushroom soup mixed with one half pint sour cream over chicken. Bake 1½ hours at 350°. Serve on bed of parsley and rice.

— Dorothy Risner

CHICKEN ENCHILADA CASSEROLE

7 qts. breast of chicken,
  cooked and diced
3 50-oz. cans cream of chicken
  mushroom soup, undiluted
2 27-oz. cans green chilies
3½ cups milk
½ cup instant minced onions

1 Tbls. garlic salt
7 doz. corn tortillas
2 cups ripe olives, chopped
3 lbs. Monterrey Jack cheese,
  shredded
2 2½-lb. containers sour
  cream

Mix chicken, chilies, soup, milk, onion and salt. Cut tortillas into bite-size pieces. Put half of tortillas in bottom of greased pans, cover with soup mixture, sprinkle with olives and cheese and remainder of tortillas. Spread sour cream on top. Bake in 325° oven for 45 minutes. Makes 2 large pans.

— Jo Oliver

A careless word may kindle strife,
A cruel word may wreck a life.
A bitter word may hate instill,
A brutal word may smite and kill.

A gracious word may smooth the way,
A joyous word may light the day.
A timely word may lessen stress,
A loving word may heal and bless.

CHICKEN À LA PERUVIAN

6 chicken breasts, boneless	6 slices Monterrey Jack cheese
6 slices bacon, thick cut	1 can Coca-Cola
6 thin slices ham	Sliced mushrooms

Cut open, flatten and leave chicken breast in one piece. Sprinkle with salt, garlic powder and a little bit of pepper. Place one slice of ham, one slice of cheese, a few mushroom slices and then roll it up. Fasten with a bacon slice. Repeat with remaining chicken breasts. Place chicken breasts on a baking pan, pouring Coca-Cola over them. Bake at 450° for 30 minutes.

—Aida Beretta

CHICKEN PARMIGIANA

6 chicken breasts, boned and skinned	¼ tsp. basil
Salt and pepper	¼ tsp. Italian seasoning
Italian flavored bread crumbs	⅛ tsp. garlic salt
Crisco oil	1 Tbls. butter
16 oz. DD	Parmesan cheese
16 oz. tomato sauce	Mozzarella cheese

Salt and pepper chicken, dip in egg and roll in bread crumbs. Brown fast in hot oil. Place in large (8½"x11" or larger) baking dish. Combine remaining ingredients except cheeses and bring to a boil. Simmer 10 minutes and pour over chicken. Sprinkle with Parmesan cheese and cover. Bake in 350° oven for 30 minutes. Remove from oven, cover with mozzarella cheese, and return to oven until cheese melts.

I passed a gleaming mirror a-shining in the sun.
'Twas but a wayside puddle for dainty feet to shun
But that small sheet of water was deep as clouds were high
For in its glinting surface was seen God's vast blue sky.

I would that I could feel assured that people passing me
Could overlook my littleness and something greater see.
That my small life with all its faults could show God's loving grace
And to the passerby reflect the beauty of His face.

ENTREES...

CHICKEN MARENGO

2½-3 lb. frying chicken, cut up
(my family likes this so
well, I use only white
meat)

1 pkg. spaghetto sauce mix
½ cup dry white wine
2 fresh tomatoes, quartered
¼ lb. fresh mushrooms

Place chicken parts in bottom of slow-cooking pot. Combine dry spaghetti sauce mix with wine; pour over chicken. Cover and cook on low 6 to 7 hours. Turn control to high, add tomatoes and mushrooms. Cover and cook on high 30 to 40 minutes or until tomatoes are done. Serve with rice, your favorite salad and your favorite bread and you have a delicious meal in minutes.

—Sue Cornelius

DOROTHY'S BAKED CHICKEN SALAD

4 Tbls. flour
4 Tbls margarine
1¼ cups chicken broth
1 cup celery, diced
2 tsp. green onion, minced
½ cup almonds or pecans,
chopped
2 eggs, hard-boiled and
chopped

½ tsp. salt
¼ tsp. pepper
¼ tsp. Worcestershire sauce
1½ Tbls. lemon juice
¾ cup mayonnaise
2-2½ cups cooked chicken
2 cups crushed potato chips,
divided use
Paprika

Make cream sauce with flour, margarine and broth. Add chicken and then other ingredients and mix thoroughly. Line baking dish with half of potato chips. Pour in chicken mixture and top with remainder of potato chips and paprika. Bake uncovered at 400° for 15 to 20 minutes. Serves 6 to 8.

—Dorothy Herbertson

Nothing in life is to be feared. It is only to be understood.
—Marie Curie

OLD-FASHIONED CHICKEN RAVIOLI

FILLING

1 lg. stewing chicken
1 lg. onion
3 stalks celery and leaves
Salt and pepper to taste
1½ loaves Italian bread,
   3 days old
½ lb. Romano cheese, grated
6 eggs
2 Tbls. fresh parsley, chopped
1 tsp. allspice or ½ tsp.
   nutmeg, optional

BASIC NOODLE DOUGH

4 cups flour
½ tsp. salt
2 eggs
5 Tbls. cold water
1 Tbls. milk
1 tsp. oil

Boil chicken with onion, celery, salt and pepper to taste until chicken is done. Add enough water to cover chicken. Simmer until tender or falls off bones. Cut 1½ loaves Italian bread into chunks and add enough broth to soften bread. Remove chicken meat from bone and chop to fine texture with knife. Mix and mash bread with hands. If too much broth, add more bread crumbs. Add chopped chicken to bread mix. Add the cheese, eggs, parsley, salt, pepper and allspice. Mix to meatball consistency.

Sift flour and salt into a large bowl. Make a well in center of flour. Add eggs, one at a time, mixing slightly after each addition. Gradually add the water, milk and oil. Mix well to make a stiff dough. Turn dough onto a lightly floured surface and knead.

To make ravioli, divide dough into fourths. Lightly roll each fourth ⅛" thick to form a rectangle. Cut dough lengthwise with pastry cutter into strips 5" wide. Place 2 teaspoons filling 1½" from narrow end in center of each strip. Continuing along the strip, place 2 teaspoons filling 3½" apart. Fold each strip in half lengthwise, covering the mounds of filling. To seal, press the edges together with the tines of a fork. Press gently between mounds to form rectangles about 3½" long. Cut apart with a pastry cutter and press the cut edges of rectangles with tines of fork to seal.

Bring to boiling in large sauce pan 7 quarts of water and 2 tablespoons salt. Gradually add 10 ravioli at a time. Boil rapidly uncovered for about 20 minutes or until tender. Remove with slotted spoon to drain. Place on a warm platter and top with tomato meat sauce. Sprinkle with Romano cheese. This recipe has been in my family for 150 years.

—Angela Alix

CHICKEN ENCHILADAS

4 chicken breasts, cooked and
    diced
1 can cream of chicken soup,
    undiluted
1 can cream of mushroom
    soup, undiluted
1 can green chilies, chopped
½ cup milk

1 Tbls. garlic salt
1 Tbls. instant minced onions
1 pkg. corn tortillas
1 sm. can chopped black
    olives
½ lb. Monterey Jack cheese,
    shredded
1 lg. carton sour cream

Mix chicken, soups, chilies, milk, onions, and garlic salt. Cut tortillas into bite-sized pieces. Put half of tortillas in bottom of greased 9"x13" pan. Cover with soup mixture. Sprinkle with olives, cheese and the rest of the tortillas. Spread sour cream over top. Bake at 325° for half an hour.

—*Jo Ann Engels*

CHICKEN SALAD CASSEROLE

3 cups chicken, diced
    (1 stewed chicken,
    deboned)
½ cup Miracle Whip
¼ cup mango, chopped
½ cup celery, chopped
½ cup onion, chopped

6 slices bread
1 can mushroom soup
2 eggs
1½ cups milk
1 cup cheese, grated
Salt and pepper
Grated cheese

Grease casserole dish. Tear up 3 slices of bread and put in bottom of dish. Combine chicken, Miracle Whip, mango, celery, and onions and pour over bread. Tear up 3 slices of bread for top. Mix together the eggs and milk and pour evenly over the casserole. Refrigerate overnight. Just before baking, cover the casserole with soup. Bake in 325° oven for 40 minutes. Remove from oven and put the cheese on top. Return to oven for 20 minutes more baking time.

MANICOTTI

BATTER

4 eggs
1 cup flour
1 cup water

FILLING

1½ lbs. ricotta cheese
4 Tbls. Parmesan cheese
2 pkgs. mozzarella cheese
1 tsp. salt
½ tsp. pepper
3 eggs
1 Tbls. parsley

SAUCE

1 lg. can Italian tomatoes
1 lg. can Italian tomato sauce
2 sm. cans tomato paste
2 Tbls. oil
½ tsp. garlic powder
½ tsp. onion powder
1 Tbls. Italian seasoning
1 Tbls. sugar
1 lb. ground beef
1 tsp. parsley flakes
Parmesan cheese
Mozzarella cheese

Combine eggs, flour and water. Beat well until smooth consistency. Using a small fry pan — on medium high heat, grease pan lightly with paper towel (use oil or margarine). Pour 2 tablespoons of batter into pan. Rotate so it is a circular "pancake"; cook ½ minute on one side and then flip over with fork; shake pan and transfer to paper towel. Layer each batch of two or three and continue to use paper towels to grease pan.

To make the filling, mix all ingredients together. Fill manicotti by spreading the filling over "pancake" leaving ½" empty around edge. Then roll pancake.

To make the sauce, combine all sauce ingredients except beef, tomato paste and cheese in a large pot. Cook ground beef in a pan separately — chopping and separating beef in a little bit of oil. Put tomato paste in this pan and stir well adding two cans of water (from tomato paste cans). Stir well and cook for 3 to 4 minutes. Add this to tomato sauce mixture and cook for at least one hour. Add water if consistency is too thick. Place sauce in baking pan. Place filled manicotti on top of sauce. Sprinkle with Parmesan cheese and Mozzarella cheese; cover with sauce and more Parmesan cheese. Bake in moderate oven (375°) for 40 minutes until you see "bubbling" of sauce. Let stand at least 15 minutes before serving.

—Rita Garbarini

NOODLE MANIA

1 16-oz. pkg. egg noodles	1 16-oz. pkg. Velveeta cheese
3 lbs. lean ground beef	Cashew nuts
2 medium onions, chopped	Milk
3 cans mushroom soup	
1 lg. jar pimento/olive pieces, chopped	

Cook noodles according to directions. Brown ground beef and onions. Add soup and pimento/olive pieces. Melt cheese and add milk to give right consistency. Mix all together. Add cashew nuts on top. Bake at 350° for 1 hour covered and ½ hour uncovered. Great for a crowd.

CROCKPOT PASTA

1 lb. box small shell macaroni	1 16-oz. can tomatoes
24 oz. mozzarella cheese, grated	2 lbs. ground beef
1 48-oz. can Prego spaghetti sauce	

Brown ground beef and drain. Add to spaghetti sauce and tomatoes. Simmer for a short while. Cook shells. Layer in crockpot as follows: Sauce, shells, more sauce, cheese. Repeat these layers until you use all ingredients, ending with grated cheese. Cook until hot and cheese is melted.

—Mary Lou Mickey

CHILI EGG PUFF

10 eggs	½ cup flour
1 tsp. baking powder	½ tsp. salt
1 pt. small curd cottage cheese	1 lb. Monterrey Jack cheese, grated
½ cup butter, melted	2 4-oz. cans green chilies, chopped
1 lb. sausage, browned	

Beat eggs until light and lemon-colored. Add remaining ingredients. Turn into a greased 13"x9"x2" pan and bake in 350° oven for 35 minutes. Serve with picante sauce.

PARTY SANDWICH

2 pkg. party rolls (Pepperidge
    Farm)
1 lb. ham, sliced paper thin
1 stick margarine, soft
1 small onion, grated

3 Tbls. poppy seeds
3 Tbls. Worcestershire sauce
3 Tbls. mustard
8-10 oz. Swiss cheese, grated

Combine margarine, onion, poppy seeds, Worcestershire sauce and mustard. Mix. Slice rolls and spread mixture. Layer cheese and ham, usually 3 or 4 layers of each. Cut sandwiches in two before baking. Cover with foil. Bake at 350° for 15 to 20 minutes. If freezing, cover with foil and return to bags.

—Carolyn Garbe

SCALLOPED OYSTERS

2 cans oysters
2 cups cracker crumbs
½ cup melted butter
½ tsp. salt

¾ cup cream
¼ cup juice from oysters
¼ tsp. Worcestershire sauce
Dash of pepper

Drain oysters, save juice. Combine cracker crumbs with butter, salt, pepper and Worcestershire sauce. Layer oysters in bottom of pan. Add layer of crumb mixture. Make three layers like this ending with the top layer cracker crumbs. Mix cream and oyster juice and pour over top of layers. Bake at 350° for 40 minutes.

—Andrea Crumly

HAPPY is the person:
    Who possesses unbounded enthusiasm for life,
    Who practices unlimited forgiveness toward others,
    Who expresses unending gratitude toward God,
    Who wages uncompromising war on injustice.

From *"Be Somebody"* by Mary Crowley

SPAGHETTI AND MEATBALLS

SAUCE

3 Tbls. cooking oil
1 medium onion
3 cloves garlic
3 cans tomato paste
8-9 cans water
3 Tbls. sugar
½ tsp. pepper
1 tsp. salt
½ lb. piece of pork (or 2 pork chops)

MEATBALLS

1 lb. ground veal or beef
½ lb. pork, ground
4-5 eggs
½ cup grated Italian cheese
1 cup bread crumbs
2 cloves garlic, finely chopped
1 sprig parsley, chopped
1 tsp. salt
¼ tsp. pepper

Macaroni (linguine)

Sauce: Chop onion and garlic and brown evenly in oil, add tomato paste and thin with water. Bring to rolling boil. Add sugar, salt, pepper, lower heat and simmer. Brown the pork and add to simmering sauce. Simmer for 1 hour or more (best if simmers all day!)

Meatballs: Mix all ingredients thoroughly, shape into balls and brown in oil. Add to simmering sauce and cook for 1 hour or more.

Macaroni: Break macaroni (linguine) in half. Cook macaroni in boiling salted water until tender (approx. 15 minutes after water comes to boil again). Run cold water over macaroni and drain well. Add sauce and sprinkle with grated cheese. Serve hot.

BREAKFAST BEFORE

1 lb. sausage, browned
1 tsp. salt
1 cup cheddar cheese
2 cups milk

6 eggs
1 tsp. mustard powder
4 slices bread

Layer bread, then layer browned sausage and cheese in baking dish. Combine remaining ingredients and pour mixture over bread. Cover and let set for at least 8 hours. Bake at 350° uncovered for 45 minutes.

—*Linda Hollinshead*

ENTREES...

PIZZA
DOUGH

1 cup milk (scald)
1 pkg. yeast
¼ cup hot tap water
4 cups flour

3 Tbls. sugar
3 Tbls. Crisco
1 tsp. salt
2 eggs

SAUCE

1 Tbls. sugar
Fried onion
Whole tomato

Celery leaves
Sausage, cheese, whatever you
 like in toppings

Cream together sugar, Crisco and salt. Add eggs and mix well. Add milk, mix well. Add 2 cups flour and mix well. Add 2 more cups of flour and yeast and stir well. Let dough rise 1 hour. Roll dough out (place a little oil in the pizza pan). Simmer sauce ingredients together. Pour 2 tablespoons sauce to cover dough. Add fried sausage or whatever on top. Sprinkle with a little oregano and Italian cheese. Bake at 400° for 15 minutes. Add some mozzarella cheese and return to oven until melted.

—Barbara Fanara

PIZZA CASSEROLE

2 lbs. ground beef
½ cup onion, chopped
2 cups twisted macaroni
½ tsp. sugar
1 can pizza sauce
1 can tomato paste
1 sm. can tomato sauce

Oregano
Onion salt
Garlic salt
Mozzarella cheese
Parmesan cheese
Pepperoni

Brown ground beef and onion. Meanwhile cook macaroni. To browned ground beef add the sugar, pizza sauce, tomato paste and tomato sauce. Season with oregano, onion salt and garlic salt. Add macaroni to the meat mixture. In casserole dish layer ½ the meat mixture. Cover with mozzarella cheese. Repeat. Top with Parmesan cheese and pepperoni. Put in microwave oven to heat through (about 5 minutes) or conventional oven preheated to 350° for 45 minutes.

—Margie Hoff

BAR-B-Q SAUCE

1 cup ketchup
½ cup brown sugar
3 tsp. Liquid Smoke

1 Tbls. prepared mustard
1 tsp. Worcestershire sauce
1 small onion, diced very fine

Mix together in a small saucepan and bring to a boil. Spoon this over your favorite meat that has been cooking in the oven. Then simmer for ½ hour at 200°.

—Geneva Walker

TORTILLA SOUP

1 medium onion, chopped
1 jalepeño pepper, minced
2 cloves garlic, minced
2 Tbls. oil
2 lbs. stew meat, cut in small
   pieces
1 lg. can tomatoes
1 can Rotel tomatoes
1 can beef broth
1 can chicken broth

1 can tomato soup
1½ cans water
1 tsp. ground cumin
1 tsp. chili powder
3 Tbls. Tabasco
1 tsp. salt
½ tsp. lemon pepper
2 tsp. Worcestershire sauce
8-10 corn tortillas
Cheese, if desired

Combine onion, jalepeño pepper, garlic and meat and sauté in the oil. Add remaining ingredients except tortillas and cheese and cook 50 minutes. Cut tortillas into bite-size pieces and add to soup. Top with cheese when serving, if desired.

—Nancy Thomas

SUPPER ON BREAD

1½ lbs. ground beef
1 cup cheese
1 small can evaporated milk
1 egg

1 small onion
1 cup cracker meal
1 loaf French bread

Mix all ingredients except French bread together and let simmer. Pack into French bread after cutting the top center out. Wrap in foil and bake 40 minutes in 350° oven.

—Marie Keel

MEAT STORAGE TIMES

	Refrigerator (35°F, 2°C)	Freezer (0°F, −20°C)
Ground Beef or Lamb	1 to 2 days	3 months
Liver	1 to 2 days	3 months
Fresh Cut Meats	2 to 4 days	6 months
Ham Slices	3 to 4 days	2 months
Wieners	4 to 5 days	1 month
Bacon	5 to 7 days	1 month
Luncheon Meats	7 days	Not advised
Cooked Meats	4 to 5 days	3 months

Reduce storage time by half for freezer sections within refrigerators.

V
E
G
E
T
A
B
L
E
S

MY FAVORITE POTATOES

1 12-oz. box Pillsbury Potato Buds	Garlic salt to taste
1 large cream cheese	Paprika
1 large ctn. sour cream	Butter

Make potatoes according to recipe on box. Soften cream cheese and beat into potatoes along with sour cream and garlic salt. Place in casserole. Dot top with butter and sprinkle with paprika for color. Bake approximately 20-25 minutes in 350° oven. So-o-o good!

—Barbara Hammond

HOT BEAN SALAD

2 cans butter beans	½ lb. bacon, cubed and browned
1 can kidney beans	
1 can lima beans	¾ cup brown sugar
1 lg. can pork and beans	¼ cup vinegar
1 lg. onion, cubed and browned	⅓ cup catsup
	¼ tsp. dry mustard

Combine and mix beans. Make sauce of other ingredients and simmer 15 minutes; pour over beans. Bake one hour at 350°.

—Erlene Hauser

BROCCOLI CASSEROLE

2 10-oz. pkgs. chopped broccoli	2 cans cream of chicken soup
2½-3 cups cooked rice	1 large jar Cheese Whiz
	1 tsp Worcestershire sauce

Cook broccoli and add rest of ingredients except 1 can of soup. Pour it over top and bake 30 minutes at 350°.

—Billie Ramsey

SQUASH CASSEROLE

3 cups yellow squash
1 stick margarine
2 medium onions, chopped
1 2-oz. jar pimentos

1 cup sour cream
1 pkg. corn stuffing mix
1 can cream of chicken soup
1 cup milk

Slice and boil squash with ½ tsp. salt. Melt margarine and toss stuffing. Mix lightly. Mix squash, sour cream, onion, milk and chicken soup in separate bowl. Put into greased 9"x12" casserole dish and layer with stuffing mix. Bake 30 minutes for 350°.

—Fern Mears

ANTIPASTO NAPOLI

2 cups tomato wedges
2 cups fresh mushroom slices
8 oz. Polish sausage, cut into
    strips
1 cup (8½ oz. jar) artichoke
    hearts, drained and
    quartered

1 cup fresh zucchini slices
1 cup bottled Italian dressing
2 qts. torn assorted salad
    greens
Grated Parmesan cheese,
    optional

Combine tomatoes, mushrooms, sausage, artichoke hearts and zucchini. Add dressing, cover and marinate in refrigerater for 2 hours. Drain, reserving marinade. Toss vegetables with assorted greens. Serve with reserved marinade. Sprinkle with Parmesan cheese to taste. Serves 4-6.

—Nancy Perotti

CARROTS SUPREME

2 lbs. carrots
¼ cup vinegar
1 cup sugar
1 can tomato soup

1 stick margarine
1 bell pepper
1 onion

Slice and cook carrots until tender. Combine vinegar, sugar, soup and margarine and bring to boil; pour over cooked carrots and add bell pepper and onion. Serve warm. This is better the next day.

—Billie Ramsey

FIESTA-RONI SALAD

1 pkg. Chicken Rice-a-Roni
2 Tbls. wine vinegar
2 Tbls. lemon juice
1 Tbls. sugar
½ tsp. garlic salt
1 cup diced tomato
½ cup diced celery

¼ cup sliced scallion
1 cup diced green chilies
   (mild)
3 ripe avocados, diced
¼ cup chopped ripe olives,
   pitted

Prepare Rice-a-Roni according to package directions. Cool. Combine remaining ingredients and add to Rice-a-Roni. Lay on bed of lettuce in large bowl or individual salad bowls and chill.

—Virginia Turner

ASPARAGUS-PEA CASSEROLE

1 stick oleo
6 slices bread, cut into fingers
   without crust
2 cans asparagus, drained

2 cans mushroom soup
2 cans English peas
1 can water chestnuts
½ cup celery, chopped

Melt oleo in a 9"x13" pan. Soak bread in oleo and remove. Lay drained asparagus in dish. mix soup, peas, water chestnuts, and celery and pour over the asparagus. Top with bread fingers. Bake at 325° for 20 minutes or until brown on top.

—Jean Wilcox

SMOKED CHEESE CARROTS

3 cups carrots, cooked and
   mashed
2 Tbls. onion, chopped

16 soda crackers, crushed
1 cup milk
1 roll smoky cheese

Mix all ingredients together, dot with butter and bake for 35 minutes at 350°.

—Sharon Louig

KENTUCKY FRIED CORN

6 strips bacon, 1 inch cubes
4 ears corn, sweet or horse,
  scraped from cob
2 small cucumbers, thinly
  sliced

1 medium onion, minced or in
  rings
1 large egg
Salt, pepper, and sugar to
  taste

Lightly fry bacon, mix other ingredients thoroughly, pour into bacon grease. Fry slowly so as not to brown too quickly, about 25 minutes. Note: Pimento strips and green sweet pepper can also be used if desired. Yield, 4-6 servings.

—Mae Mitchell

CHOWDER PARMESAN

2 cups potatoes, diced
1 cup carrots, sliced
1/2 cup celery, sliced
1/2 cup onion, chopped
1 1/2 tsp. salt
1/4 tsp. pepper
2 cups boiling water

WHITE SAUCE
1/4 cup butter
1/4 cup flour
2 cups milk

1/2 cup Parmesan cheese

Combine all of first ingredients with boiling water. Simmer until tender. Make white sauce. Stir into cooked vegetables. Add 1/2 cup Parmesan Cheese. Variations: Add 1 can creamed corn or 2 cans shrimp, or clams. Yield: 6-8 servings.

—Joanne Roe

PEPPY POTATOES

1 pkg. seasoned coating mix
  for chicken
1/4 tsp. salt

4 unpeeled potatoes, cut in 1"
  wedges
Melted butter

Pour coating mix and salt in plastic or paper bag. Dip potatoes in melted butter, shake in bag. Place potatoes on well-greased baking sheet. Bake at 325° for 55 minutes.

—Bonnie and Shelley Dunn

MARINATED CARROTS

5 cups carrots, cooked and
    sliced
1 cup red onion, sliced
1 green pepper, sliced
1 10¾-oz. can tomato soup
½ cup salad oil

1 cup sugar
¾ cup vinegar
1 tsp. mustard
1 tsp. Worcestershire sauce
1 tsp. salt
1 tsp pepper

Cook the carrots, then mix with the pepper and onion. Mix the seasonings together. Pour over the vegetables. Cover and let sit 24 hours in refrigerator. Drain all the sauce off before serving.

— Roberta Husband

CARROT PENNIES

2 cans sliced carrots, drained
1 green pepper, sliced and
    divided
1 medium onion, sliced and
    divided
1 small jar pimentos
1 can tomato soup

½ cup salad oil
1 cup sugar
¾ cup cider vinegar
1 tsp. prepared mustard
2 tsp. Worcestershire sauce
¼ tsp. black pepper

Mix first 4 ingredients together and chill. Mix and pour remaining ingredients over vegetables. Refrigerate lightly covered. Will keep for weeks. May be served as salad.

— Martha Moore

MOM'S BEANS

2 lbs. Navy beans
2 cups sugar
1½ Tbls. salt

¾ Tbls. pepper
½ lb. lard, cut in pieces
2 Tbls. Karo syrup (dark or light)

Cook beans on top of stove in water covering beans 1 inch for 2 hours. Put in oven dish, add and mix other ingredients. Bake at 350° for 4 hours.

— Kitty Masengarb

SQUASH CASSEROLE

3 pkgs. frozen yellow squash,
   cooked
1 can cream of chicken soup
½ pint sour cream
½ cup carrots, grated
½ cup cheese, grated
1 small jar pimentos, chopped
   (optional)
1 small onion, diced

TOPPING

1 pkg. Pepperidge Farm Stuffing, Herb Seasoning
1 stick margarine, melted
1 dash poultry seasoning

Layer half of stuffing mixture in 9"x12" dish, add squash mixture. Add remaining stuffing mixture on top. Bake 30 minutes at 350°.

—*Adelene Stevens*

ZUCCHINI SQUASH DISH

2 pounds squash
1 cup butter or oleo
1 large onion
1 box cheese croutons
8 ounces sour cream

1 can creamed chicken soup
1 small jar pimentos
Parsley and seasoning of your
   choice

Cut up squash and onion. Boil until tender. Pour off liquid and let cool. Mix in sour cream, chicken soup, and pimentos. Melt butter and pour over croutons. Let sit. Put ½ of the croutons in a baking dish. Pour in squash mixture. Put remaining croutons on top. Bake at 350° until brown. A great dish to freeze.

—*Mildred Marsh*

The first four words in our Bible "In the beginning God" may be taken as the Christian's life motto. In everything we should begin with Him — in companionships, in marriage, in business partnerships and every day and always, we should begin with God, turning to Him in all circumstances and on all occasions, doing nothing without first referring to Him.

EASY BAKED BEANS

4 slices bacon
2 Tbls. bacon drippings
½ cup chopped onion
2 1-lb. cans pork and beans in
    tomato sauce

2 Tbls. brown sugar
1 Tbls. Worcestershire sauce
1 tsp. prepared mustard

Cook bacon until crisp, then crumble. Cook onion in bacon drippings until tender; add crumbled bacon, pork and beans, brown sugar, Worcestershire sauce, and mustard. Mix well. Bake uncovered in a 1½ quart casserole dish at 325° for 1½ to 1¾ hours. Serves 6.

— Carol Childress

SUPER POTATO CASSEROLE

5 large potatoes
4 Tbls. green pepper, chopped
1 cup cheese, grated
1 tsp. salt
¼ cup milk

1½ Tbls. pimento, chopped
6 Tbls. onions, chopped
½ tsp. pepper
½ stick butter

Cook potatoes with jackets, and peel while still warm, then let cool and cube them. Mix in green pepper, cheese, salt, milk, pimento, onion and pepper and mix well. Melt butter and pour over, sprinkle with parsley. Bake in pre-heated oven 45 minutes at 400°. This can be prepared a day ahead of time, removing from refrigerator at least 3 hours before putting in oven. Leave butter and parsley off until then.

— Mildred Yahr

The value of all human endeavor must be graded on this:
    Is it good for the children?
    Does it build people into better human beings?
From "Be Somebody" by Mary Crowley

123

POTATO DUMPLINGS

9 large potatoes, grated and
   drained
8-9 slices bread, soaked with
   water and squeezed out

3 large onions, grated
1½ Tbls. salt
5 tsp. baking powder
Flour

Mix together and add flour to stiffen. Drop by spoonfuls into boiling water. Boil at least 20 minutes. Good with pork roast and gravy.

—Barb Ahlers

SHAKE 'N BAKE POTATOES

6 medium potatoes, peeled
   and quartered
Milk

1 envelope original flavor
   Shake 'n Bake
Sour cream

Dip potatoes in milk and coat with Shake 'n Bake. Salt to taste. Bake on cookie sheet that has ⅛" cooking oil. Bake at 400° for 30 minutes. Turn two or three times. Serve with sour cream.

—Cheryl Purington

AU GRATIN POTATOES

8 large potatoes
¼ cup butter
¼ cup onion, finely chopped
¼ cup flour
4 cups milk
1 tsp. salt

¼ tsp. hot pepper sauce
¼ tsp. marjoram
¼ lb. cheddar cheese,
   shredded
Paprika and parsley for garnish

Cook potatoes unpeeled, then peel and cube. Saute onion in butter, blend in flour, then remove from heat. Stir in milk, return to heat to thicken. Stir in salt, pepper sauce, marjoram and cheese. Add potatoes to sauce. Bake in casserole dish for 25 minutes at 350°. Garnish with paprika and parsley.

—Joanne Roe

124

HOT GERMAN POTATO SALAD

9 slices bacon
1 cup onions, sliced
2 Tbls. flour
2 Tbls. sugar
2 tsp. salt
½ tsp. celery seed

1 cup water
⅓ cup vinegar
9 medium potatoes, (boiled
    with skins on, then peeled
    and sliced.)
Dash pepper

Fry bacon in a large skillet until crisp. Remove and drain. Cook onions in bacon drippings until golden brown. Blend in flour, sugar, salt, celery seed, pepper. Cook over low heat, stirring until bubbly. Remove from heat and add water and vinegar. Boil and stir for 1 minute. Pour warm sauce over sliced potatoes. Crumble bacon and stir in just before serving. This goes great with fresh baked ham.

—*Marilyn Lambie*

SOUR CREAM POTATOES

8 medium sized potatoes
3 Tbls. parsley flakes
1½ cup sour cream
1 cup cheddar cheese, grated

1 small onion, minced
1 stick margarine
¾ tsp. salt

Peel and dice potatoes. Cook until tender. Pour off water. Saute onion in margarine. Add parsley, cooking slowly. Add salt and pour over diced and cooked potatoes. Fold in sour cream lightly. Top with cheese. Bake at 350° until cheese is melted and bubbly.

YUMMY BUFFET POTATOES

2 lbs. frozen hash brown
    potatoes
1 8-oz carton sour cream
1 10-oz. pkg. grated cheese

2 cans cream of chicken soup
¼ cup dried chives
½ cup margarine, melted

Thaw potatoes. Combine all ingredients and pour into a greased baking dish. Bake for 1 hour a 350°.

—*Linda Hollinshead*

SCALLOPED POTATOES

2 lbs. frozen hash brown
   potatoes
10 oz. cheddar cheese, grated
1 medium onion, minced
1 pt. sour cream

1 can cream of chicken (or
   mushroom) soup
1 stick margarine, melted
Salt and pepper to taste

Combine all ingredients and bake for 45 minutes to 1 hour in 350°
oven.

— Mary Ann Morton

SWEET POTATO CASSEROLE

3 cups sweet potatoes,
   mashed
¾ cup white sugar
2 eggs, beaten
1 tsp. vanilla
½ tsp. almond extract

½ cup milk
½ cup margarine (1 stick)
4 Tbls. cooking wine
Pinch of salt
Grated orange peel

TOPPING

1 cup brown sugar
1 cup chopped nuts (walnuts
   or pecans)

1 cup plain flour
⅓ cup butter

Mix casserole ingredients and put in greased dish. Bake at 350°
for 30 to 35 minutes. To make topping, cut butter into flour, add
sugar and nuts, spread on top of baked potatoes and bake until
it looks good.

— Shirly Dixon

SWEET POTATOES AND COCONUT

4 cups sweet potatoes, cooked
4 eggs
¼ cup flour
1 cup coconut

2 tsp. vanilla
2 cups sugar
1 cup milk
1 stick butter, melted

Blend all ingredients and bake in moderate oven until firm. Use
as a vegetable or dessert.

— Rosa Garner

126

CORINNE'S WHITE BEAN AND BROCCOLI SOUP

4 cups cooked white beans,
either Great Northern or
Navy beans
1 bunch broccoli, steamed and
chopped
3 carrots, sliced
3 lg. stalks celery, sliced

3-4 Tbls. parsley, chopped
3 cloves garlic, crushed
3 Tbls. olive oil
2 qts. chicken stock, vegetable
stock, or water
Salt, freshly ground pepper,
and dried oregano to taste

Saute the vegetables in olive oil. Add this mixture to the beans
and add stock or water to the consistency that you desire. Cook
about 2 hours to allow the flavors to marry. Just before you are
ready to eat, add the steamed broccoli. Add a few drops of olive
oil to each bowl before serving. Eat with a crisp green salad and
toasted French bread.

—Corinne Kasten

CORN CASSEROLE

1 can mexicorn, drained
1 can whole kernel corn,
drained
1 can cream of celery soup

1 stick margarine
1 cup cheddar cheese, grated
1 cup cooked rice, yellow
Salt and pepper to taste

Cook rice. Add margarine and stir until melted. Add all other ingredients to rice mixture and bake in casserole dish for 30 to 35
minutes at 350°.

—Dot Hopkins

MARINATED CARROTS

2 lbs. carrots, chopped
1 green pepper, sliced
½ cup oil
¾ cup sugar

¾ cup vinegar
1 cup tomato soup
Dash of salt

Cook carrots until slightly tender. Add remaining ingredients and
refrigerate. Great for summer!

—Linda Hollinshead

SPINACH CASSEROLE

1 can spinach, drained
2 eggs, beaten
1 cup cottage cheese
½ tsp. seasoned salt

¼ tsp. pepper
¼ cup cheese, shredded
1 tsp. sesame seed, toasted

Combine eggs, cottage cheese, pepper and salt; mix well. Stir in spinach. Spoon mixture into lightly greased 1-quart casserole dish. Bake, uncovered, at 350° for 20 minutes. Sprinkle cheese and sesame seeds. Bake for an additional 5 minutes.

—Cathy Gilmer

COPPER PENNIES

2 lbs. carrots
1 can tomato soup, undiluted
½ cup cooking oil
½ cup sugar
½ cup vinegar

1 lg. onion, sliced and
   separated
1 green pepper, sliced in
   circles

Slice carrots, cook and drain. In saucepan, heat tomato soup, oil, sugar, and vinegar to a boil. Add onion and green pepper to the carrots. Pour hot tomato mixture over top. Let set an hour or more. May be served hot or cold.

DRESSING

1 can Campbell onion soup
1 can Campbell celery soup
1 can Campbell mushroom
   soup

4 eggs
2-3 cans chicken broth
Cornbread
Sage to taste

Mix all ingredients and bake at 350° until light brown. An easy but delicious dressing.

—Charlotte Matthews

128

LIGHT GRITS SPOONBREAD

2 cups skim milk
1/3 cup uncooked regular grits
1/2 tsp. salt

3 eggs, separated
Vegetable cooking spray

Combine milk, grits and salt in a heavy 3-quart saucepan. Bring to boil; reduce heat and cook, stirring constantly, for 10 to 12 minutes or until very thick. Beat egg yolks until thick and lemon-colored. Gradually stir in about 1/4 of hot mixture, stirring constantly. Beat egg whites (at room temperature) until stiff peaks form; fold into grits mixture. Coat a 1 1/2-quart casserole dish with cooking spray; spoon grits mixture into casserole dish. Bake in 375° oven for 35 to 40 minutes or until lightly browned. Yields 6 servings (about 85 calories per serving).

—Sue Cornelius

I like God's mathematics — He can take nine-tenths and do more with it than I can with ten-tenths.

Tithing takes the worry out of living.

From *"Be Somebody"* by Mary Crowley

B R E A D S

OATMEAL BREAD

1 cup oatmeal
¼ cup sugar
1 Tbls. salt
¼ cup shortening
3 Tbls. light molasses

1 cup boiling water
1 pkg. dry yeast
1 cup warm water
4-4½ cups flour

In large bowl, combine oatmeal, sugar, salt, shortening, and molasses with boiling water. Cool to lukewarm. Add yeast, warm water and half of the flour. Beat until smooth. Add rest of the flour and knead until smooth. Place dough into greased bowl. Cover, let rise until double. Punch down. Cover and let rise 15 minutes. Shape into two loaves. Bake approximately 35 minutes.

—Ardith Anderson

STUFFED HARD ROLLS

1 dozen hard rolls
1 lb. grated cheddar cheese
½ cup chopped green pepper
¼ cup sliced green onions
2 chopped hard-boiled eggs

½ pint sliced stuffed olives, green
1 8-oz. can tomato sauce
¾ cup oil

Slice hard rolls in half, scoop out centers. Spoon mixture into rolls. Wrap individually in foil. Bake at 350° for 20-25 minutes. Yield, about 12.

—Joanne Roe

CARROT BREAD

1 cup sugar
¾ cup oil
2 eggs
2 cups flour
1 tsp. cinnamon

1 tsp. baking powder
1 tsp. soda
1¼ cups carrots, shredded
½ cup nuts or raisins

Cream sugar and oil together. Blend in eggs. Add alternately dry ingredients with shredded carrots. Grease and flour three 6"x3" pans. Bake 1 hour in 325° oven.

—Dorothy Cummings

BREADS...

SUN BREAD

This is a simple bread, whose beginnings were in a time long gone by. And it is simple to make as it uses ingredients that are common to almost every household. It comes from the lands of the "Fertile Crescent" and it will help to make a treasure of your table. Very simply put, this requires more muscle than imagination, but like many of the Lord's creations, it is a labor of love, and the rewards are the enjoyment of His bounty!

2 cups yellow cornmeal
4-5 cups whole grain wheat
1 cup millet
1 cup chopped sunflower
   seeds
½ cup golden raisins
½ cup chopped almonds
2 cups water
¼ cup sesame oil
Salt

Simply stir all the ingredients together until they are very well mixed. Form into two loaves, making certain that the dough is thick enough so the loaves won't fall apart when baking. Bake at about 350° for about 1½ hours. Those who prefer health food will find this filled with nutrition and it can be eaten with Grace from the Lord's table.

Millet: A generic term somewhat loosely applied to a group of small grain cereals. In the early days of the world's history, millet held a very high place as a food grain.

ZUCCHINI BREAD

3 eggs, beaten
2 cups sugar
1 tsp. salt
¼ tsp. baking powder
3 tsp. cinnamon
1 cup oil
3 cups flour
½ tsp. nutmeg
1 tsp. soda
2 cups zucchini squash,
   peeled and grated

Mix the eggs, oil, sugar and zucchini. Add remaining ingredients. Bake in 325° oven for 1 hour. Candied cherries, nuts and raisins may be added for extra festive occasions.

—Marty Cunningham

134

MONKEY BREAD

1 qt. scalded milk	1 cup flour
1 cup sugar	3 tsp. salt
1 cup oleo	2 tsp. baking powder
2 pkgs. dry yeast	1 tsp. soda
8 cups flour	Melted oleo

Dissolve yeast in ½ cup water. Pour milk over sugar and oleo. Cool. Add dissolved yeast, add 8 cups flour, one at a time, let rise double, add 1 cup flour and other ingredients. Let rise double. Punch down and store in refrigerator in covered container. Will keep up to two weeks. When ready to make bread, roll out thin. Cut into strips. Melt oleo in pan and then fill pan one half full with strips dipped in melted oleo. Let rise and bake at 425° 10-15 minutes.

—Faye Shumway

POPPY SEED BREAD

3 cups flour	1½ tsp. baking powder
1½ cups milk	1½ Tbls. poppy seeds
1½ tsp. vanilla	1½ tsp. salt
2½ cups sugar	1 cup plus 2 Tbls. salad oil
3 eggs	1½ tsp. almond extract

GLAZE:

¾ cup powdered sugar	2 tsp. butter, melted
¼ cup orange juice	½ tsp. almond extract

Combine all ingredients except glaze and beat 2 minutes. Pour into 2 greased loaf pans, bake 1 hour at 350°. Pour glaze over loaves while still warm.

—Sharon Lovig

Then I will give you rain in due season, and the land shall yield her increase, and the trees of the field shall yield their fruit, and your threshing shall reach unto the vintage, and the vintage shall reach unto the sowing time and ye shall eat your bread to the full, and dwell in your land safely.

Leviticus 26:4-5

QUICK ROLLS

1 tsp. baking powder
½ tsp. salt
¼ cup shortening
¼ cup lukewarn water
4 cups flour, minimum

2 Tbls. sugar
¼ tsp. soda
1 pkg. or cake yeast
sour milk or buttermilk

Sift 3 cups flour with baking powder, sugar, salt, and soda. Cut in the shortening. Dissolve yeast in the water and add enough sour milk to make 1 cup of liquid. Add to the dry ingredients. Stir in additional flour to make a stiff dough. Turn out on board and knead for 1 minute. Roll out ½ inch thick and cut with biscuit cutter. Place in pan and let rise 1 hour. Bake about 15 minutes at 425°.

—Barbara McDonald

HOT ROLLS

¼ cup sugar
¼ cup oil or melted
   shortening
1 tsp. salt

1 egg
½ cup boiling water
1 pkg. yeast
3 cups flour

Dissolve yeast in ½ cup lukewarm water. Put sugar, oil, salt, and egg in bowl and mix together. Add boiling water to above, then add yeast, and 3 cups flour. Let rise 45 minutes. Bake at 350° until brown.

—Sue Engman

Ring in the love of truth and right,
Ring in the common love of good.
Ring out old shapes of foul disease,
Ring out the narrowing lust of gold;
Ring out the thousand wars of old.
Ring in the thousand years of peace.
Ring in the valiant man and free,
The larger heart, the kindlier hand;
Ring out the darkness of the land,
Ring in the Christ that is to be.

—Alfred Lord Tennyson

YEAST ROLLS

1 cup Crisco	1 cup lukewarm water
1 cup sugar	2 pkgs. dry yeast
1 tsp. salt	2 beaten eggs
1 cup water, boiling	6-7 cups flour

Mix Crisco, sugar, salt and boiling water together, let stand until cool. Combine lukewarm water, yeast and eggs; mix with first mixture. Add flour to liquid mixture. Place on floured board. Knead about 12 times. Make into clover leaf rolls, let rise only once. Bake in moderate oven at 375° until brown. Yield 36. You can refrigerate for 2-3 days in a large bowl with loose-fitting lid.

—Janie Reeves

NO-KNEAD YEAST ROLLS

2 large or 3 small eggs	3 cups warm water
2 tsp. salt	2 pkgs. dry yeast
¾ cup sugar	8-10 cups flour
¾ cup shortening, half butter	

Mix together eggs, salt, sugar, and shortening. Dissolve yeast in water and add to above mixture. Add flour 2 cups at a time and stir well. Don't get dough too stiff, add just enough for easy handling. Place in greased bowl and let rise for several hours, punching down when it gets to top of bowl. Roll out about ½ inch for cinnamon rolls, spread with mixture of 1 cup sugar, ½ cup melted butter, and 3 tsp. cinnamon; then roll up and cut into 1 inch slices. Put into pan cut sides down and let rise until double and bake 20 minutes. This recipe can be used for 4 loaves of bread; shape dough into four loaf pans, let rise until double and bake 375° for about 35 minutes. This recipe makes good dinner rolls and sweet rolls with your favorite glaze.

—Donna Ruckman

BREADS...

UNA'S BREAD

4 eggs, well beaten
1 cup milk
½ cup Wesson oil
½ cup honey

1 pkg. dry yeast
1 tsp. salt
2 cups flour
2½ cups flour

Combine liquid ingredients, then add yeast, salt, and 2 cups flour. Beat with electric mixer. Add 2½ cups flour, work with hands, shape and grease and leave in covered bowl 2 hours. Turn out on floured board, shape (rolls, or roll out thin, cover with butter and shape into butterhorn) and let rise. Bake 20 minutes at 350°.

—Una Jarvis

PEG ROLLS

¾ cup shortening
2 eggs
⅔ cup sugar
1 cup warm potatoes, mashed

1 yeast cake in ½ cup
    lukewarm water
1 tsp. salt
1 cup warm water
7½ cups unsifted flour

Cream shortening and sugar; add eggs to mixture, then add beaten potatoes. Add yeast cake, salt and water and flour alternately. Let rise once. Punch down and put in refrigerator if you don't want to bake until the next day. Otherwise, let rise once more and make into biscuits. Let rise again and bake in 375° oven.

—Genevieve Bowers

A famous Chinese proverb:

If you are planning for one year, sow grain,
ten years, plant trees;
but when planning for one hundred years, grow men.

HOT ROLLS

½ cup sugar
¾ tsp. salt
1 pkg. or cake yeast

½ cup shortening
2 eggs, beaten
5 cups flour, approx.

Add sugar, salt and shortening to hot water and let cool. Dissolve yeast in ¼ cup of warm water, then add this to the sugar mixture. Add the beaten eggs and 3 cups of flour. Mix well with hands, then put on board and knead well. (Probably will take about 2 cups of flour.) Roll out, cut with biscuit cutter, put in greased pan to rise for about 2 hours. Bake at 400° for 12 minutes.

—Barbara McDonald

BUBBLE BREAD

1 cup milk, scalded
½ cup shortening
½ cup sugar
1 tsp. salt
2 cakes yeast
2 eggs, beaten

4½ cups flour
1 stick butter, melted
1 Tbls. sugar
1 cup sugar
½ cup nuts, chopped
(optional)

Mix scalded milk, shortening, sugar and salt together. Let cool to lukewarm then crumble the yeast into mixture. Add beaten eggs and flour. Mix to soft dough, turn out on a floured board and knead until smooth and not sticky. Place in a greased bowl and cover with a damp cloth. Let rise until double in bulk. Punch down and let set for 10 minutes. While dough is setting, combine the butter, sugar, and nuts.

Make dough into small balls, about the size of a walnut. Roll each ball in butter, then into the sugar mixture. Place in greased angel food cake pan, in staggered rows and layers until all dough is used. Let rise again, then bake in 350° oven about 45 minutes. Turn out on board or plate and pull off luscious pieces one by one.

—Sharon Wienandt

BREADS . . .

ZUCCHINI BREAD

3 cups flour
2 cups sugar
1 tsp. salt
1 tsp. baking soda
1 tsp. baking powder
1 tsp. cinnamon
3 eggs, beaten

2 cups zucchini, chopped, fine
   seeds and all
2 tsp. vanilla
1 small can crushed pineapple, drained
1 cup salad oil
1 cup nuts

Combine flour, sugar, salt, soda, baking powder and cinnamon in a large bowl. Add other ingredients. Mix well. Bake in greased and floured 9"x5"x3" loaf pan for 1 hour in 350° oven.

—Clair Griffith

ZUCCHINI BREAD

3 eggs
1 cup oil
2 cups sugar
2 cups zucchini, peeled and
   grated
1 tsp. vanilla

¼ tsp. baking powder
1 cup nuts
3 cups flour
1 tsp. salt
3 tsp. cinnamon
1 tsp. soda

Beat eggs, sugar and oil. Add vanilla and stir in zucchini. Sift flour, salt, cinnamon, soda and baking powder. Stir into the first mixture. Fold in nuts. Pour into 2 well-greased 9"x5"x3" loaf pans. Bake in 325° oven for 60 to 75 minutes.

—Sally Jerore

Decorating your home is a little like falling in love. It's full of excitement, anticipation and delight. And while on one hand, it sets you to daydreaming, on the other, it makes you more aware of everything around you. Helping you to create a warm and beautiful environment is what we believe in.

140

BRAN MUFFINS

1 cup Nabisco 100% Bran
2 cups Kellogg's All-Bran
1 cup boiling water
½ cup oil
1 cup brown sugar
2 eggs, beaten
2 cups buttermilk

2¼ cups wheat flour
2½ tsp. soda
½ tsp. salt
⅔ cup dates, chopped
  (optional)
⅔ cup walnuts (optional)

Combine Bran and All-Bran with boiling water and let stand. Add remaining ingredients. Bake in oiled muffin tins in 400° oven for 15 minutes. Cover unused batter and store in refrigerator. Use as needed. Will keep at least 2 weeks. Yields 2 dozen muffins.

—Joanne Roe

CORNMEAL ROLLS

2 cups milk
⅔ cups white cornmeal
½ cup sugar
1 stick butter or margarine
1½ tsp. salt

3 eggs, beaten
2 pkgs. yeast
½ cup warm water
6 scant cups white flour

Slowly add milk to cornmeal. Cook until thick and remove from heat. Add sugar, butter or margarine, and salt. Let cool. Dissolve yeast in water and let stand 10 minutes. Add yeast to beaten eggs and cornmeal. Add flour and knead to a very soft dough. Let rise once. Roll out ¾" thick and cut with cookie cutter and let rise. Use for hamburger buns, or for rolls of any type. Bake at 350° until golden brown.

—Jane Alexander

What we learn with pleasure, we never forget.
—Alfred Mercier

PUMPKIN BREAD

2 cups pumpkin
4 eggs
1 cup oil
⅓ cup water
·3½ cups flour

3 cups sugar
1 Tbls. pumpkin spice
2 tsps. soda
1½ tsps. salt
1 cup nuts, optional

Preheat oven to 350°; grease and flour pans. Combine pumpkin, eggs, oil and water and mix well. Sift together dry ingredients and add to pumpkin mixture a little at a time. Mix well. Place in greased and floured loaf pans. Makes 2 regular loaves or 3 small loaves. Bake in 350° oven for 1 hour to 1 hour and 20 minutes.

—Dinah Houfek

PUMPKIN BREAD

2¾ cups sugar
2 sticks margarine
3 eggs
2 cups pumpkin
2¾ cups flour
1 tsp. baking soda
2 tsp. baking powder

1 Tbls. cinnamon
1 Tbls. vanilla
1 tsp. nutmeg
1 tsp. cloves
½ tsp. salt
1 cup nuts, chopped

Using largest bowl, cream together sugar and margarine. Add eggs one at a time and beat using electric mixer. Sift flour and measure accurately. Sift again with the baking soda, baking powder, cinnamon, nutmeg, cloves and salt. Add the flour mixture to the sugar, margarine and egg mixture. Blend well with a wooden spoon. Add the pumpkin, vanilla and nuts. Blend well after each addition, but do not beat. Bake in 325° oven for 1 hour in loaf or tube pans which have been lightly greased and floured. Fill pans two-thirds full.

—Kathy Wallace

God will mend a broken heart if we give Him ALL the pieces.
From *"Be Somebody"* by Mary Crowley

SOUR CREAM CORN BREAD

2 cups Martha Gooch
   complete corn bread mix
1 egg, beaten
1 Tbls. shortening, melted
½ cup cream style corn

½ cup sour cream
½ small can green chili
   peppers, drained and
   chopped
½ cup grated cheese

Preheat oven to 300°. Mix egg and corn bread mix thoroughly with a fork. Stir in shortening, corn, sour cream and peppers. Spoon half of the mixture into a greased piping hot 6" heavy skillet or an 8"x8"x2" pan and then spread with cheese. Cover with remaining corn bread mixture. Bake about 40 minutes. Serves 4 to 6.

—Evelyn Wood

NEVER FAIL ICE BOX ROLLS

2 pkgs. dry yeast
¼ cup lukewarm water
1 tsp. sugar
⅓ cup sugar
½ cup shortening (do not
   use oil)

1 egg
1 cup warm water
4 cups plain flour
1 tsp. salt

Dissolve yeast in ¼ cup lukewarm water. Add 1 teaspoon sugar. Let stand as you cream shortening and one-third cup sugar. Add egg and 1 cup of warm water. Beat. Add yeast cake mixture. Beat in flour and salt. Let rise until doubled. Then roll out and put in refrigerator. Use as needed. Remove from refrigerator approximately 2 hours before baking. These can be frozen and always rise well. Bake in 350° oven for 15 minutes. Yields about 2½ dozen. May be dipped in butter before refrigeration.

—Jackie Ragland

PRAYER

Grant me the bread of Thy wisdom, Lord; let it be the staff that sustains my life. Teach me to walk always in your righteous ways, to be your servant, that I may be free. Send out your light and truth in the land, so that all men may know and love Thee.

BREADS...

BASIC YEAST DOUGH

1 cup milk	1 Tbls. sugar
½ cup sugar	½ cup water, lukewarm
2 tsp. salt	2 cups flour
4 Tbls. margarine	2 eggs
2 pkg. yeast	3½-4 cups flour

Heat milk to scald — use cooking thermometer. Pour hot milk over ½ cup sugar, salt and margarine. Stir to melt. In another bowl, soften the yeast in 1 tablespoon sugar and the lukewarm water. Cover and set aside to rise. When milk mixture is cooled add 2 cups flour and mix well. Add the yeast mixture and the eggs, mixing well after each addition. Stir in 3½ to 4 cups flour. Knead well, using as little flour as possible. Shape into a ball and place in a bowl and cover. Set in warm place to rise.

SWEDISH TEA RING

Basic yeast dough recipe	Brown sugar
Melted butter	Chopped nuts
Cinnamon	Powdered sugar glaze

Separate dough into 3 parts. Roll each part in a rectangle approximately ¼" thick. Spread generously with melted butter. Sprinkle with lots of cinnamon and brown sugar. Add chopped nuts, if desired. Roll the dough like a jelly roll and form a ring on greased pizza pan. Cut into dough with scissors about every ¾". Turn each cut to shape tea ring. Cover and let rise to double. Bake approximately 25 minutes in 375° oven. While still warm, glaze with powdered sugar glaze.

YEAST ROLLS

Basic yeast dough recipe

When dough is double in bulk, shape into your favorite shape rolls. Let rise and bake. You can follow any yeast roll directions in a cookbook.

144

BREADS...

MASTER MIX DEVELOPED AT PURDUE UNIVERSITY

5 lbs. all purpose flour
2½ cups dry milk solids
¾ cup double acting baking
   powder

3 Tbls. salt
2 Tbls. cream of tartar
½ cup sugar
2 lbs. vegetable shortening

Sift dry ingredients together. Then cut in shortening until mix looks like cornmeal. Store at room temperature in giant canister or two Econo Canisters. (Tupperware). Yield: 29 cups.

1 DOZEN BISCUITS
3 cups mix, ¾ cup water. Blend and knead for 10 strokes. Pat out and cut. Bake at 450° for 10 minutes.

18 MEDIUM PANCAKES OR 6 WAFFLES
3 cups mix, 1 egg, 1½ cups water. Blend, bake as usual.

1 DOZEN MUFFINS
3 cups mix, 2 Tbls. sugar, 1 egg, 1 cup water. Mix water and eggs, add to dry ingredients. Bake at 450° for 45 minutes.

8" x 8" GINGERBREAD
2 cups mix, ¼ cup sugar, 1 egg, ½ cup water, ½ cup molasses, ½ tsp. each: cinnamon, ginger, cloves. Beat egg, water and molasses, mix with dry ingredients. Bake in 350° oven for 40 minutes.

9" ROUND COFFEE CAKE
3 cups mix, 1 cup sugar, 1 egg, ⅔ cup water. Blend, put in pan and cover with topping: ½ cup brown sugar, 3 Tbls. melted butter, ½ tsp. cinnamon. Nuts and raisins (½ cup) are optional. Bake at 400° for 25 minutes.

DROP COOKIES
3 cups mix, 1 cup sugar, 1 egg, ⅓ cup water, 1 tsp. vanilla, ½ cup nuts and/or chocolate chips. Bake in 375° oven for 10 minutes.

SHORTCAKE
2 cups mix, ½ cup water, ¼ cup melted butter, 2 Tbls. sugar. Mix and knead a few strokes. Roll ½" thick. Cut into six 3" cakes or bake in 8"x8" pan.

(Continued on next page)

MASTER MIX DEVELOPED AT PURDUE UNIVERSITY

The Master Mix can be used successfully in any recipe calling for biscuit mix, using water in the place of milk. Here are a few others:

2 8" LAYERS, YELLOW OR CHOCOLATE CAKE

3 cups mix, 1½ cups sugar, 3 eggs, 1 cup water, 1 tsp. vanilla, (½ cup cocoa for chocolate cake). Blend sugar into mix. Beat eggs and water and add half of mix. Beat 2 minutes. Add remainder of mix and beat an additional 2 minutes. For chocolate cake, add cocoa to dry ingredients. Bake at 325° for 25 minutes.

FRITTERS

2 cups mix, ⅔ cup water, 1 egg, 2 cups fruit or cooked vegetable. Mix ingredients. Stir in pineapple chunks, peach chunks, or whole kernel corn (drained). Drop by small teaspoons into hot deep fat and fry until golden brown. Drain. Serve hot with confectioner's sugar.

1-2-3 COOKIES

1 cup peanut butter, ¼ cup margarine, ½ cup water, 1 cup granulated sugar (or brown sugar). Mix until smooth, then add 2 cups mix. Drop by teaspoon onto lightly greased cookie sheet. Flatten with fork dipped in flour. Bake 8-10 minutes in 400° oven. Makes 6½ dozen cookies.

BANANA COFFEE CAKE

2 cups mix, 1 egg, 1 Tbls. sugar, 1 cup fully ripened mashed bananas. No additional liquid is required. Mix well. Bake in 8"x8" greased pan for 25 minutes in 400° oven.

MONEY SAVING MILK RECIPE

Mix 5 cups powdered milk and 11 cups water in the jumbo canister. When mixed, add ½ gallon whole milk. Let stand, sealed in refrigerator overnight. Put into 2 qt. beverage containers for easy serving.

ANGEL BISCUITS

2 pkgs. dry yeast, dissolved in 1 cup lukewarm water. Add 2 Tbls. sugar, 2 tsp. salt, 1 tsp. soda, ¾ cup cooking oil or 1 cup shortening, about 5 cups self-rising flour and 2 cups buttermilk. Mix until consistency of rolls. Seal and store in refrigerator. Lasts about 1 week. Pinch off desired amount and bake at 400° for 10 to 12 minutes.

D
E
S
S
E
R
T
S

DESSERTS...

PUMPKIN COOKIES

3 cups sugar
5 cups flour
3 tsp. baking soda
3 tsp. cinnamon
1½ cups shortening

3 tsp. vanilla
3 Tbls. baking powder
3 cups canned pumpkin
1 cup nuts, chopped
1 cup raisins

Mix all ingredients except nuts and raisins. Fold in nuts and raisins and drop by spoonful on ungreased cookie sheet. Bake at 325° for 15 minutes. Yields approximately 6 dozen cookies.

—Dorothy Bailey

EASY TARTS

4 Tbls. butter
8 oz. cream cheese
2 tsp. lemon juice
1 tsp. vanilla
⅓ cup sugar

1 egg
1 can cherry pie filling
Vanilla wafers
Butter

Put a vanilla wafer in the bottom of each cupcake paper and put a dab of butter on top. Mix together cream cheese, lemon juice, vanilla, sugar and egg until smooth. Spoon this mixture into cupcake paper on top of the vanilla wafer and butter until it is about half full. Bake at 375° for 15 minutes. Remove from oven and place 1 Tbls. of canned cherry pie filling on top.

—Edith Jericke

Thus saith the Lord,
Let not the wise man glory in his wisdom,
Neither let the mighty man glory in his might,
Let not the rich man glory in his riches;
But let him that glorieth glory in this,
That he understandeth and knoweth me,
That I am the Lord which exercise
Loving-kindness, judgment, and righteousness, in the earth:
For in these things I delight, saith the Lord.

—Jeremiah 9:23-24

BANANA OATMEAL COOKIES

1½ cups flour
1 cup white sugar
1 tsp. salt
½ tsp. baking soda
¼ tsp. nutmeg
¾ tsp. cinnamon

1¼ cups oil or soft shortening
1 egg
3 large bananas, mashed (or 4 small ones)
½ cup walnuts
1¾ cups uncooked oatmeal

Mix all ingredients together and drop by spoonfuls on ungreased cookie sheet. Bake at 350° until golden brown. Makes a nice moist cookie.

—Deanna Burr

SEVEN LAYER BARS

¼ cup butter
1 cup graham cracker crumbs
1 cup coconut, shredded
1 6-oz. pkg. semisweet chocolate bits

1 6-oz. pkg. butterscotch bits
1 can sweetened condensed milk
1 cup walnuts, chopped

Preheat oven to 350°. Melt butter in 13"x9"x2" pan. Sprinkle cracker crumbs evenly over butter and press down. Sprinkle with coconut, chocolate bits, then butterscotch bits. Pour milk evenly over all. Sprinkle on nuts, press lightly. Bake 30 minutes. Cool and cut in ½" bars. Makes 48 bars.

—Darlene Quinlan

WALNUT BARS

1 lb. light brown sugar
4 eggs
1¼ cups flour

1½ cups walnuts
½ tsp. baking powder
Powdered sugar

Preheat oven to 350°. Beat eggs until light. Add remaining ingredients. Spread in greased and floured 9"x13" pan. Bake 25 to 30 minutes. DO NOT OVERBAKE. Cut into bars while warm. Roll in powdered sugar. Makes approximately 18 bars.

—Ada Dalley

HAIRY RANGER COOKIES

1 cup butter (must be real butter)
1½ cups sugar
1 cup brown sugar, packed
2 eggs
1 cup flour
1 tsp. baking soda
½ tsp. baking powder
½ tsp. salt
1½ tsp. vanilla
2 cups oatmeal (regular, not instant)
2 cups cornflakes
½ cup coconut, shredded
1 cup raisins or dates
½ cup nuts

Cream the butter, then add both sugars and cream some more. Then cream in the eggs and vanilla. In a separate mixing bowl, thoroughly mix the flour, baking powder and salt. Add to creamed mix and beat. Mix remaining ingredients in a dish pan. Gently stir the beaten mix into this stuff. It will be very thick and hard to stir, but try not to crush the cornflakes. Pat into flat baking pans, about 1 inch thick. You don't have to do a beautiful job of it since it spreads out while baking. Bake at 325° for about 30 minutes or until medium brown on top. Watch it carefully, as the raisins on bottom tend to burn. Remove from oven and cool. Run a knife around edges and turn onto a plate. Pick out the black raisins as they will give a burned taste if left in. You can vary the big ingredients, like using more or less nuts and coconut or raisins, dates, or currants, etc.

—Patty White

SCALLOPED PINEAPPLE

1 cup oleo
2 cups sugar
3 eggs
2½ cans crushed pineapple
4 cups dry bread, cubed
½ cup milk

Combine oleo and sugar. Mix and add eggs. Fold in pineapple. Moisten bread cubes with milk and add to mixture. Bake in a loaf pan in 350° oven for 45 minutes.

—Corinne Kasten

PECAN TARTS

1 cup flour
1 stick butter
1 3-oz. pkg. cream cheese

FILLING
1 large egg, beaten
1 cup brown sugar
2 Tbls. butter, melted
1 cup pecans

To make tarts, mix all three ingredients together to make pastry. Form little tarts in tart pan. Chill.

Mix all the filling ingredients together and fill tart shells. Bake at 350° for 20 minutes.

CRUNCHY BARS

1 pkg. crescent rolls
1 can sweetened condensed
   milk

1 pkg. coconut pecan frosting
   mix
¼ cup butter or margarine,
   melted

Press rolls to cover 9"x13" pan (do not leave any holes) and come up on the sides about ½". Pour milk to cover dough. Sprinkle frosting mix evenly over this, then drizzle melted butter over the top. Bake in 400° oven for 12 to 15 minutes. Cool at room temperature. Cut into squares.

—*Marian Rasmussen*

QUICK CHOCOLATE COOKIES

¼ cup butter
2 cups sugar
¼ cup Hershey's cocoa
½ cup evaporated milk

3 cups Mother's oats
1 tsp. vanilla
½ cup peanut butter

Combine butter, sugar, cocoa and milk and bring to boil. Boil for one minute and remove from heat. Add remaining ingredients and mix well. Drop by teaspoonful on waxed paper. Let cool and serve.

—*Polly Gregor*

BROWNIES

¾ cup shortening
4 oz. (or 8 Tbls.) cocoa
1 cup brown sugar, firmly
    packed
1 cup granulated sugar
3 eggs

1 tsp. vanilla
1¼ cup flour
1 tsp. baking powder
½ tsp. salt
½ cup nuts
Marshmallow cream

Melt shortening and cocoa together and cool. Mix remaining ingredients except marshmallow cream with shortening and cocoa mixture and pour onto cookie sheet. Bake in 350° oven for 15 minutes. Remove from oven and spread marshmallow cream on top.

—Louella Smith

EASY BROWNIES

2 sticks butter or margarine,
    melted
¾ cup cocoa
2 cups sugar
4 eggs

1½ cups flour
½ tsp. baking soda
½ tsp. salt
2 tsp. vanilla
½ cup nuts, chopped

Measure and sift together dry ingredients into bowl. Add melted butter or margarine, eggs and vanilla and beat until smooth. Fold in nuts. Pour into greased and floured 10½"x15½" pan and bake for 20 minutes in 350° oven. Cool for 5 minutes and frost.

—Georgia Schmeckpeper

I met God in the morning, when my day was at its best,
And His presence came like sunrise, like a glory in my breast.
All day long the presence lingered, all day long He stayed with me.
And we sailed in perfect calmness, o'er a very troubled sea.

Other ships were blown and battered, other ships were sore distressed.
But the wind that seemed to blow them brought to us a peace and rest.

Then I thought of other mornings, with a keen remorse of mind,
When I, too, had loosed the moorings, with His presence left behind.
So I think I know the secret. . . learned from many a troubled way;
You must seek Him in the morning, if you want Him through the day.

CONGO BARS

1 lb. brown sugar	½ tsp. salt
3 eggs	1 cup nuts, chopped
⅔ cup oil	1 6-oz. pkg. chocolate chips
2¾ cups flour	1 6-oz. pkg. butterscotch chips
2½ tsp. baking powder	1 tsp. vanilla
1 tsp. baking soda	

Mix sugar, eggs and oil together. Sift together flour, baking powder, soda and salt and add to first mixture. Then add nuts, chips and vanilla and mix well. Spread on ungreased cookie sheet and bake in 375° oven for 15 minutes. DO NOT OVERBAKE.

—Sophie Zagar

DELICIOUS PEANUT BUTTER BALLS

1 18-oz. jar crunchy peanut butter	1 cup margarine, room temperature
4 cups powdered sugar	1 8-oz. milk chocolate bar
	½ bar paraffin

Mix peanut butter, sugar and margarine and form into one-inch balls. Place on a cookie sheet and chill for a few minutes. Melt chocolate and paraffin in top of double boiler. Dip each ball into chocolate. Keep chocolate at low temperature while dipping. These freeze beautifully and taste great right out of freezer.

Tastes just like peanut butter cups!

—Linda Read

To believe only in possibilities is not faith, but mere philosophy. If anything can be done, experience and skill can do it. If a thing cannot be done, only faith can do it. Faith is fear that has said its prayers. Faith is not contrary to reason, but rather, reason grown courageous.

—Elton Trueblood

TOPPED COOKIES

2 cups sifted flour
½ tsp. soda
¼ tsp. salt
1 egg

1 cup brown sugar
½ cup butter
1 tsp. vanilla

TOPPING

1 cup walnuts, chopped
½ cup brown sugar, firmly
    packed

¼ cup dairy sour cream

Combine flour, soda and salt in mixing bowl. Gradually add butter and sugar, creaming until light and fluffy. Add egg and vanilla. Beat well. Shape into one-inch balls and place 2" apart on ungreased cookie sheet. Combine the topping ingredients. Make a depression in the center of each ball with thumb and place one teaspoon topping in each depression. Bake in 350° oven for 12 to 14 minutes.

—Nancy Scott

LEMON COOLERS

1 pkg. lemon cake mix*
1 large container Cool Whip

1 egg
½ cup powdered sugar

Preheat oven to 350°. Ingredients do not need to be room temperature. Mix cake mix, Cool Whip and egg in large bowl by hand. Drop mixture by teaspoon into powdered sugar to coat. Place on greased cookie sheet and bake for 10 to 15 minutes. Let cool on sheet for 5 minutes before removing. Makes approximately 4 dozen.

* Spice or applesauce cake mix may be used. Omit ½ cup powdered sugar and use ½ cup sugar and cinnamon mixture. Chocolate mix is used with powdered sugar.

—Katie Stuedemann

155

FIVE LAYER COOKIES

1 stick butter, melted
1¼ cups graham crackers, crushed
½ can coconut

1 6-oz. bag chocolate chips
1 6-oz. bag butterscotch chips
1 can Eagle Brand milk
Chopped pecans

Combine butter and cracker crumbs and pat into 9"x13" pan. Sprinkle coconut over crumbs. Layer chocolate chips over coconut, then layer butterscotch chips over chocolate chips. Cover all with Eagle Brand milk. Sprinkle chopped pecans over all. Bake 35 to 40 minutes in 350° oven.

—Sharon Anderson

MAYONNAISE COOKIES

¾ cup mayonnaise
1 cup sugar
3 tsp. cocoa
1 cup raisins or dates
1 cup nuts

1 tsp. baking soda
1 cup boiling water
2 cups flour
½ tsp. salt
1 tsp. vanilla

Cream mayonnaise, sugar and cocoa. Add raisins or dates, nuts, baking soda and boiling water and mix well. Add flour, salt and vanilla. Bake in an 8"x8"x2" pan or make drop cookies. Bake at 325° for 12 to 15 minutes.

—Nettie Brown

MARSHMALLOW COOKIES

2 cups sugar
½ cup cream
1 jar marshmallow cream

¼ lb. margarine
2 cups graham cracker crumbs

Combine sugar and cream and cook on medium heat to soft ball stage. Remove from heat and add marshmallow cream and margarine. Stir until melted. Add crumbs. Drop at once on waxed paper.

—Kathy Darlene Carver

POTATO CHIP COOKIES

2 cups brown sugar
1 cup shortening
2 eggs
2 cups flour

1 tsp. baking soda
1 tsp. pure vanilla
1 cup potato chips, crushed
1 cup nuts, chopped

Cream together sugar, shortening and eggs. Stir in flour, baking soda and vanilla. Mix well. Add chips and nuts. Mix well to distribute evenly. Drop by teaspoonsful onto ungreased cookie sheet. Bake in 350° oven for 10 to 12 minutes.

— Glorie Mello

OLD-FASHIONED SUGAR COOKIES

2 cups flour
½ tsp. baking soda
½ tsp. salt
½ cup shortening
1 cup sugar

1 egg yolk
½ cup buttermilk
1 tsp. vanilla
1 egg white

Mix flour, baking soda and salt. Mix shortening, sugar and egg yolk and add to flour mixture alternately with buttermilk. Add vanilla and egg white. Drop by spoonful and flatten.

— Marvis Johnson

MERINGUE SURPRISES

2 egg whites
1 tsp. vanilla
⅛ tsp. salt

½ cup sugar
1 6-oz. pkg. chocolate chips

Combine egg whites, vanilla and salt. Beat until stiff. Beat in sugar gradually until stiff and satiny. At Christmas, divide mixture into two parts and add red and green food coloring. Fold half of chocolate chips into each mixture. Drop by teaspoonful onto greased cookie sheet and bake 30 minutes in 300° oven.

— Norma Juriek

BROWNIES

1 1-lb. can Hershey syrup
½ cup butter, softened
1 cup sugar
1 cup flour
1 dash salt
4 eggs
½ cup walnuts

FROSTING
½ cup butter
1½ cups sugar
⅓ cup milk
½ cup chocolate chips

To make brownies, mix butter and sugar in large bowl. Add remaining ingredients (except nuts) and beat with mixer. Then add nuts. Bake in 9"x13" pan for 20 minutes in 350° oven. Using medium-sized pan, combine all frosting ingredients (except chocolate chips) and boil for one minute. Take off heat and add chocolate chips. Stir often and frost while brownies are still warm.

—Darlene Menneke

BROWNIES

2 Tbls. cocoa
1 cup sugar
¾ cup self-rising flour
1 stick butter, melted
2 eggs
½ tsp. vanilla
½ cup pecans
Pinch of salt

ICING
1 stick butter
3 Tbls. cocoa
6 Tbls. milk
1 lb. confectioner's sugar
½ tsp. vanilla
Pinch of salt

Combine all ingredients for brownies and bake in 350° oven for 20 minutes. Make icing by combining butter, cocoa, milk and salt. Bring to boil and add the sugar and vanilla. Pour over brownies when removed from oven.

—Faye Hoke

DESSERTS...

QUICK BROWNIES

1 cup sugar
4 Tbls. cocoa
5 Tbls. oil
¾ cup plain flour
⅓ cup milk
2 eggs
1 tsp. vanilla
Pinch of salt

FROSTING

2 cups powdered sugar
½ stick margarine, melted
2 Tbls. cocoa
3-4 Tbls. evaporated milk
1 tsp. vanilla
½ cup pecans, optional

Put all brownie ingredients into medium mixing bowl and mix well. Pour into greased and floured 9"x13" pan and bake in 350° oven for 20 minutes.

Mix all frosting ingredients except pecans in bowl until smooth. Fold in pecans, if desired. Spread on brownies while hot.

—Janice McCalip

BUTTERSCOTCH BROWNIES

½ cup butter
2 cups brown sugar
2 eggs
1 tsp. vanilla
2 cups flour

2 tsp. baking powder
¼ tsp. salt
1 cup coconut
1 cup walnuts

Melt butter, remove and stir in brown sugar. Add eggs, one at a time, stirring until smooth. Stir in vanilla; add all other ingredients. Stir well. Bake on greased cookie sheet for about 25 minutes in 350° oven.

—Connie Reimers

Stress is really an integral part of life. We set our whole pattern of life by our stress end-point. If we hit it exactly, we live dynamic, purposeful, useful, happy lives. If we go over, we break. If we stay too far under, we vegetate.

—H. M. Marvin, M.D.

HERSHEY BROWNIES

½ cup shortening
1 cup sugar
4 eggs
1 cup flour
½ tsp. baking powder
1 1-lb. can Hershey's syrup
¾ cup nuts
½ tsp. vanilla
Dash of salt

FROSTING
6 Tbls. butter
6 Tbls. milk
1½ cups sugar
1 cup chocolate chips
½ bag miniature
   marshmallows
Nuts if desired

To make brownies, cream shortening with mixer. Add remaining ingredients and beat well. Pour into large greased pan. Bake at 350° for 20 to 25 minutes. For frosting, mix butter, milk and sugar and cook only until dissolved. Add remaining ingredients and beat until smooth.

—*Gwen Pigott*

CHOCOLATE MARSHMALLOW COOKIES

1¾ cups flour
½ tsp. salt
½ tsp. baking soda
½ cup cocoa
½ cup shortening
1 cup sugar

1 egg
1 tsp. vanilla
¼ cup milk
½ cup nuts, chopped fine
1 pkg. large marshmallows

Sift dry ingredients together. Beat well by hand the shortening, sugar, egg, vanilla and milk. Add to the dry ingredients. Add the nuts. Preheat oven to 350°. Drop mix by spoonsful onto greased cookie sheet. After baking 8 minutes, remove from oven and press ½ a large marshmallow into each cookie. Return to oven and bake 2 minutes longer. Cool and frost with your favorite chocolate frosting. Makes approximately 3 dozen cookies.

—*Margaret Hamler*

Mothers as well as fools sometimes walk where angels fear to tread.

press ball with fork
like peanut.
butter cookies

bake 325° for
about 12-15 min
cool & sprinkle with
powdered sugar.

Enjoy !
:)

White Choc or Semi Sweet

Copyfast *Printing Center*

Choc Chip
Butter cookies

1 lb butter
   Softened

2 C pdr sugar
_____
   cream
2 tsp Vanilla
1 tsp Salt
4 1/4 C flour
1 cup nuts / 12 oz bag of chips

It will be crumbly form small balls
   over

CHOCOLATE CHIP COOKIES

½ cup butter	½ tsp. baking soda
½ cup sugar	½ salt
¼ cup brown sugar	¼ tsp. hot water
1 egg, beaten	1 6-oz. pkg. chocolate chips
1 cup plus 2 Tbls. flour	½ tsp. vanilla

Cream butter and sugars. Add egg and beat well. Sift dry ingredients and add to creamed mixture. Add hot water and mix well. Add chocolate chips and vanilla. Drop by rounded teaspoonful on ungreased cookie sheet and bake in preheated 350° oven for 10 to 12 minutes. Yields 3½ dozen.

—*Karen Rohrbaugh*

M & M COOKIES

1 cup margarine	2¼ cups flour
1 cup brown sugar	1 tsp. baking soda
½ cup sugar	½ tsp. salt
2 tsp. vanilla	M & M's
2 eggs	

Blend shortening and two sugars. Beat in vanilla and eggs. Mix baking soda and salt and ¼ cup flour. Beat into first mixture. Add the rest of the flour and mix well. Drop by teaspoon (scant) on cookie sheet. Decorate each cookie with 3, 4, or 5 M & M candies. Bake 8-10 minutes in 375° oven.

—*Dolores Arsenault*

The greatest discovery of my generation is that people can alter their lives by altering their attitudes of mind.

—William James

CHOCOLATE SQUARES

2 cups sugar
2 cups flour
½ tsp. salt
1 stick oleo
½ cup salad oil
¼ cup cocoa

1 cup water
2 eggs
1 tsp. vanilla
½ cup sour milk (or 1 tsp.
    vinegar and 1 tsp. soda
    dissolved in sweet milk)

Mix sugar, flour and salt together in bowl. Mix oleo, oil, cocoa and water in pan and bring to a boil. Pour hot mixture over dry ingredients and stir. Add remaining ingredients and beat well. Pour into a greased and floured 12"x18" pan and bake in 350° oven for 30 minutes.

—JoAnn Weber

CHOCOLATE BUTTERSWEETS

½ cup butter or oleo
½ cup powdered sugar
¼ tsp. salt

1 tsp. vanilla
1-1¼ cups flour

FILLING
1 3-oz. pkg. cream cheese
1 cup powdered sugar
1 tsp. vanilla
2 Tbls. flour
½ cup nuts

ICING
½ cup Nestle's semi-sweet
    chocolate chips
2 Tbls. butter
2 Tbls. water
½ cup powdered sugar, sifted

To make the cookies, combine all ingredients and mix well. Make into small balls, the size of a walnut and put on a cookie sheet. Press thumb in center of each for the topping. Bake in 350° oven for 10 to 12 minutes.

For the creamy nut filling, soften the cream cheese and blend in the sugar and vanilla. Add the flour; then cream well. Stir in the nuts and put on cookie while still warm.

For the chocolate icing, melt the chocolate chips and butter with 2 Tbls. water over low heat stirring occasionally. Add the powdered sugar and beat until smooth. Put the icing over the cream filling.

—Helen Marie Rossi

MISTI'S SUGAR COOKIES

¾ cup shortening (not butter)
1 cup sugar
2 eggs
1 tsp. vanilla

Food coloring, if desired
2¼-2½ cups flour
1 tsp. baking powder
1 tsp. salt

ICING

Milk
Powdered sugar

Pinch of salt
½ tsp. vanilla

Mix shortening, sugar, eggs, vanilla and food coloring until fluffy. Mix flour, baking powder and salt together in a separate bowl. Combine the two mixtures and chill for one hour. Heat oven to 400° and roll dough ⅛" thick on a lightly floured board. Cut with a cookie cutter and place on an ungreased baking sheet. Bake just until the cookies are set (about 6 minutes). Set cookies aside to cool.

Combine all icing ingredients and beat well. Ice cookies when cool. Makes about 3 dozen cookies.

—Julie Wallis

RYAN'S SNICKERDOODLES

1 cup shortening (part butter)
1 cup sugar
2 eggs
2½ cups flour

1 tsp. baking soda
½ tsp. salt
2 Tbls. sugar
2 tsp. cinnamon

Heat oven to 400°. Mix shortening, 1 cup sugar and eggs until fluffy. In a separate bowl mix flour, baking soda and salt thoroughly and add to the shortening mixture. Make sure the dough is not too dry. It should just barely form into nearly golf sized balls. Mix 2 tablespoons sugar and 2 teaspoons cinnamon together and roll balls in mixture. Place on an ungreased cookie sheet and bake just until the cookies are set (about 10 minutes). Yields 2 dozen cookies.

—Julie Wallis

APPLE BARS

1 cup sugar
1 cup water
2 Tbls. cornstarch
1 tsp. vanilla
1½ cups oatmeal

1 cup brown sugar
2 cups flour, sifted
¾ cup shortening, softened
4-5 apples
Salt

Combine sugar, water, cornstarch and vanilla and bring to a boil. Cook about 5 minutes. Cool. In a separate bowl, mix oatmeal, brown sugar, flour, shortening and salt with fork. Grease 9"x13" cake pan. Cover bottom and sides with dry ingredients, reserving some of the dry ingredients for top. Cover crumbed pan with apples, sliced thin. Pour cooked filling over apples. Sprinkle the reserved crumbs over filling. Bake in 375° oven for 45 minutes to 1 hour.

—Bettie Leustek

MICHIGAN APPLE COOKIES

½ cup butter or oleo
1⅓ cup brown sugar
1 egg
¼ cup apple juice (use baby's can for economy)
2 cups flour
½ tsp. salt

½ tsp. cloves
1 tsp. cinnamon
1 tsp. baking soda
1 cup apples, peeled and chopped
1 cup raisins
1 cup nuts, chopped

GLAZE

½ cup powdered sugar
1 Tbls. butter

2 Tbls. apple juice or water

Cream together the first 4 ingredients. Combine all dry ingredients and add to cream mixture. Stir in apples, raisins and nuts. Drop on cookie sheet and bake 13 minutes in 350° oven. Combine glaze ingredients and spread a little glaze on each cookie while still warm.

—Doris Roper

YUM YUM COOKIES

1 cup shortening
1½ cups sugar
3 eggs
3 cups self-rising flour (if
    plain, add 1 tsp. baking
    soda and ¼ tsp. salt)

1 tsp. cinnamon
1 Tbls. water
1 8-oz. pkg. dates, chopped
1 cup nuts

Blend shortening with sugar until light and fluffy. Add eggs one at a time, beating well after each addition. Combine dry ingredients and add to sugar mixture. Add water to dates and add with nuts to flour mixture. Drop by teaspoons onto greased cookie sheet. Bake at 375° for 12 to 15 minutes. Yields 6 dozen cookies.

—Barbara McDonald

REFRIGERATOR DATE COOKIES

1 cup shortening
2 cups brown sugar
2 eggs
1 cup nuts, ground

1 cup dates, ground
3½ cups cake flour
1 tsp. salt
1 tsp. baking soda

Cream shortening and sifted sugar thoroughly. Add eggs 1 at a time and beat well after each addition. Add nuts and dates which have been put through food chopper. Sift dry ingredients together, add to creamed mixture and mix well. Shape into rolls 2 inches in diameter. Wrap in waxed paper and store in refrigerator until firm. Slice thin and bake 8 minutes in 400° oven. Makes 11 to 12 dozen cookies.

—Evelyn Lord

MAY WE RESOLVE ALWAYS

May we be a little less impatient with those we deem too slow,
A little less arrogant because of all we know,
A little more forgiving and swifter to be kind,
And a little more eager — to be sweeter all the time!

DATE BARS

1 cup flour	1 egg
½ tsp. salt	⅔ cup milk
1 tsp. baking powder	1¼ cups dates, chopped
1 cup sugar	1 cup nuts, chopped
1 tsp. cinnamon	

Sift dry ingredients. Add nuts and dates. Beat egg, add milk and mix well. Add gradually to dry mixture and combine. Pour into 9"x13" shallow pan. Bake in 350° oven for 25 to 30 minutes. Cut into squares.

— JoAnn Weber

ORANGE DROP COOKIES

1½ cups brown sugar, firmly packed	3 cups flour, sifted
1 cup margarine	½ tsp. salt
2 eggs	2 tsp. baking powder
1 Tbls. orange peel, grated	1 tsp. baking soda
1 tsp. vanilla	¾ cup buttermilk

FROSTING

1 Tbls. orange peel, grated	3 Tbls. margarine
3 Tbls. orange juice	Powdered sugar

Cream brown sugar and margarine. Add eggs, orange peel and vanilla. Beat until fluffy. Add flour, baking soda, baking powder and salt, alternating with buttermilk. Drop by teaspoonsful on ungreased cookie sheet. Bake in 350° oven for 10 to 12 minutes. Prepare frosting by combining orange peel, orange juice and margarine, adding enough powdered sugar to make a good frosting consistency. Frost cookies while still warm.

— Debbie Wark

Luck is preparation meeting opportunity . . .
The harder I work . . . the luckier I get!
From "Be Somebody" by Mary Crowley

FROSTY STRAWBERRY SQUARES

1 cup flour
¼ cup brown sugar
½ cup walnuts, chopped
½ cup butter or oleo, melted
2 egg whites
⅔ cup sugar

1 pkg. Dream Whip, prepared
   according to pkg. directions
1 10-oz. pkg. frozen strawberries, partially thawed
Whole strawberries for garnish

Stir together flour, brown sugar, walnuts, and butter or oleo. Spread evenly in shallow baking pan. Bake in 350° oven for 20 minutes, stirring occasionally. Sprinkle ⅔ of these crumbs in 13"x9"x2" pan. Combine egg whites, sugar, and berries in a large bowl. With electric mixer beat at high speed to stiff peaks (about 10 minutes). Fold in prepared Dream Whip. Spoon over crumbs and top with remaining crumbs. Freeze 6 hours or overnight. Cut in squares and trim with whole strawberries.

—JoAnn Weber

HOLIDAY FRUIT DROPS

1 cup shortening
2 cups brown sugar
2 eggs
½ cup buttermilk
3½ cups flour
1 tsp. baking soda

1 tsp. salt
1½ cups pecans, broken
2 cups candied cherries,
   chopped
2 cups dates, chopped
Pecan halves

Mix shortening, sugar and eggs well. Stir in buttermilk, add dry ingredients. Stir in pecans, cherries and dates. Chill one hour. Drop rounded teaspoonsful of dough onto greased cookie sheet. Place pecan halves on top of each cookie. Bake in 400° oven for 8 to 10 minutes.

—Florence Pruiett

Curiosity is the wick in the candle of learning.
—William A. Ward

CREAM WAFERS

1 cup butter, softened   2 cups flour
⅓ cup whipping cream   ½ cup sugar

FILLING

¼ cup soft butter   1 tsp. vanilla
¾ cup powdered sugar   Food coloring, optional
1 egg yolk

Mix butter, whipping cream and flour and chill one hour. Roll ⅛"
thick. Cut into small shapes 1½" in diameter. Transfer onto plate
with ½ cup sugar on it. Coat both sides with sugar. Place on
ungreased baking sheet. **Important:** Prick 4 times with fork. Bake
at 375° for 7 to 9 minutes. To make filling, combine all the filling
ingredients and mix well. Place filling between two wafers.

— Judy Sandberg

BROWNIES

2 cups sugar   1 cup water
2 cups flour   ½ cup milk
1 stick margarine   2 eggs, beaten
½ cup shortening   1 tsp. baking soda
4 Tbls. cocoa   ½ tsp. salt

Sift sugar and flour together in a bowl and set aside. In a saucepan,
mix margarine, shortening, cocoa and water. Bring to a rapid boil
and pour over sugar and flour mixture. Add milk, eggs, baking
soda and salt. Pour into a well-greased brownie pan. Bake for 20
minutes at 400°.

— Jan Setsodi

BONNIE'S YOGURT POPSICLES

1 3-oz pkg. Jello, prepared and   1 8-oz. carton yogurt
   chilled   1 Tbls. honey

When Jello has thickened, add yogurt and honey. Pour into cups
and freeze.

— Bonnie Dunn

BISCOCHITOS (Cookies)

1 cup sugar	1 cup shortening
3 eggs	4 cups flour
2 tsp. vanilla	3 tsp. baking powder
2 tsp. anise seed	

Mix thoroughly sugar, eggs, vanilla and anise seed. Add shortening and stir. Sift flour and baking powder and blend into mixture. Roll out about ⅛" thick, cut with cookie cutter and place on a slightly greased baking sheet. Bake at 400° for 6 to 8 minutes.

—Aurora De La O

CRUNCHY KISSES

½ cup white sugar	3 cups corn, wheat, or bran
½ cup corn syrup	flakes, raisin squares
⅔ cup peanut butter	(Captain Crunch is also
	good)

Mix sugar and syrup in saucepan and bring to a boil over medium heat. Turn off heat and add peanut butter. Using a wooden spoon, blend thoroughly. Pour over flakes in large bowl. Stir lightly until coated. Drop by tablespoons onto waxed paper. Let cool.

—Norma Haney

SUMMER CAKE

1 lg. box Jello (any flavor, but	Cool Whip
red is best)	
1 Duncan Hines white cake	
mix, prepared as directed	

Prepare Jello as directed, but omit the cold water. DO NOT refrigerate. Let set at room temperature. Bake cake, using a 9"x13" pan. Let cool. Poke holes in cake. Pour Jello over cake and refrigerate at least two hours. Frost with Cool Whip before serving.

—Darlyne Hastins

"GRANDMA'S FIG COOKIES"

FILLING FOR COOKIES

This filling makes enough filling for 4 batches of cookies. Cut into fourths for dough recipe.

5 lbs. figs	3 cups wine or orange juice
2 lbs. raisins	1 12-oz. can crushed
1 lb. dates	pineapple
4 tsp. cinnamon	2 ground oranges
4 tsp. nutmeg	2 cups pecans
1 tsp. cloves	2 cups walnuts
1 tsp. black pepper, crushed	2 cups almonds
1 cup honey or jelly	

Mix all ingredients together and let set while mixing dough.

DOUGH

6 cups flour	3 sticks margarine
1 cup sugar	3 eggs, beaten
3 tsp. baking powder	1 cup milk
1 tsp. salt	1 Tbls. vanilla

Mix flour, sugar, baking powder and salt together. Work in margarine. Beat eggs well. Add milk and vanilla. Add to flour mixture. Roll dough into long, 2-inch wide strips. Fill the center of the strips with filling. Bring sides together to form a roll. Roll lightly to seal the seam. Cut into approximately 2" pieces (cut diagonally). Bake in 400° oven for 15 minutes.

ICING

1 lb. powdered sugar	1 tsp. vanilla or lemon extract
1 stick margarine, softened	Milk

Cream together sugar, margarine and vanilla. Add milk a little at a time, mixing together with mixer. Icing should be slightly runny. Add extract to flavor icing. **These cookies are wonderful!**

— *Barbara Fanara*

DESSERTS...

FRESH APPLE CAKE

2 cups sugar
1 cup shortening or butter
4 eggs
2½ cups flour
½ cup cold water
1 tsp. cloves
1 tsp. cinnamon

1 tsp. nutmeg
1 tsp. baking soda
1 tsp. salt
1 cup nuts
2 cups fresh apples, chopped
   finely

Mix sugar and shortening until creamy. Add eggs, then add water and vanilla. Sift flour, spices and salt together. Add to sugar mixture, then add apples and chopped nuts. Bake at 350° for 45 minutes to 1 hour.

—Katie Havard

MANDARIN ORANGE CAKE

1 yellow cake mix (disregard
   directions on box)
1 cup oil

4 eggs
1 small can Mandarin oranges,
   juice and all

TOPPING

1 lg. can crushed pineapple,
   with juice

1 pkg. instant vanilla pudding
1 9-oz. container Cool Whip

Combine cake mix, oil, eggs and oranges and mix well. Put in greased and floured 9"x13" pan. Bake in 350° oven for 35 minutes. Stir together pineapple, pudding and Cool Whip until thoroughly mixed. Spread on cake. Keep refrigerated.

—Sharon Anderson

HUSBAND'S HOMECOMING

I scrubbed the kitchen floor today, and washed the woodwork, too...
I refereed the children's play, until I'm black and blue...
I washed the dishes, and baked a cake, and cleaned the linen chest,
And now I'll just lie down and take a little, teeny rest.
That's just when you walk in and say, "So this is what you do all day?"

LEMON CHEESECAKE

1 3-oz. pkg. lemon Jello
1 cup boiling water
3 Tbls. lemon juice
1 8-oz. pkg. Philadelphia
    cream cheese

1 cup granulated sugar
1 tsp. vanilla
1 13-oz. can Milnot (or
    evaporated milk)

CRUST

½ lb. graham crackers   ½ stick oleo

To make filling, combine all ingredients except milk and chill. Beat milk and add partially thickened Jello, cheese and sugar mixture. To make crust, crush graham crackers and pour melted butter over them. Mix well and press into bottom of pie pan. Pour in the filling and chill.

—*Crystal Sronce*

JUICE CAKE

1 Duncan Hines yellow cake
    mix

3 eggs
1½ cans apricot nectar

ICING

1½ cups powdered sugar   1 8-oz. can apricot nectar

Empty contents of cake mix into mixing bowl; add eggs and apricot nectar. Preheat oven to 350°. Beat ingredients at medium speed for 3 to 5 minutes. Pour ingredients into cake pan and bake for 45 minutes. To make the icing, combine sugar and nectar in saucepan. Bring to boil and stir until thick. Let cool and pour over cooled cake.

—*Pearlie Williams*

Judge not another — from your high and lofty seat. Step down into the arena, where he and his problems meet.

From *"Be Somebody"* by Mary Crowley

FRUIT CAKE

1 cup sugar
1½ cups flour
½ tsp. salt
1 tsp. baking powder
4 eggs

1 lb. candied cherries
1 lb. candied pineapple
1 lb. pitted dates
1 lb. pecans

Chop fruit and nuts and mix with ½ cup flour. Mix together other dry ingredients. Add eggs to make a batter. Mix batter mixture with fruit and nut mixture. Bake at 325° for 1½ hours.

—Gladys B. Phelps

MELT-IN-YOUR-MOUTH BLUEBERRY CAKE

2 eggs, separated
1 cup sugar
¼ tsp. salt
½ cup shortening
1 tsp. vanilla

1½ cups all purpose flour, sifted
1 tsp. baking powder
⅓ cup milk
1½ cups blueberries

Beat egg whites until stiff. Add about ½ cup of the sugar to keep them stiff. Cream shortening and add salt and vanilla. Add remaining sugar gradually. Add unbeaten egg yolks and beat until light and creamy. Add sifted dry ingredients alternately with the milk. Fold in the beaten whites. Take a bit of the flour called for in the recipe and coat the blueberries so they won't settle. Fold in the fresh blueberries. May also use canned berries. Turn into a greased 8"x8" pan. Sprinkle top of batter lightly with granulated sugar. Bake 50 to 60 minutes in 350° oven.

—Linda Pelotte

HOMEMADE ICE CREAM

2½ cups sugar
1 tsp. vanilla
6 eggs

1 qt. half & half
2 cups Cool Whip
2½ cups fruit

Mix all together and pour into ice cream freezer.

—Marie Keel

173

BELVILLE GOOEY BUTTER CAKE

1 Duncan Hines yellow butter
   cake mix
1 stick butter
1 egg

1 8-oz. pkg. cream cheese
2 eggs
¾ box confectioner's sugar

Mix cake mix, butter and 1 egg by hand and press into 8"x12" baking dish. Combine cream cheese, 2 eggs and confectioner's sugar and beat with mixer until creamy. Pour over first mixture and bake at 350° for 30 to 35 minutes. Sprinkle confectioner's sugar over cake when baked. Cool and refrigerate (better if refrigerated overnight). Cut in bars or squares.

—Rosalyn Dowling

MAYONNAISE CAKE

2 cups flour
1 cup sugar
½ tsp. salt
1 tsp. soda
1 tsp. vanilla

1 tsp. baking powder
4 Tbls. cocoa
1 small jar or ½ cup
   mayonnaise
1 cup water

Mix all dry ingredients together; add mayonnaise, vanilla and water. Mix until smooth. Bake at 350° for 30 minutes. To make sheet cake, double recipe and bake about one hour.

—Linda McGuckin

I have just a minute with sixty seconds in it,
Forced upon me, can't refuse it.
Didn't seek it, didn't choose it.
But, it's up to me to use it.

I must suffer if I lose it.
Give account if I abuse it.
Just a tiny, little minute . . .
But, ETERNITY is in it.

—Unknown

"RED RED" CHRISTMAS CAKE

½ cup shortening or oleo
1½ cups sugar
2 eggs
2 cups flour
2 Tbls. cocoa
1 tsp. salt

1 Tbls. vinegar (reserve)
1 tsp. baking soda (reserve)
1 cup buttermilk
1 tsp. vanilla
1 2-oz. bottle red food
   coloring

Stir together flour, cocoa and salt. Cream shortening (or oleo) and sugar. Add eggs, one at a time. Beat until fluffy. Add sifted dry ingredients alternately with buttermilk. Add vanilla and food coloring. Beat well. Fold in soda and vinegar, which have been mixed together. Bake at 350° for 30 minutes if using two round pans — 35 minutes for oblong pan.

CREAMY WHITE FROSTING

1 cup milk
¼ cup flour
1 cup sugar

1 stick oleo
1 cup shortening
Coconut, if desired

Combine milk and flour. Cook until thick and let cool. Beat sugar, oleo and shortening until fluffy. Add to first mixture and beat until ready to spread. Cover with red coconut if desired. To color coconut, just add a couple of drops of red food coloring to bowl of coconut and stir until well coated.

—Joan Van Dyke

POPPY SEED CAKE

1 pkg. white cake mix
1 oz. poppy seeds
1 Tbls. cooking oil
2 Tbls. more moisture than
   cake mix calls for

Vanilla filling
Whipped cream or whipped
   topping

Bake cake in 2 layers for 30 minutes at 350°. Put layers together with favorite vanilla filling. Top with whipped cream or other whipped topping just before serving.

—Kay Oberlitner

PINEAPPLE DREAM CAKE

2 cups flour
2 cups sugar
1 tsp. vanilla

2 tsp. baking soda
2 eggs
1 lg. can crushed pineapple

ICING

1 8-oz. pkg. Philadelphia
　　cream cheese
½ stick oleo

1 tsp. vanilla
½-¾ box powdered sugar

Mix all cake ingredients together and pour into baking pan. Bake in 350° oven for 1 hour or until done. Combine all icing ingredients and ice cake. This makes a very moist and rich cake and is very EASY!

—Mary Jane Spencer

PINEAPPLE CAKE

3 eggs
2 cups sugar
1 tsp. vanilla
1 #2 can crushed pineapple,
　　with juice

2 cups flour
2 tsp. soda
½ tsp. salt

ICING

1½ cups sugar
1 cup evaporated milk
¾ stick butter

1½ cups flaked coconut
1 cup nutmeats

To make the cake, beat eggs, add sugar and mix well. Add vanilla, then pineapple and juice. Add flour sifted with soda and salt. Pour into large greased and floured pan. Bake 45 minutes in 350° oven. (Batter should not be more than 1 inch thick.)

Ten minutes before the cake is done begin icing. Mix sugar, milk and butter and bring to a boil. Cook 2 minutes. Add coconut and nuts. Spread on hot cake and return to oven 10 minutes, or under broiler for 2 to 3 minutes.

—Ann Burkes

DESSERTS . . .

STRAWBERRY CAKE

1 box white cake mix
1 10-oz. pkg. strawberries,
   thawed
1 3-oz. pkg. wild strawberry
   Jello

¾ cup oil
½ cup water
3 Tbls. flour
3 eggs

FROSTING

1 10-oz. pkg. Cool Whip

1 10-oz. pkg. strawberries,
   thawed

Mix all cake ingredients together and bake in 350° oven for 40 to 45 minutes. For the frosting, mix the Cool Whip and strawberries, juice and all. Spread on cooled cake. Keep refrigerated.

—Sue Chandler

SWEET AND SAUERKRAUT CAKE

½ cup butter or margarine
1½ cups sugar
3 eggs
1 tsp. vanilla
2 cups all-purpose flour, sifted
1 tsp. baking powder
1 tsp. baking soda

¼ tsp. salt
½ cup cocoa powder
1 8-oz. can (1 cup) sauerkraut,
   drained, rinsed, finely
   chopped
1 cup water

In large mixing bowl, cream butter or margarine and sugar until light. Beat in eggs, one at a time, and add vanilla. Sift together flour, baking powder, baking soda, salt and cocoa. Add to creamed mixture alternately with water, beating after each addition. Stir in kraut. Turn into greased and floured 13"x9"x2" baking pan. Bake at 350° for 35 to 40 minutes.

—Bethany Fowler

Real joy comes not from ease or riches or from the praise of men, but from doing something worthwhile.

—Sir Winfred Grenfell

177

DESSERTS...

DREAM CAKE

1 angel food cake, broken into
   pieces
2 pkgs. Dream Whip
1 cup cold milk

1 cup confectioner's sugar
1 8-oz. pkg. cream cheese
1 can cherry pie filling

Beat Dream Whip and milk together. Add sugar and mix. Beat cream cheese until smooth. Add Dream Whip mixture to cream cheese a little at a time. Place layer of cake pieces in 13"x9" pan, then layer of Dream Whip mixture, another layer of cake, then Dream Whip mixture. Put cherry pie filling on top and chill overnight. Serves about 12.

—Connie Henry

SOUR CREAM CAKE

½ cup Wesson oil
1 cup butter
3 cups sugar
6 eggs
3 cups flour

1 cup sour cream
1 tsp. vanilla
1 tsp. baking powder
Pinch of salt

GLAZE

1 cup confectioner's sugar

2 Tbls. lemon juice or milk

Cream oil, butter and sugar. Add eggs, one at a time. Add flour with sour cream to first mixture. Mix well. Add flavoring and bake one hour in greased tube pan at 350°. Combine glaze ingredients and glaze cake.

—Faye Hoke

Where we are wrong, make us willing to change; and where we are right, make us easy to live with. Deliver us, we pray, from the tyranny of trifles. Teach us how to listen to the prompting of Thy Spirit, and thus save us from floundering in indecision that wastes time, subtracts from our peace, divides our efficiency and multiples our troubles.

—Peter Marshall

DESSERTS...

POLKA DOT CAKE

3 cups flour
2 cups sugar
1 tsp. salt
½ cup cocoa
2 tsp. baking soda

1 tsp. vanilla
2 Tbls. white vinegar
2 cups cold water
⅔ cup oil

TOPPING

1 8-oz. pkg. cream cheese
1 egg
⅓ cup sugar

½ tsp. vanilla
1 6-oz. pkg. chocolate bits

To make the cake, mix all dry ingredients, and then add liquids. Mix well. Pour into greased and floured 13"x9"x2" pan. Bake in 350° oven for 45 to 60 minutes. May have to bake a little longer, but it is worth it. This is a delicious cake.

Make the topping by combining all the ingredients, stirring in chocolate bits last. Drop by spoonsful over the cake.

—Patricia Boyer

PINEAPPLE CREAM CAKE

1 lg. pkg. lemon Jello
1½ cups boiling water
2 8½-oz. cans crushed
   pineapple, with juice

3 egg yolks
¾ cup powdered sugar, sifted
1½ cups heavy cream
1 angel food cake

Dissolve Jello in water. Add pineapple, chill until slightly thickened. Beat egg yolks, gradually adding sugar. Beat until thick and yellow colored. Whip cheese. Fold in egg mixture and cream into Jello. Chill until of spreading consistency. Purchase or make an angel food cake. With a sharp knife, cut into three layers. Spread topping between layers and over top and sides. Chill until ready to serve.

—Alberta Crowell

MILNOT CHEESECAKE

1 3-oz. pkg. lemon Jello
1 cup boiling water
1 8-oz. pkg. cream cheese
½ cup sugar
1 tsp. vanilla

1 13-oz. can Milnot
3 cups graham cracker crumbs
½ cup butter or margarine,
   melted

Dissolve gelatin in boiling water. Chill until slightly thickened. Cream together cheese, sugar and vanilla. Add gelatin and blend well. Fold in stiffly whipped Milnot (this can be done with electric mixer). Mix graham cracker crumbs and melted butter. Pack ⅔ of mixture on bottom and sides of 9"x13"x2" pan, or larger. Add filling and sprinkle with remaining crumbs. Chill overnight. Cut in squares and serve plain or garnish with fruit. Serves 12 to 16.

—Lee and Mary Chorey

LEMON CHEESECAKE

FILLING

2 8-oz. pkgs. cream cheese
1 6-oz. box lemon Jello
1 lg. can crushed pineapple

1 lg. container Cool Whip
2 cups sugar

CRUST

2½ sticks oleo, melted

2 pkgs. graham crackers,
   crushed

Make Jello with 2 cups of very hot (but not boiling) water. Set aside to cool. Drain crushed pineapple. Cream together cream cheese and sugar. Add cooled Jello and mix until well blended. Add pineapple. Fold in Cool Whip and pour into prepared crust.

To prepare the crust, combine the ingredients and press ⅔ of mixture into bottom of oblong pan. Pour in cream cheese mixture. Sprinkle remaining ⅓ of graham cracker mixture on top. Chill well before serving. Can be made the day before.

—Virginia Rosloniec

PISTACHIO INSIDE OUTSIDE CAKE

1 pkg. white or yellow cake mix
1 pkg. pistachio flavor Jello
   instant pudding
3 eggs

1 cup club soda
1 cup oil
½ cup chopped nuts

FROSTING

1½ cups cold milk
1 envelope Dream Whip

1 pkg. pistachio flavor Jello
   instant pudding
Chopped nuts for garnish

Blend all cake ingredients. Bake in greased and floured 10" bundt pan in 350° oven for 50 minutes. Cool 15 minutes. Remove from pan and cool. Split into 3 layers.

Blend all the frosting ingredients together and whip until thickened, about 5 minutes. Spread about 1 cup of frosting between each layer. Spoon remainder of frosting into center of cake. Chill, garnish with chopped nuts.

—*Susan Sherman*

PISTACHIO CAKE

1 lg. box yellow cake mix
1 3½-oz. box instant pistachio
   pudding
1 cup oil
½ pt. sour cream

4 eggs
½ cup nuts, chopped
1 Tbls. cinnamon
1 tsp. nutmeg
½ cup sugar

Combine cake mix, pudding, oil and sour cream, and add eggs in large mixing bowl. Combine well. Pour one-half cake batter into greased and floured 10" tube pan. Combine nuts, sugar and spices. Sprinkle one-half the nut mixture evenly over batter. Pour in remaining batter and top with remaining nut mixture. Press nut mixture into batter with the back of a spoon. Bake at 350° for 50 to 60 minutes. Let cake cool at least 30 minutes before removing from pan.

—*Maureen Fugate*

WATERGATE CAKE

1 box white cake mix
1 box instant pistachio
   pudding
1 cup cooking oil

3 eggs
1 cup soda water
½ cup nuts

FROSTING

1 box pistachio instant
   pudding

1 envelope Dream Whip
1¼ cups cold water

To make the cake, mix first 5 ingredients with electric mixer at medium speed for 2 minutes. Fold in nuts. Pour in greased and floured tube pan. Bake 45 to 55 minutes in 350° oven. Mix frosting ingredients according to directions on Dream Whip box.

—Vickie Ambrose

WATERGATE CAKE

1 box Duncan Hines Deluxe II
   cake mix
1 box instant pistachio
   pudding

3 eggs
½ cup nuts, chopped
1 cup Wesson oil
1 cup soda water

ICING

2 pkgs. Dream Whip
1¼ cups milk
1 pkg. pistachio instant
   pudding

Coconut
Chopped nuts
Cherries

In a large mixing bowl put cake and pudding mixes. Combine and add other ingredients. Beat 4 minutes. Grease and flour bundt pan. Bake 45 minutes to 1 hour. Cool.

Combine 2 packages Dream Whip and the milk. Beat until stiff, then add 1 box instant pistachio pudding mix. Ice the cake with mixture and garnish with coconut, chopped nuts and cherries.

—Linda Abel

Watergate Cake recipes were also contributed by Judy Griffin, Kathy Parbel, Lillie Mae Keener, and Metta Ray Biehler.

DESSERTS...

JELLO-PUDDING CAKE

1 box yellow cake mix, prepare
   according to pkg. directions
1 small pkg. strawberry Jello
1 10-oz. strawberry soft drink

1 medium sized container
   Cool Whip
2 cups cold milk
1 lg. box instant vanilla
   pudding

Bake cake in one layer in oblong pan. Let cool and pierce with fork. Mix Jello with 1 cup hot water and strawberry soft drink. Pour over cake. Mix Cool Whip, 2 cups milk and vanilla pudding together and pour over cake. Let cool in refrigerator for about two hours.

—Sylvia Verdin

VANILLA WAFER CAKE

1 12-oz. box vanilla wafers
6 eggs
1 cup walnuts, chopped
1 tsp. vanilla
1 7-oz. pkg. angel coconut

1¼ cups sugar
1 stick margarine
1 cup milk
Whipped cream, if desired

Crush vanilla wafers into fine crumbs. Add eggs and vanilla. Beat in sugar until smooth. Add walnuts and coconut. Bake at 350° for 45 minutes. Serve with whipped cream or plain.

—Jackie Hacketts

WORRY...
   ...is a misuse of the imagination.
   ...is assuming responsibility that God never intended you to have.
   ...never robs tomorrow of its sorrow.
   ...only saps today of its strength.

From "Be Somebody" by Mary Crowley

PINEAPPLE-COCONUT CAKE

1 pkg. Duncan Hines pine-
    apple supreme cake mix
1 pkg. pineapple instant
    pudding mix

4 eggs
½ cup Wesson oil
1 10-oz. bottle 7-Up

ICING

2 Tbls. flour
1½ cups sugar
1 stick oleo

1 lg. can crushed pineapple
2 eggs, well beaten
1 can coconut

Combine cake and pudding mix, eggs, oil and 7-Up and mix well. Bake in three 9" layer pans or four 8" pans in 325° oven for 20 to 25 minutes. Ice while warm.

To prepare icing, melt oleo and add sugar, flour and pineapple. Add eggs and cook until thick. Add coconut. Put between layers and on top of cake while still hot.

—Dollie Clary

COCONUT TOPPING

2 pkgs. frozen coconut
8 oz. sour cream

2 cups sugar

Mix all ingredients well and set in refrigerator overnight. Make butter cake in 3 pans and ice them with the icing. Wrap in foil or cover, and let set 3 days, if possible.

—Nellie Smith

DUMP CAKE

1 #2 can crushed pineapple
1 can instant cherry pie filling
1 box yellow cake mix

1 cup pecans, chopped
1 stick margarine

Spread the pineapple, juice included, in a 13"x9" pan. Next, spoon the cherry pie filling on top and sprinkle the dry cake mix over this. Spread the pecans over all and dot with margarine. Do NOT stir any of the ingredients. Bake at 350° for 1 hour.

—Joy Skinner and Susan Bahner

DESSERTS . . .

FRESH APPLE CAKE

2 cups sugar
2 eggs
1½ cups oil
2 tsp. vanilla
3 cups apples, peeled and
    chopped

3 cups flour
1 tsp. cinnamon
1 tsp. soda
½ tsp. salt
Whipped cream, if desired

Blend sugar, eggs, vanilla and oil. Sift dry ingredients together and blend with sugar mixture. Add chopped apples. Pour into greased and floured pan and bake one hour until done in 350° oven. The cake mixture will be very thick, almost like paste. However, the result is a very moist delicious cake. You may add a whipped cream topping if desired.

— Judy Keller

DELICIOUS DUMP CAKE

1 can cherry pie filling
1 can crushed pineapple
1 two-layer white cake mix

1 stick margarine
Whipped topping

Mix pie filling and pineapple together and pour in a buttered 9"x12" pan. Sprinkle with cake mix. Dab margarine over top. Bake at 350° until golden brown. Serve warm with whipped topping.

— Bea Fiala

BANANA SAILBOATS

1 pkg. vanilla pudding, large size
Vanilla wafer cookies

Bananas
Miniature marshmallows

Prepare pudding according to package directions. Line individual serving dishes with vanilla wafers. Slice bananas over wafers. Spoon cooled pudding over this. Decorate with marshmallows and additional banana slices if desired.

— Deb Willis

185

RAW APPLE CAKE

½ cup butter
1 cup sugar
2 cups apples, chopped
2 cups flour
½ tsp. salt
1 tsp. cinnamon

¼ tsp. nutmeg
1 cup raisins
1 cup nuts
1 tsp. soda
1 Tbls. hot water
1 egg

Cream butter and sugar. Add the egg and then the apples. Dissolve the soda in hot water and add to apple mixture. Sift flour with salt, nutmeg and cinnamon. Mix the raisins and nuts in the flour mixture and add to apple mixture. Stir well and bake in a 9"x12" pan in 350° oven until done.

—Velma Kugler

APPLE CAKE

1 cup cooking oil
2 cups sugar
3 eggs
2 cups self-rising flour
3 cups fresh apples, chopped

1 tsp. vanilla
1 cup pecans or black walnuts
½ cup raisins, optional
1 tsp. cinnamon
1 tsp. nutmeg

TOPPING

1 cup sugar
1 Tbls. white syrup
1 tsp. vanilla

1 stick margarine
½ cup buttermilk
½ tsp. baking soda

To make cake, combine oil, sugar and eggs. Beat well. Add flour, beat thoroughly, and add remaining ingredients. Stir to blend well (be sure to flour nuts). Pour into greased 11"x7"x2" or 8"x8"x2" pan. Bake at 350° for 40 to 45 minutes. Combine all topping ingredients except vanilla and cook over medium heat to soft ball stage. Add vanilla and remove from heat. Beat until slightly thickened. Pour over cake.

—Linda Guill

MARSHA'S PARTY APPLE CAKE

2 eggs
2 cups sugar
2 tsp. baking soda
⅛ tsp. salt
2 tsp. cinnamon

1 tsp. vanilla
4 cups apples, diced
2 cups flour
½ cup cooking oil
1 cup walnuts, chopped

CREAM CHEESE FROSTING

1½ cups powdered sugar
2 3-oz. pkgs. cream cheese
3 Tbls. butter

½ tsp. vanilla
Pinch of salt
Chopped nuts

Beat eggs, add sugar and cream well. Add vanilla. Sift together flour, soda, salt and cinnamon. Add alternately with oil. Stir in apples and nuts. Pour mixture in 15"x9"x1½" pan which has been greased. Bake in 350° oven for 1 hour. Cool and frost.

To make the cream cheese frosting, mix cream cheese and butter till it blends easily. Sift in powdered sugar. Add vanilla and salt. Blend and spread on cake. Top with nuts, if desired.

—Marsha Sisneros

INDIAN APPLE CAKE

1 cup shortening
1½ cups brown sugar
2 eggs
2 cups flour
1 tsp. baking soda
1 tsp. baking powder

2 tsp. cinnamon
1 cup buttermilk
2 medium apples, diced
(reserve 2 or 3 Tbls. for topping)

TOPPING

½ cup brown sugar
½ cup nuts, chopped

½ tsp. cinnamon
Reserved apples

Mix shortening and sugar. Add eggs and sift in dry ingredients. Add 1 cup buttermilk, then add apples. Place in a 9"x13" greased pan. Combine topping ingredients and place on top of batter. Bake in 350° oven for 40 to 45 minutes.

—Colleen Tolle

FRESH APPLE CAKE

4 cups apples, chopped
2½ cups sugar
½ cup water
1 cup butter, melted
2 eggs
3 cups flour
1 tsp. baking soda

½ tsp. salt
4 tsp. cinnamon
2 tsp. nugmeg
4 tsp. allspice
2 cups pecans, chopped
2 cups light raisins

CARAMEL FROSTING

2 cups light brown sugar
1 stick butter

⅔ cup milk or cream
3 cups confectioner's sugar

Combine the apples, sugar, and water and mix well. This is liquid for cake. Combine butter, eggs and flour and mix with liquid. Add remaining ingredients and blend well. Bake in 300° oven for 1½-2 hours until done. Most of the time it takes 2 hours. Make the frosting by combining the brown sugar, butter, and milk or cream. Bring to a boil for one minute and stir in the three cups confectioner's sugar (or enough to thicken).

People also use this cake at Christmas instead of fruit cakes. It stays moist and is better 2 or 3 days longer.

—Sharon Cobb

APPLE NUT CAKE

2 cups sugar
2 eggs
½ cup Mazola oil
2 cups flour
2 tsp. baking soda
¼ tsp. salt

1 tsp. vanilla
2 tsp. cinnamon
3 cups chopped apples
    (Jonathan)
1 cup nuts

ICING

1½ cups powdered sugar
2 3-oz. pkgs. cream cheese
2 Tbls. butter

Salt
Vanilla

Combine all cake ingredients and bake for 45 minutes in 350° oven in a 9"x13" greased pan. Combine icing ingredients and top cake. Do not cover cake.

—Genevieve Bowers

DESSERTS . . .

FRESH APPLE CAKE

1¼ cups oil
2 cups sugar
2 eggs
1 tsp. vanilla flavoring
½ tsp. black walnut flavoring
4-5 cups apples, chopped

1 cup walnuts, chopped
3 cups flour
1 tsp. baking soda
1 tsp. salt
1½ cups cinnamon

TOPPING

1 cup sugar
½ cup buttermilk
½ tsp. baking soda
1 tsp. dark corn syrup

1 stick margarine
1 tsp. vanilla flavoring
Dash of salt

Mix together the oil, sugar, eggs and flavorings. Add the chopped apples and chopped nuts. Stir in the flour, soda, salt and cinnamon. Spread in ungreased 9"x13" pan. Bake for 1 hour and 15 minutes at 300°.

Combine all topping ingredients and cook for 10 minutes, stirring occasionally. Pour over warm cake.

—Melody Nuesch

APPLE CHIP CAKE

3 eggs
1¾ cup sugar
¾ cup oil
1 cup pecans or English walnuts
2 cups flour
1 tsp. baking soda

1 tsp. cinnamon
1 tsp. salt
1 tsp. vanilla
2 cups apples, chopped or grated
Whipped cream or ice cream, if desired

Combine eggs, sugar and oil. Mix well; then add nuts. Add remaining ingredients and mix well. Bake in a 9"x10" pan at 375° until done, about 25 minutes. Top with whipped cream or ice cream. this cake is also delicious without a topping.

—Sandy Mattern

Apple Cake recipes were also contributed by Donna Schneider, Sue Chandler and Ann Sorrell.

189

BEEFSTEAK CAKE

This recipe has been handed down through four generations of my family. My great-grandmother once declared it was "good as any beefsteak" and the name just hung on.

THREE WHITE LAYERS

2 cups sugar
1 cup butter (2 sticks)
3 cups plain flour
1 tsp. baking powder

1 cup milk
1 tsp. vanilla flavoring
6 egg whites, beaten

Cream together sugar and butter. Sift together flour and baking powder. Add flour mixture to sugar mixture, alternating with milk. Bake in three 9" round pans at 350° for 25 to 30 minutes, or until done.

THREE DARK LAYERS

2 cups sugar
1 cup butter (2 sticks)
3 cups plain flour
1 tsp. baking powder
1 tsp. cinnamon

1 tsp. allspice
1 tsp. nutmeg
1 cup milk
1 box raisins
6 egg yolks, beaten

Cream together sugar and butter. Sift together flour, baking powder and spices. Add flour mixture to sugar mixture, alternating with milk. Add raisins, then fold in egg yolks. Bake in three 9" round pans at 350° for 25 to 30 minutes, or until done.

LAYER FILLING

2 cups sugar
1 cup flour
3 cups boiling water

2 coconuts, grated
Vanilla

Mix sugar and flour together and add boiling water. Boil until thick as starch and add coconut. Flavor with vanilla as desired.

SEVEN MINUTE FROSTING

2 egg whites, unbeaten
1½ cups sugar
5 Tbls. water

1½ tsp. corn syrup
1 tsp. vanilla

Combine all ingredients except vanilla in top of double boiler. Beat until thoroughly mixed. Place over boiling water, beating constantly. Cook 7 minutes or until frosting will stand in peaks. Remove from heat and add the vanilla. Beat until thick enough to spread.

—Fay Bownan

190

CINNAMON TWIST POUND CAKE

2½ cups flour
2 cups sugar
½ tsp. soda
½ tsp. salt

1 tsp. vanilla
1 cup (2 sticks) margarine,
    softened
3 eggs

TWIST TOPPING

2 tsp. cinnamon

4 Tbls. brown sugar

GLAZE

1 cup powdered sugar
1 Tbls. lemon juice

Nuts

Combine all cake ingredients in a large bowl. Blend 3 minutes at medium speed. Pour half the batter into a greased and floured bundt pan. Sprinkle twist topping over the batter and add the remaining batter. Bake at 325° for 55 to 60 minutes. After cooling for one hour, pour the glaze over the cake and sprinkle with nuts.

— *Carol Ruiz*

CHOCOLATE CRAZY CAKE

2 cups sugar
3 cups flour
⅓ cup cocoa
1 tsp. salt
2 tsp. baking soda

1 tsp. vanilla
2 Tbls. vinegar
¾ cup oil
2 cups cold water

Combine sugar, flour, cocoa, salt and baking powder. Mix together and add remaining ingredients. Mix, but do not beat. Bake in 350° oven for 35 minutes using a 9"x13" pan.

— *Bonnie Dehne*

Our opinions become fixed at the point we stop thinking.
— Joseph Ernest Renan

LOW CALORIE CHEESECAKE

2 envelopes unflavored gelatin
¾ cup sugar
¼ tsp. salt
2 medium eggs, separated
1 cup skim milk
1 tsp. lemon rind, grated
3 cups small curd cottage
   cheese

1 Tbls. lemon juice
1 tsp. vanilla
½ cup ice cold water
½ cup nonfat dry milk
⅓ cup graham cracker crumbs
⅛ tsp. cinnamon
⅛ tsp. nutmeg

Mix gelatin, sugar and salt in top of double boiler. Beat egg yolks and skim milk; add to gelatin mixture. Cook, stirring constantly, until gelatin is thoroughly dissolved. Remove from heat. Add lemon rind and cool. Sieve cottage cheese and stir into gelatin mixture. Add lemon juice and vanilla. Chill, stirring occasionally, until mixture mounds slightly when dropped from spoon. Beat egg whites stiffly; fold into gelatin mixture. Beat water and dry milk until stiff and mixture stands in peaks. Fold into gelatin mixture. Turn into 8" pan. Spread top with mixture of graham cracker crumbs, cinnamon and nutmeg. Chill until firm. Yields 6 servings.

—Francis O'Neal

CREAM CHEESE CAKE

5 8-oz. pkgs. cream cheese
¼ tsp. vanilla
¾ tsp. grated lemon
1¾ cups sugar
¼ tsp. salt

5 eggs
2 egg yolks
¼ cup whipping cream
1 can cherry pie filling
1 box graham crackers

Beat egg whites until stiff. Beat cream cheese until creamy. Add vanilla and lemon peel. Mix sugar, flour and salt together, gradually blend in cream cheese and eggs and egg yolks one at a time. Blend gently. Stir in whipped cream. Use **large** spring cake pan. Put in 450° oven for 12 minutes, then reduce temperature to 300° for 55 minutes or until knife comes out clean.

CHRISTMAS APPLESAUCE CAKE

CAKE

1½ cups sugar
1 tsp. cinnamon
½ tsp. nutmeg
½ tsp. cloves
2 cups plain flour
2 tsp. baking soda

3 eggs
1½ cups applesauce
½ cup dates
2 cups nuts, chopped
½ cup butter
Pinch of salt

To make cake, cream butter and sugar, then add eggs, one at a time. Sift dry ingredients together, reserving a little flour to put over dates and nuts. Add applesauce, nuts, dates, and last, the dry ingredients to the sugar mixture. Bake in 2 layers, 30 minutes in 375° oven. Remove from oven and cool.

FRUIT FILLING

¼ cup water
1 Tbls. sugar
2 Tbls. flour
2 Tbls. butter

3 Tbls. dates
2 Tbls. nuts, chopped
3 Tbls. raisins

To make filling, mix all ingredients and cook until thick. Spread filling between layers after layers have cooled.

CARAMEL ICING

1 cup brown sugar
1 cup white sugar

¾ cup evaporated milk
½ stick butter

To make icing, combine sugar and milk. Cook to soft ball stage. Remove from heat and add butter. Let stand till cool and then beat to spreading consistency.

Note: This cake may be filled, frosted, and frozen weeks ahead.

—Ruth Roberts

People's minds are changed through observation, not through argument.

—Will Rogers

DESSERTS . . .

STRAWBERRY JELLO CAKE

1 cup miniature marshmallows
2 10-oz. pkgs. frozen strawberries, sliced and in syrup
1 3-oz. pkg. strawberry Jello
2¼ cups flour
1½ cups sugar
½ cup shortening
3 tsp. baking powder
½ tsp. salt
1 cup milk
1 tsp. vanilla
3 eggs

Grease a 9"x13" pan. Sprinkle marshmallows over bottom of pan. Set aside. Combine strawberries and syrup with dry Jello. Mix and set aside. Combine remaining ingredients, beat until moistened. Beat 5 minutes. Pour over marshmallows, then spoon berry mixture over batter and bake in 350° oven for 45 to 50 minutes.

—Doris Dyer

KENTUCKY STACK CAKE

¾ cup shortening or butter
1 cup sugar
1 cup molasses
1 cup buttermilk
4 cups all purpose flour
3 eggs
1 tsp. baking soda
½ tsp. salt
2 tsp. baking powder
½ tsp. of several spices, use at
   least 2 or 3 such as cinnamon, cloves, allspice,
   nutmeg, etc.
3 cups thick applesauce
Lemon
Vanilla

Make the applesauce for filling from dried apples if you have them (sweetened and spiced). Cream shortening and sugar. Blend well and blend in molasses and stir well. Add eggs, one at a time, stirring well after each. Add milk alternately with sifted dry ingredients. The mixture will be stiff. Divide into six balls. Place each one in 8" cake pan, pat out to fill pan (I flour my hands to do this). Bake in 350° oven for 18 minutes. When cool, stack layers with applesauce. Can be iced with favorite icing.

—Mae Mitchell

DESSERTS . . .

ANGEL FOOD SURPRISE

1 angel food cake and pan
1 lg. pkg. Jello (any flavor)
1 pkg. Dream Whip, prepared

2 cups drained fruit (reserve 2
cups juice for later)

Dissolve Jello in a bowl with 2 cups hot water. Add fruit and re-maining juice with part water to make 2 cups. Pour into angel food pan, place angel food cake upside down in Jello mixture. As cake will float, put heavy mugs on cake to hold down in pan. Let set in refrigerator until firm. Remove cake from tin onto plate and frost with Dream Whip.

Variations: Strawberry Jello and strawberries; orange Jello and crushed pineapple; black cherry Jello with cherries. Fruit cocktail can also be used.

— Martha Bendall

FRUITED INTERIOR CAKE

1 lg. size sponge or angel food
cake
1 lg. can fruit cocktail, drained

1 lg. bowl Cool Whip, or
equivalent

Fruit cocktail should be cold before using. Drain off juice and mix in large bowl with Cool Whip. Slice cake in half to make two layers. Spread fruit mixture over bottom layer about ¼" thick and add top layer. Fill the "interior" of cake with mixture and spread over the top of cake making a lush topping. Keep refrigerated until ready to serve. Makes 12 servings.

— Carolyn Drawdy

Nothing is more efficient than honesty: those who break the law or abuse the basic moral code in the name of profit are doing more to make "profit" a dirty word than all of the critics of the free-enterprise system put together.

—William Simon

STRAWBERRY DELIGHT

1 small box frozen strawberries   **1 large box white frosting mix**
1 large box white cake mix

Thaw strawberries, drain off liquid and save. Mix cake according to directions on box. Stir in strawberries. Pour into pans and bake according to directions on box. Mix frosting according to directions on box, substituting liquid from strawberries for water. Frost cake when cool and garnish with strawberries if desired.

—Linda Maroney

STRAWBERRY ANGEL FOOD CAKE

2 cups fresh strawberries,
  crushed
1 large angel food cake (from
  bakery)
1 large container Cool Whip
  topping

1 pkg. Knox gelatin
1 Tbls. cold water
½ cup boiling water
1 cup sugar

Crush strawberries and add sugar. Dissolve gelatin with cold water and add boiling water. Mix with strawberries and let thicken in refrigerator about 30 minutes. While mixture is setting, cube angel food cake into 1-inch cubes and set aside. Blend ½ the Cool Whip with thickened strawberries. Lind a 9"x9" pan with waxed paper. Put layer of cake cubes, then one of strawberries, alternating each, but ending with cake on top. Put waxed paper on top of cake layer. then place another pan of about the same size on top of waxed paper and weight it down with something heavy (a full milk carton or the equivalent). This blends the layers together. Refrigerate for 2 hours, then pull off the top waxed paper and turn out onto a serving plate. Pull off the other waxed paper and frost with the remaining Cool Whip. Cut in squares and serve.

—Rolanda Allgood

JEWISH APPLE CAKE

3 cups flour	2½ tsp. vanilla
2½ cups sugar	3 tsp. baking powder
1 cup cooking oil	6 apples, chopped
4 eggs	2 tsp. cinnamon
½ tsp. salt	3 Tbls. sugar
⅓ cup orange juice	

Combine flour, 2½ cups sugar, oil, eggs, salt, orange juice, vanilla and baking powder in one bowl. In another bowl combine the apples, cinnamon and 3 Tbls. sugar. If you add more apples, add more sugar and cinnamon. Use greased and floured tube pan. Layer batter, then apples, etc. Bake 1½ to 2 hours, until done in preheated 350° oven.

—Linda S. Abel

APPLESAUCE BUNDT CAKE

CAKE MIXTURE

1 pkg. yellow cake mix	1 tsp. vanilla
1 pkg. instant vanilla pudding mix	¾ cup cooking oil
	¾ cup water
4 eggs	⅓ cup applesauce

SUGAR MIXTURE

½ cup nuts, chopped	¼ cup sugar
1 tsp. cinnamon	

ICING

Powdered sugar	Milk

Combine cake ingredients and beat with electric mixer for 9 minutes. Combine ingredients for sugar mixture. Preheat oven to 350°. Grease and flour bundt pan. In bottom of pan spread one-third of the batter. Then sprinkle one-half of the sugar mixture on top. Add another one-third of the batter and remaining sugar mixture. Top with remaining batter. Bake for 50 minutes. Let cake cool for 15 minutes and remove from pan. Drizzle with glaze of powdered sugar and milk.

—Billie Leader

197

BANANA SPLIT CAKE

2 cups graham cracker
  crumbs, crumbled
1 stick butter, melted
2 sticks margarine
2 eggs

1 box powdered sugar
7 bananas
1 lg. can crushed pineapple,
  drained
1 med. size carton Cool Whip

Mix graham cracker crumbs and butter and press into bottom of 9"x12" pan. Bake in 350° oven for 5 minutes. Cool thoroughly. Combine margarine, eggs, and powdered sugar and whip until fluffy. Spread over graham cracker crust. Slice bananas lengthwise and layer over crust mixture. Put crushed pineapple on top of bananas. Top with Cool Whip.

—Esther Graham

BANANA SPLIT CAKE

1 stick margarine, melted
2 cups graham crackers,
  crushed
2 eggs
2 sticks margarine, melted
2 cups powdered sugar

3-5 bananas
1 20-oz. can crushed pineapple, well drained
2 cups whipped cream
½ cup maraschino cherries
¾ cup nuts, chopped

Combine 1 stick margarine and crushed graham crackers and press into bottom of 9"x13" pan. Combine eggs, 2 sticks of margarine and sugar and beat 15 minutes. Spread over graham cracker crumbs. Slice bananas and put over top of sugar mixture. Spread pineapple next. Put whipped cream over the pineapple. Place cherries and nuts over the whipped cream.

—Elaine Schwarting

*Man's mind stretched by a new idea never
goes back to its original dimensions.*

—Oliver Wendell Holmes

BANANA BREAD

1 cup sugar *2*	½ tsp. salt *1*	
½ cup margarine *1*	1 tsp. baking soda *2*	
2 eggs, beaten *4*	3 bananas, mashed *6*	
2 cups flour *4*	½ cup nuts, chopped *1*	

Beat eggs well. Cream sugar and margarine. Add to eggs and stir. Sift flour, salt and baking soda. Add to creamed mixture. Beat in bananas, stir in chopped nuts. Bake in large loaf pan in 350° oven for 40 to 45 minutes.   *2 Small Pans*

CARLENA JULIAN

BANANA NUT BREAD

1¾ cups flour, sifted	2 eggs
1¼ tsp. baking powder	1 cup bananas, mashed
½ tsp. baking soda	½ cup walnuts, chopped
⅓ cup shortening	¾ tsp. salt
⅔ cup sugar	

Sift flour, baking powder, baking soda and salt. Cream shortening and sugar thoroughly. Add eggs, one at a time. Beat well. Add dry ingredients alternately with mashed bananas. Stir just enough to blend. Do not beat. Add nuts with last addition of flour. Put batter in an oiled loaf pan and bake in 350° oven for one hour.

— Carol Horine

Mary C. Crowley's pattern for living:

Fret not thyself because of evildoers, neither be thou envious against the workers of iniquity. For they shall soon be cut down like the grass, and wither as the green herb.

Trust in the Lord, and do good; so shalt thou dwell in the land, and verily thou shalt be fed.

Delight thyself also in the Lord; and he shall give thee the desires of thine heart. Commit thy way unto the Lord; trust also in him; and he shall bring it to pass.

Psalm 37:1-5

PINEAPPLE CAKE AND TOPPING

CAKE

1 tsp. vanilla
2 cups flour
2 tsp. baking soda
2 eggs

2 cups sugar
½ cup water
1 #2 can crushed pineapple
and juice

Mix first 6 ingredients well. Fold in pineapple and juice. Grease and flour pan. Bake at 350° for 25 to 30 minutes.

TOPPING

1 stick butter
1 8-oz. package cream cheese

1 cup powdered sugar
1 tsp. vanilla

Combine and cream all ingredients well. Spoon over cake right out of oven.

—Bea Kirchinger

PINEAPPLE SURPRISE

1 box Washington cake mix
2 pkgs. instant vanilla pudding
1 8-oz. pkg. cream cheese,
softened

1 lg. can crushed pineapple,
drained
1 lg. box Dream Whip
Slivered almonds

Mix cake mix according to directions. Make vanilla pudding according to directions. Put thin layer of cake mix in 13"x9"x2" pan (you might not use it all). Bake and cool. Cream together pudding and cream cheese. Refrigerate for one hour. Layer pudding mixture onto cooled cake, then pineapple. Prepare Dream Whip according to directions on package and layer over pineapple. Top with nuts and refrigerate until used.

—Linda Abel

True strength does not depend on the size of one's biceps. It is related to a sense of purpose, the ability to think and analyze, and the proper respect for human response.

—Unknown

CARROT CAKE

2 cups sugar
1½ cups oil
4 eggs
2 cups flour
2 tsp. soda

1 tsp. salt
2 tsp. cinnamon
3 cups carrots, finely grated
½ cup coconut, shredded
¾ cup nuts, chopped

FROSTING

1 3-oz. pkg. cream cheese
1¾ cups powdered sugar, sifted

¼ cup butter
1 tsp. vanilla

To make the cake, mix sugar, oil, and eggs until thoroughly blended. Sift together flour, soda, salt and cinnamon. Add to first mixture and beat until smooth. Stir in carrots, coconut and nuts. Pour into greased 13"x9½"x2" pan and bake in 325° oven for 55 minutes. Combine all frosting ingredients and mix until smooth.

— Gayle McMasters

PINEAPPLE UPSIDE-DOWN CAKE

⅓ cup butter
½ cup brown sugar, packed
8 pineapple rings
8 maraschino cherries
⅓ cup pecan halves
2 eggs

⅔ cup sugar
6 Tbls. pineapple juice
1 tsp. vanilla
1 cup enriched flour, sifted
⅓ tsp. baking powder
¼ tsp. salt

Melt butter in a heavy 10" skillet. Evenly spread the brown sugar over the butter and arrange pineapple over the brown sugar and butter mixture. Put a maraschino cherry in the center of each pineapple ring and arrange pecan halves between the rings. Beat eggs until thick and lemon colored. Beat in sugar gradually, then beat in pineapple juice and vanilla. Sift flour, baking powder, and salt together and beat into sugar mixture. Pour batter over pineapple rings in skillet. Bake in moderate oven for 45 minutes at 350°. Immediately turn upside down on serving plate.

— Jean Wilson

BROWN SUGAR POUND CAKE

3 sticks butter	2 tsp. vanilla
1 lb. light brown sugar	3 cups flour
½ cup white sugar	½ tsp. baking powder
5 eggs	1 cup milk

Cream butter and sugars thoroughly. Add eggs, one at a time, beating at medium speed. Add flavoring. Sift dry ingredients together; add to creamed mixture alternately with milk. Mix well. Place in large tube pan and bake in 325° oven for 1½ hours.

—Rosa Garner

COLD OVEN POUND CAKE

½ cup shortening	5 eggs
1 stick margarine	1 cup milk
3 cups plain flour	1 tsp. vanilla
3 cups sugar	1 tsp. butternut flavoring
½ tsp. baking powder	

Cream sugar and shortening well. Add melted margarine (let cool). Add eggs, one at a time, beating after each. Sift flour and baking powder well. Add milk, flour and flavoring alternately. Beat 10 minutes. Pour into greased and floured tube or bundt pan. Put in cold oven and turn heat to 350° and bake 1 hour and 15 minutes.

—Mary Ruth Cox

POUND CAKE

3 sticks butter	6 eggs
1 lb. box powdered sugar	1½ tsp. butter flavoring
1 lb. box Swans Down cake flour	

Preheat oven to 350°. Cream butter until creamy. Add sugar and flavoring. Add eggs one at a time. Beat until smooth and creamy. Pour batter in a greased and floured bundt pan. Bake for 1½ hours.

—C. L. Daniels

POLISH POUND CAKE

2 sticks butter or oleo
½ cup shortening
3 cups white sugar
2 Tbls. flavoring (vanilla,
    butternut, or nutmeg)
5 large eggs
3 cups of flour

½ tsp. salt
1 cup nuts, chopped
1 10-oz. jar maraschino
    cherries, drained and
    chopped
1 small can Carnation milk

Beat butter and shortening until fluffy. Add sugar, 1 cup at a time, and beat well. Add flavoring and salt. Add eggs, one at a time, beating after each egg. Add flour and milk, alternating, with flour ending. Fold in nuts and cherries. Grease and flour angel food cake pan. Put in **cold** oven, turn heat to 300°. Bake 2½ hours. Do **NOT** open oven before 2 hours.

—Peggy Marosy

Polish Pound Cake recipe was also contributed by Vicki Ambrose.

APRICOT NECTAR CAKE

¾ cup apricot nectar
¾ cup oil
1 pkg. yellow cake mix
4 eggs

1 pkg. lemon Jello
1 tsp. vanilla
1 tsp. lemon extract

ICING

¼ cup lemon juice

1 cup powdered sugar

Mix all cake ingredients well and bake in angel food pan for 35 minutes in 350° oven. Combine the lemon juice and powdered sugar. Mix well and pour over cake that has been pierced so that icing may be absorbed.

—Maida Godwin

You cannot push anyone up the ladder unless he is willing to climb himself.
—Andrew Carnegie

CRUMB CAKE

2 cups sugar
2 cups flour
2 sticks (1 cup) butter or
   margarine
3 eggs

1 cup nuts
1 cup buttermilk
½ tsp. vanilla
1 tsp. baking soda
½ tsp. salt

Combine sugar, flour and margarine and save one cup of mixture for "crumbs". Add remaining ingredients, beat and pour into 13"x9" pan. Cover with crumbs. Bake 40 minutes in 350° oven.

—Mollie Hauf

OATMEAL CAKE

1¼ cups boiling water
1 stick butter
1 cup quick oats (instant)
1 cup brown sugar
1 cup white sugar
2 eggs

1½ cups flour
1 tsp. baking soda
1 tsp. baking powder
½ tsp. salt
1 tsp. cinnamon
1 tsp. vanilla

ICING

1 cup brown sugar
½ cup canned milk

4 Tbls. butter
1 cup coconut

Mix boiling water, butter and oats and heat until butter melts. Add remaining ingredients. Bake at 350° for 30 to 35 minutes in a 13"x9"x2" pan. Combine icing ingredients and spread on hot cake. Broil until bubbly.

—Joyce Challis

One of the best things about being a woman is I don't have to go out into the world and prove I'm a man. I speak from a full cup. . .I am deeply glad I am a woman. I do not feel complimented when men say I think like a man. I don't think like a man. I think like me.

From "Be Somebody" by Mary Crowley

DESSERTS...

ZUCCHINI CAKE

½ cup margarine
½ cup oil
⅓ cup sugar
2 eggs
1 tsp. vanilla
½ cup sour milk
4 Tbls. cocoa

2½ cups flour, unsifted
½ tsp. baking powder
1 tsp. baking soda
1 tsp. salt
½ cup chocolate chips
2 cups zucchini, grated

Cream together margarine, oil and sugar. Add remainder of ingredients, the zucchini stirred in last. Pour mixture in 9"x13" greased pan. Sprinkle chocolate chips on top and bake at 325° for approximately 50 minutes.

—Joyce Koertje

ZUCCHINI CAKE

3 cups flour
3 cups granulated sugar
1 tsp. salt
1½ tsp. baking soda
1 tsp. baking powder

2½ tsp. cinnamon
1 tsp. vanilla flavoring
4 eggs
1½ cups cooking oil
3 cups squash, grated

FROSTING

1 8-oz. pkg. Philadelphia
   cream cheese, room
   temperature

1 stick oleo, room
   temperature
1 lb. powdered sugar
1-2 tsp. vanilla

Mix all ingredients except nuts together in a bowl. Add the nuts. Stir and pour into a greased and floured 13"x9" pan, or three 9" pans. Bake at 325° approximately 35 minutes according to pan size used.

Combine frosting ingredients and beat until fluffy. Spread over cooled cake.

—Mary Stearley

RED VELVET CAKE

½ cup butter
2 eggs
2 tsp. cocoa
1½ cups sugar
2 oz. red food coloring
2 cups flour

1 cup buttermilk
1½ tsp. baking soda
1 Tbls. vinegar
1 tsp. vanilla
1 tsp. salt

Cream butter and sugar. Add eggs. Make paste with coloring and cocoa. Add to creamed mixture. Mix salt, vanilla, and buttermilk with flour. Mix soda and vinegar. Add last, folding in. Do not beat after vinegar and soda are added. Bake at 350° for 30 minutes.

—Dolly Fields

RED CAKE

4 lg. bottles red food coloring
3 Tbls. cocoa
½ cup shortening
1½ cups sugar
2 eggs
1 cup buttermilk

2¼ cups cake flour, sifted 3
    times
1 tsp. salt
1 tsp. vanilla
1 Tbls. vinegar
1 tsp. baking soda

FROSTING

1 stick butter
8 Tbls. shortening
1 cup granulated sugar

3 Tbls. flour
¾ cup milk, tepid temperature
1 tsp. vanilla

Mix food coloring and cocoa together and set aside. Cream shortening and sugar with mixer and add eggs and the coloring paste. Add buttermilk alternately with cake flour, then add salt and vanilla. Remove from mixer and add vinegar and baking soda. Stir by hand. Bake 30 to 35 minutes in two small layer pans in 350° oven.

To make the frosting, cream butter and shortening together and add sugar. Add flour one tablespoonful at a time. Add milk and vanilla and beat 15 minutes at high speed. Spread on cake.

—Sherry Muhlbach

CRAZY CAKE

1½ cups flour	1 tsp. vanilla
1 cup white sugar	1 Tbls. vinegar
1 tsp. baking soda	6 Tbls. salad oil or melted
½ tsp. salt	shortening
2 Tbls. cocoa	1 cup cold water

Use square or large round layer cake pan. Do not grease. Put flour, sugar, soda, salt and cocoa into sifter and sift once. Return to sifter and sift into cake pan. Make three depressions in dry ingredients. Put vanilla in one depression, vinegar in another, and salad oil or shortening in the third depression. Pour cold water over all. Mix well with fork. Bake until done in medium 350° oven approximately 30 minutes. Cool in pan.

—Toni McCracken

COKE CAKE

2 cups sugar	1 cup Coke
1½ cups miniature	3 Tbls. cocoa
marshmallows	2 eggs, beaten
2 cups flour, unsifted	½ cup buttermilk
2 sticks (1 cup) butter or	1 tsp. soda
margarine	1 tsp. vanilla

COKE ICING

½ cup margarine	1 box confectioner's sugar
3 Tbls. cocoa	1 cup nuts
6 Tbls. Coke	

In a bowl combine flour and sugar. Let Coke, cocoa and margarine come to a boil in double boiler. Pour over flour mixture and mix thoroughly. Add eggs, buttermilk, soda and vanilla. Beat well. Bake in 13"x9" pan in 350° oven for 30 minutes or until done.

Make the icing by combining the margarine, cocoa and Coke. Heat to boiling and pour in sugar. Add nuts. Pour onto **hot** cake.

—Trecy Nanney

COCA-COLA CAKE

2 cups sugar
2 cups flour
1 cup Coca-Cola
3 Tbls. cocoa
2 sticks butter

½ cup buttermilk
1 tsp. baking soda
2 eggs, beaten
1½ cups miniature
    marshmallows

COCA-COLA TOPPING

6 Tbls. Coca-Cola
3 Tbls. cocoa
1 stick butter

1 box confectioner's sugar,
    sifted
1 cup nuts
1 tsp. vanilla

To make the cake, sift together the sugar and flour. Bring butter, cocoa and Coca-Cola to a boil. Pour into flour mixture. Dissolve baking soda in buttermilk. Stir in marshmallows, buttermilk and eggs. Pour into a 9"x13" pan and bake in 350° oven for 35 minutes. Make the topping by bringing the butter, cocoa and Coca-Cola to a boil. Add remaining ingredients. Top cake while hot.

—Sharon Ann Spivey

COKE CAKE

2 cups sugar
2 cups flour
1 tsp. baking soda
½ lb. margarine
1 cup Coke
3 Tbls. cocoa

½ cup buttermilk
1½ cups miniature
    marshmallows
2 eggs, beaten
1 tsp. vanilla

ICING

1 stick margarine
6 Tbls. cocoa
6 Tbls. Coke

1 box confectioner's sugar
1 cup pecans

Combine flour, sugar and soda in bowl. Heat butter, cocoa and Coke to boiling. Pour over flour and sugar mixture. Add buttermilk, marshmallows, eggs and vanilla. Mix well. Bake 35 minutes in 350° oven. Combine first three icing ingredients and bring to a boil. Pour into sugar. Beat, add nuts, and spread over warm cake.

—Beverly Crane

HOT WATER CHOCOLATE CAKE

1½ cups flour
1½ cups sugar
1 tsp. salt
4 Tbls. cocoa
1 stick butter

1½ tsp. baking powder
1 tsp. baking soda
1½ cups water, divided use
1 egg
2 tsp. vanilla

BOILED ICING FOR HOT WATER CAKE

1 cup sugar
¼ cup cocoa
¼ cup oleo

¼ cup Milnot (or evaporated
    milk)
2 tsp. vanilla

Mix flour, sugar, salt, cocoa and butter together. Add 1 cup hot water and beat until smooth. Mix soda and baking powder with ½ cup hot water. Add egg and vanilla to mixture. Beat well. This makes a thin batter. Bake at 350° for 20 to 30 minutes. To make the icing, combine sugar, cocoa, oleo and milk. Bring to a boil and boil for 1 minute. Add vanilla. Beat for a short time.

—Betty Shaw

CRAZY CHOCOLATE CAKE

3 cups flour, unsifted
⅓ cup cocoa
1 tsp. salt
2 cups sugar
2 tsp. baking soda

2 Tbls. vinegar
⅔ cup or 12 Tbls. oil
2 tsp. vanilla
2 cups cold

Sift the flour, cocoa, salt, sugar and baking soda into a 9"x13" cake pan. Then add remaining ingredients. Stir with fork to blend. Do not beat. When well mixed, bake at 350° for 25 to 35 minutes. Cool in pan. If mixed in a bowl, this recipe will make two 9" layers, three 8" layers or 2½ dozen cupcakes.

—Pam Layer

MISSISSIPPI MUD CAKE

2 cups sugar
1 cup margarine, softened
4 eggs
1½ cups plain flour
⅓ cup cocoa

2 tsp. vanilla
¼ tsp. salt
1 cup chopped nuts
1 bag small marshmallows

ICING

1 stick margarine
⅓ cup cocoa
1 box confectioner's sugar
½ cup evaporated milk

1 tsp. vanilla
1 cup nuts, chopped
Dash of salt

Mix sugar, margarine and eggs. Then blend in other ingredients *except* marshmallows. Grease and flour oblong pan and bake 30 minutes at 350°. Remove and spread marshmallows on top. Return to oven for 10 minutes or until marshmallows are melted. (Watch closely.) To make the icing, mix all icing ingredients and spread on cake.

—Billie Ramsey

BROWNIE MARSHMALLOW CAKE

1 cup pecans
2 cups sugar
2 sticks oleo
4 eggs
1½ tsp. butter flavoring

1 tsp. vanilla flavoring
1½ cups flour
⅔ cups cocoa
1 5½-oz. pkg. marshmallows

ICING

½ box powdered sugar
½ cup cocoa
½ stick oleo, melted

½ cup evaporated milk
1 tsp. butter flavoring
1 tsp. vanilla flavoring

Combine all ingredients except marshmallows, adding eggs one at a time. Bake in 350° oven for 30 minutes in a greased 9"x13" pan. When cake is done, take out of oven and put marshmallows on hot cake. Return to oven to melt marshmallows. When melted, take out of oven and pour icing over the whole cake. To make the icing, combine all icing ingredients. Beat until creamy and spread on cake.

—Jean M. Koncar

CHOCOLATE CHIP CAKE

1 stick margarine	1½ tsp. baking powder
1 cup sugar	1 tsp. baking soda
2 eggs	¼ tsp. salt
1 cup sour cream	Cinnamon mixture of ¼ cup
1 tsp. vanilla	sugar and 1 tsp. cinnamon
2 cups flour	1 lg. pkg. chocolate chips

Cream margarine, sugar and eggs together. Add sour cream, vanilla, flour, baking powder, baking soda and salt. Grease and flour 13"x9" pan. Pour half of batter into pan and spread out. Sprinkle half the cinnamon mixture over batter and half the chocolate chips. Spread the rest of the batter over chips and sprinkle with the remaining cinnamon mixture. Lightly press the remaining chocolate chips into batter. Bake at 350° for 30 minutes.

—Peggy Marosy

DEVIL'S FOOD CAKE

This recipe was passed along from a cookbook over 50 years old, with a clipping from The Kansas City Star *"About Town" column, not dated. The story goes that a young woman from Kansas after a visit to New York couldn't forget the flavor of the devil's food cake served by a top-notch hotel, so she wrote asking the hotel for the recipe. They sent it, along with a bill for $100.00. She must have thought it worth it because she paid the bill, and here is the recipe.*

½ cup butter	1 cup nuts
4 oz. bitter chocolate	2 tsp. vanilla
2 eggs	2 cups sugar
1½ cups milk	2 cups flour
2 tsp. baking powder	

Cream butter and one cup of sugar. Melt chocolate. Beat eggs and add to butter mixture. Add second cup of sugar. Beat mixture well. Add melted chocolate. Mix dry ingredients and add to butter mixture, alternately with milk. Add vanilla and nuts. Bake in loaf pan at 350° for 50 minutes. Frost with choice of frosting.

—Mildred Yahr

CHOCOLATE OATMEAL CAKE

1½ cups boiling water	2 eggs, lightly beaten
1 cup quick oatmeal	1 tsp. baking soda
1 cup margarine	1 tsp. cream of tartar
1 cup brown sugar	½ cup bitter cocoa
1 cup granulated sugar	1⅓ cups flour

FUDGY FROSTING

½ cup sugar	6 Tbls. margarine
2 tsp. brown sugar	1 cup nuts, chopped
1 cup coconut	1 6-oz. pkg. chocolate chips
¼ cup evaporated milk	

Pour water over oats and margarine and let stand 15 minutes. Stir and add both sugars and eggs that have been slightly beaten. Blend. Sift baking soda, cocoa, cream of tarter and flour together and add to batter. Stir until well blended. Put into greased and floured 9"x13" pan and bake at 350° for 30 to 40 minutes. To make the frosting, put all ingredients in top of double boiler and heat over boiling water until melted. Spread over warm cake and return to oven and bake until frosting becomes bubbly. Cool two hours before serving.

—*Barbara Stecker*

SURPRISE CAKE

2 cups sugar	2 tsp. instant chocolate
2 cups flour	2 eggs
2 tsp. baking soda	1 lg. can fruit cocktail

FROSTING

½ stick margarine	1 cup canned milk
1 cup sugar	1 heaping tsp. chocolate
1 cup coconut	

To make the cake, mix dry ingredients. Add eggs and fruit cocktail. Bake at 325° for 50 to 60 minutes. To make the frosting, mix all together and boil about 8 minutes, or until thick.

—*Patricia Lormand*

WHITE CHOCOLATE CAKE

¼ lb. white chocolate
½ cup hot water
1 cup butter
2 cups sugar
4 egg yolks
1 tsp. vanilla

2½ cups cake flour
1 tsp. baking soda
1 cup buttermilk
4 egg whites, beaten
1 cup pecans
1 cup coconut

ICING

⅔ cup evaporated milk
1 cup sugar
4 Tbls. butter
3 egg yolks

1 tsp. vanilla
1 cup pecans
1 cup coconut

Melt chocolate in hot water and cool. Cream butter and sugar. Add egg yolks, one at a time, beating after each addition. Add chocolate mixture and vanilla. Sift flour and baking soda together and add alternately with buttermilk. Don't overbeat. Fold in 4 beaten egg whites. Gently stir in nuts and coconut. Bake in 3 layers in 350° oven for 25 to 30 minutes. Let cool. To make the icing, bring to a boil the milk, sugar and butter. Beat egg yolks well and add to mixture. Add vanilla. Cook over low heat until thick. Remove from heat and add the nuts and coconut. Beat until spreading consistency.

—*Geneva Stroup*

EASY CHOCOLATE CAKE

3 cups flour
2 cups sugar
2 tsp. baking soda
1 cup salad oil
2 tsp. vinegar

1 tsp. salt
6 Tbls. cocoa
2 tsp. vanilla
2 cups cold water

Combine all ingredients and mix well with a fork. Pour in baking pan and bake in 350° oven for 40 minutes. Can be mixed in greased pan and then baked, or this recipe will make 24 to 28 cupcakes.

—*Sandy Wicht*

WHITE CHOCOLATE SHEET CAKE

1 stick butter or margarine	1 tsp. cinnamon
4 Tbls. (1 square) white chocolate	½ tsp. salt
½ cup shortening	1 cup buttermilk
1 cup water	2 eggs
2 cups white sugar	1 tsp. baking soda
2 cups all-purpose flour	1 tsp. vanilla

ICING

1 stick butter	1 lb. powdered sugar
1 Tbls. white chocolate	1 tsp. vanilla
6 Tbls. milk	1 cup pecans, chopped

Combine butter or margarine, chocolate, shortening and water together and bring to a rolling boil in a saucepan. Combine chocolate mixture with sugar, flour, cinnamon and salt in a large bowl. Mix well and add the buttermilk, eggs, soda and vanilla. Mix well again and pour into jelly roll pan. Bake in 400° oven for 20 minutes. To make the icing, bring butter, chocolate and milk to a boil. Add other ingredients. Spread on cake as it comes from oven. Iced cake freezes great.

—Janice Blackburn

CHOCOLATE LUSH

1 cup flour	2 small pkgs. instant pudding mix
1 stick margarine	3 cups milk
1 12-oz. container Cool Whip	Nuts
1 8-oz. pkg. cream cheese	
1 cup confectioner's sugar	

Mix flour and margarine together and press on bottom of pan (spray pan with Pam to avoid sticking). Bake in 350° oven for 15 to 20 minutes. Allow to cool. Combine 1 cup of Cool Whip, cream cheese, and sugar. Spread on top of cooled crust. Combine pudding mix and milk. Spread on top of cream cheese mixture. Top with remaining Cool Whip. Sprinkle nuts on top.

—Janie Hoff

CHOCOLATE MARBLE CAKE

2½ cups cake flour, sifted
1½ tsp. baking powder
½ tsp. baking soda
1 tsp. salt
1⅔ cups sugar
¾ cup shortening
1 square chocolate, melted

2 Tbls. hot water
¼ tsp. baking soda
1 Tbls. sugar
1 cup sour milk or buttermilk
3 eggs
1 tsp. vanilla

Sift together the cake flour, baking powder, ½ teaspoon baking soda, salt and 1⅔ cups sugar. Measure into a mixing bowl the shortening, melted chocolate, hot water, ¼ teaspoon baking soda, and 1 tablespoon sugar. Sift flour mixture into shortening mixture. Add the sour milk or buttermilk and beat two minutes and add vanilla and eggs and beat one minute at slow speed. Add chocolate mix to ¼ of batter, mixing only to blend. Bake at 350° for 35 to 40 minutes.

–Pollyanna Core

ENTHUSIASM!!

That certain something that makes us great — that pulls us out of the mediocre and commonplace — that builds into us Power. It glows and shines — it lights up our faces — ENTHUSIASM, the keynote that makes us sing and makes men sing with us.

ENTHUSIASM — the maker of friends — the maker of smiles — the producer of confidence. It cries to the world, "I've got what it takes." It tells all men that our job is a swell job — that the house we work for just suits us — the goods we have are the best.

ENTHUSIASM — the inspiration that makes us "Wake Up and Live." It puts spring in our step — spring in our hearts — a twinkle in our eyes and gives us confidence in ourselves and our fellow men.

ENTHUSIASM — It changes a pessimist to an optimist, a loafer to a go-getter.

ENTHUSIASM — If we have it, we should thank God for it. If we don't have it, then we should get down on our knees and pray for it.

MISSISSIPPI MUD CAKE

2 sticks margarine
2 cups sugar
⅓ cup cocoa
4 eggs

1 cup nuts, chopped
1 cup coconut
1 cup flour
Miniature marshmallows

ICING

1 stick margarine
⅓ cup cocoa
⅓ cup milk

1 tsp. vanilla
1 lb. powdered sugar

Mix the two sticks of margarine with the sugar and cocoa and cream well. Beat the eggs one at a time (beat them well). Add to the sugar and margarine mixture. Add chopped nuts, coconut and flour and mix well again. Pour into greased and floured 9"x13" pan. Bake in 350° oven for 30 minutes or until done. Take from oven, cover with miniature marshmallows and return to oven until marshmallows are brown and puffy. To make the icing, combine one stick margarine, cocoa and milk. Stir and let mixture come to a boil. Then add vanilla and 1 pound of powdered sugar and mix. Pour the hot icing over warm cake. Serve warm with vanilla ice cream.

—Andrea McCoy

CHOCOLATE POUND CAKE

1 cup butter or margarine
   (cold)
½ cup shortening (cold)
3 cups sugar
5 eggs (cold)
1½ cups cake flour, sifted

1½ cups regular flour
1 tsp. baking powder
½ tsp. salt
½ cup cocoa
1 cup milk
1 tsp. vanilla

Cream butter, shortening, eggs, and sugar together. Sift dry ingredients together, then add all other ingredients. Bake 1½ hours at 325° or until done. Do not overcook. May be cooked in tube pan or loaf pans. Freezes well.

—Sondra Simmons

CHOCOLATE BAR CAKE

2 cups flour	1 tsp. baking soda
2 cups sugar	1 cup cooking oil
1/2 cup cocoa	1 tsp. vanilla
1 cup buttermilk	1 cup boiling water

CHOCOLATE FROSTING

1/2 cup butter or margarine	5 cups powdered sugar
4 Tbls. cocoa	1/2 cup nuts, chopped
6 Tbls. cream or milk	Vanilla

Sift flour, sugar and cocoa into a bowl. Combine buttermilk and the baking soda and add to the flour mixture. Add cooking oil and vanilla. Mix well, then add the boiling water. Batter is thin. Pour onto large cookie sheet and bake 20 minutes in 350° oven. Frost while warm with chocolate frosting.

To make the frosting, combine butter or margarine, cocoa, and cream or milk. Bring to a boil then pour into the powdered sugar. Mix well and add the nuts and vanilla.

—Frances Holdbrook

CHOCOLATE ZUCCHINI (OR CARROT) CAKE

1/2 cup butter or margarine	1/2 tsp. baking soda
1/2 cup oil	1/2 tsp. cinnamon
1 3/4 cups sugar	1/2 tsp. cloves
2 eggs	1/2 tsp. salt
1 tsp. vanilla	2 cups semi-sweet chocolate
1/2 cup canned milk or sour	pieces
milk if preferred	1/4 cup nuts, chopped
2 1/2 cups flour	2 cups zucchini (or carrots, if
4 Tbls. cocoa	preferred), shredded

Cream margarine, oil and sugar together. Add eggs, vanilla and milk and blend. Sift flour, cocoa, soda, cinnamon, cloves and salt. Blend with creamed mixture. Stir in zucchini (or carrots). Spoon into greased and floured loaf pan. Sprinkle chocolate pieces and nuts on top. Bake in 325° oven for 40 to 45 minutes.

—Nellie Wray

RTS . . .

TEXAS SHEET CAKE OR BROWNIES

2 cups sugar
½ tsp. salt
1 cup water
½ cup sour cream
1 tsp. baking soda

2 cups flour
2 sticks (1 cup) butter or
  margarine
4 Tbls. cocoa
2 eggs

BUTTERNUT FROSTING

6 Tbls. canned milk
1 cup butter or margarine
4 Tbls. cocoa

1 lb. powdered sugar
1 tsp. vanilla
1 cup nuts

In a large bowl put sugar, flour and salt. In heavy pan bring butter, water and cocoa to a boil. As it boils, immediately add dry ingredients. Add sour cream. Add eggs and soda. Mix until well blended after each addition. Batter will be thin. Bake in greased cookie sheet with high sides in 350° oven for 20 to 25 minutes. May use two 9"x13" pans. Prepare frosting while cake is baking. To make the frosting, boil milk, butter and cocoa in heavy pan until bubbly. Stir in sugar and vanilla until smooth. Add nuts. Spread over hot brownies. Serves 24 to 48 2" squares.

—Wilma Taylor

NO BAKE BROWNIES

1 cup evaporated milk
2 cups miniature
  marshmallows
1 6-oz. pkg. Toll House
  chocolate bits
½ cup sugar

¼ tsp. salt
1 Tbls. butter or margarine
1 tsp. vanilla
1 cup walnuts, chopped
2 pkgs. Nabisco graham
  crackers

Cook first five ingredients until melted. Cook and stir to a full boil for 5 to 6 minutes. Remove from heat and gradually stir in remaining ingredients. Press into 9" buttered pan. Chill 1 hour.

—Sue Noble

218

CHOCOLATE SHEET CAKE

2 cups sugar
2 cups flour
½ cup margarine
½ cup Crisco oil
¼ cup cocoa
1 cup water

2 eggs
½ cup buttermilk
1 tsp. baking soda
1 tsp. vanilla
Pinch of salt

FROSTING

1 cup sugar
¼ cup canned milk
¼ cup margarine

½ cup chocolate chips
Pinch of salt

Mix sugar, flour and salt in a large bowl and set aside. Combine margarine, shortening, oil, cocoa and water and bring to a boil. Add to flour mixture and stir. Add remaining ingredients. Pour into greased and floured sheet cake pan. Frost while cake is still very hot. Combine all frosting ingredients except chocolate chips. Bring to a boil and add the chocolate chips.

—Suzanne Leavens

FUDGE MARBLE POUND CAKE

1 pkg. fudge marble cake mix
½ cup Crisco oil (use Crisco
    as some other oils may
    cause the cake to fall)

4 eggs
1 pkg. instant vanilla pudding
    mix (4-serving size)
1 cup water

Preheat oven to 350°. Blend all the ingredients except the pudding in a large bowl. Beat at medium speed for 2 minutes. Pour ¾ of the batter into a greased and floured bundt pan. Blend pudding into remaining batter. Spoon dark batter here and there over light batter. Pull knife through batter in wide curves several times. Bake at 350° for about 45 to 55 minutes until center springs back when touched lightly. Cool right side up for about 25 minutes, then remove from pan. If desired, dust top of cooled cake with confectioner's sugar or drizzle with chocolate glaze.

—Deloris Heminger

NO ICING CHOCOLATE CHIP CAKE

1 cup raisins
1 cup plus 3 Tbls. hot water
1 tsp. baking soda
1 cup white sugar
1 cup shortening
2 eggs

2 cups flour
½ tsp. salt
1 Tbls. cocoa
1 tsp. vanilla
½ cup nuts, chopped
1 cup chocolate chips

Preheat oven to 350°. Pour hot water over raisins. Remove enough water to dissolve soda and return to raisins. Cream sugar and shortening. Add beaten eggs, flour, salt, cocoa and vanilla. Beat well. Add ½ cup chocolate chips, raisins and water mix and stir. Pour into greased and floured 9"x13" pan. Sprinkle remaining chocolate chips and nuts on top. Bake for 40 minutes.

—Vicki Freeman

ROCKY ROAD BROWNIES

1 cup butter
8 Tbls. cocoa
2 cups sugar
4 eggs

1 cup self-rising flour
2 tsp. vanilla
1 cup nuts, chopped
1 cup miniature marshmallows

FUDGE FROSTING

4 Tbls. cocoa
1 stick butter

½ cup Pet milk
1 box powdered sugar

Melt butter and blend in cocoa. Add sugar and eggs and stir well. Add flour and vanilla. Bake in 350° oven in greased and floured 9"x13" pan for 25 to 30 minutes. Do not overcook. Brownies will be shiny and may sink slightly in center. As soon as brownies are removed from oven top with miniature marshmallows and sprinkle with nuts. Frost with fudge frosting.

To make the frosting, melt butter over medium heat and add cocoa. Stir well. Add milk and sugar. Cook, stirring constantly, until sugar is well blended, approximately 1 minute. Pour over brownies. Carefully smooth frosting over marshmallows and nuts.

SOUR CREAM GERMAN CHOCOLATE CAKE

⅔ cups sugar
½ cup milk
1 egg, slightly beaten
3 1-oz. squares unsweetened
    chocolate
½ cup shortening
1 cup sugar

1 tsp. vanilla
2 eggs
2 cups flour
1 tsp. baking soda
½ tsp. salt
1 cup sour cream

Combine first four ingredients in saucepan and cook. Stir over medium heat until chocolate melts and mixture comes just to boiling. Cream together shortening and sugar until fluffy. Add vanilla. Add eggs one at a time, beating well after each. Sift dry ingredients and add to creamed mixture alternately with sour cream. Beat until smooth after each addition. Blend in cooled chocolate mixture. Bake in two greased and floured 9" round pans at 350° for 25-30 minutes. Cool ten minutes before removing from pans. Cool and frost with chocolate frosting and garnish with chocolate curls.

—Gladys Zuehlke

MATHILDA'S ONE-PAN CAKE

1 box yellow cake mix
2 eggs
1 lg. pkg. strawberry gelatin
1 lg. pkg. vanilla instant pudding

1 carton whipped topping
    (8-oz. size)
Water

First generously grease a long sheet cake pan. Preheat oven to 350°. Prepare cake mix according to package directions adding two eggs and water. Bake for 40 minutes. Remove from oven immediately, prick cake with fork all over to make little holes. Mix gelatin with 2 cups hot water and pour over cake so gelatin will go into holes and saturate the cake. Allow the cake to cool. Prepare pudding according to directions and spread over cake. Top with whipped topping. Place in refrigerator to cool, and keep refrigerated.

—Patricia R. Lormand

CARROT PINEAPPLE CAKE

3 cups cake flour, sifted
2 cups sugar
2 tsp. cinnamon
1½ tsp. baking soda
1½ tsp. salt
1 tsp. baking powder
1 8-oz. can crushed pineapple
3 eggs, beaten

¾ cup cooking oil
¾ cup buttermilk
2 tsp. vanilla
1½ cups walnuts, chopped
2 cups raw carrots, grated and
    loosely packed
3½ oz. coconut, shredded

BUTTERMILK GLAZE

½ tsp. baking soda
1 tsp. white corn syrup
1 stick butter (½ cup)

1 cup sugar
½ cup buttermilk
½ tsp. vanilla

Mix together all dry ingredients. Drain pineapple; reserve syrup. Add pineapple syrup to dry mixture, add eggs, cooking oil, buttermilk, and vanilla; beat 3 minutes. Stir in pineapple, nuts, carrots and coconut. Bake in greased and floured 12-cup bundt pan at 325° for about 1½ hours or until cake tests done. Cool in pan 10-15 minutes, turn out onto wire rake or serving plate. Top with Buttermilk Glaze.

To make the glaze, mix first 5 ingredients in saucepan. Bring to a boil and boil for 5 minutes. Remove from heat and add vanilla. Prick cake all over with fork and pour glaze over hot cake. Cover cake completely.

—Pat Bettenhausen

Carrot Cake recipes were also contributed by Maralee Lemke, GeorgeAnn Dyer, Rose Hoing, Ferta Duke, Kathy Chavez, and Elaine Kaufman.

There is no such thing as moral neutrality. Those who do not stand up forthrightly in behalf of their convictions, by their inaction are supporting the opposite view. On any scale whatever a person perceives right and wrong, silence turns out to be a vote for wrong.

—John A. Howard

BANANA SPLIT CAKE

3 sticks margarine, melted, divided use
2 cups graham crackers, crushed (may need a little more)
3 eggs
2 cups powdered sugar

3-5 bananas
1 20-oz. can crushed pineapple, well drained
2 (or more) cups whipped cream
½ cup maraschino cherries
¾ cup nuts, chopped

Combine 1 stick of margarine and the graham crackers and place in bottom of 9"x13" pan. Beat together the eggs, the 2 remaining sticks of melted margarine and the sugar for 15 minutes. Spread over the graham cracker crumbs. Slice bananas and put on top of sugar mixture. Put pineapple over the bananas. Put whipped cream over the pineapple. Place cherries and nuts over the whipped cream.

—Cathy Gilmer

VANILLA WAFER CAKE

1 stick margarine
1½ cups sugar
5 eggs
1 lb. vanilla wafers
¾ cup milk

1 tsp. vanilla
1 sm. can Baker's coconut
1 cup pecans
2 tsp. baking powder

ICING

1 lb. confectioner's sugar
1 stick butter

1 1-lb. can crushed pineapple, drained

Cream margarine and sugar. Add the eggs. In a separate bowl, crush vanilla wafers (makes about 5 cups). Add vanilla wafers to other mixture with baking powder, milk and vanilla. Add coconut and pecans. Bake in square pan in 300° oven for 40 minutes. Gently mix icing ingredients together and ice cake.

This cake stays great in refrigerator approximately 5 weeks. Tastes even better after being in refrigerator one week.

—Nancy Tillotson

CARROT CAKE

2 cups sugar
1½ cups Wesson oil
4 eggs
2 tsp. baking soda
2 cups flour

1 tsp. salt
2 tsp. cinnamon
3 cups carrots, grated raw
½ cup nuts, chopped

Beat sugar and oil, add eggs and cream well. Sift flour, soda, salt and cinnamon; add to first mixture and fold in carrots and nuts. Pour into greased and floured pan and bake in 300° oven for 40 minutes.

—Denise Gore

PHILADELPHIA CREAM CHEESE ICING

1 box confectioner's sugar
¼ cup margarine

1 8-oz. pkg. Philadelphia
   cream cheese
1 tsp. vanilla

Combine ingredients in one bowl and beat until smooth. Makes enough icing for three layers, top and sides, or a nice thick coating on a rectangular cake.

—Denise Gore

THREE LAYER CAKE

1 cup flour
½ cup margarine
½ cup nuts
1 8-oz. pkg. cream cheese
1 cup powdered sugar

1 cup Pet Whip
2 pkgs. lemon instant pudding
   mix
3 cups milk

Combine flour, margarine and nuts. Press into 9"x13" pan. Bake 15 minutes at 350°. Cool. Cream together cream cheese, powdered sugar and Pet Whip. Place on top of cooled first layer. Combine and beat pudding mix and milk until thick. Place on top of second layer. Top the last layer with Pet Whip. Make the day before and refrigerate.

—Arlou Ripplemeyer

DESSERTS...

ITALIAN CREAM CAKE

1 stick butter
½ cup vegetable shortening
2 cups sugar
5 egg yolks
2 cups self-rising flour
1 tsp. baking soda

1 cup buttermilk
1 tsp. vanilla
1 small can coconut
1 cup nuts, chopped
5 egg whites

CREAM CHEESE FROSTING

1 pkg. cream cheese, softened
1 box powdered sugar
1 tsp. vanilla

Nuts and coconut to suit taste
Pet milk

Cream butter and shortening, add sugar and beat until smooth. Add egg yolks and beat well. Combine flour and soda and add mixture alternately with buttermilk. Stir in vanilla and add coconut and nuts. Fold in egg whites, pour in greased pans. Bake at 350° for 25 minutes.

—*Charlotte Matthews*

SOUR CREAM COFFEE CAKE

½ cup butter or margarine
1 cup sugar
2 eggs
2 cups flour
1 tsp. baking powder

1 tsp. baking soda
½ tsp. salt
1 tsp. vanilla
1 cup sour cream

TOPPING

1 cup pecans, chopped
¾ cup light brown sugar

¼ cup white sugar
1 tsp. cinnamon

Cream butter with sugar and add eggs one at a time. Mix thoroughly. Add vanilla to sour cream and add alternately with sifted dry ingredients. In a separate bowl, combine topping ingredients. pour ½ cake batter into lightly greased 9"x13" pan. Add ½ of the topping, the rest of the batter, then the remaining topping. Use a table knife and slightly "marble", so topping is woven through cake. Bake in 350° oven.

—*Joyce Bright*

OATMEAL CAKE

1½ cups boiling water
1 stick butter or margarine
1 cup oatmeal
1 cup brown sugar
1 cup white sugar

1 tsp. salt
2 eggs
1 tsp. vanilla
1½ cups flour
1 tsp. soda

FROSTING

1 stick butter or margarine
1 cup brown sugar
1 cup coconut

½ cup canned milk
1 tsp. vanilla
1 cup nutmeats

Stir water, butter and oatmeal until butter has melted; let stand 30 minutes. Mix sugars, salt, flour, soda and add eggs and vanilla. Combine with oatmeal mixture. Bake at 350° for 35 minutes. For frosting, beat butter, brown sugar, coconut, milk, vanilla and nuts until dissolved. Broil a few minutes under broiler on warm cake. Oatmeal cake is only good with this frosting on it.

—Jeannine Westmoreland

BANANA NUT CAKE

½ cup margarine or
   shortening
1½ cups sugar
3 eggs, separated
1 tsp. soda

4 Tbsp. buttermilk
3 ripe bananas, mashed
1½ cups flour
1 tsp. vanilla
1 cup nuts

ICING

1 8-oz. pkg. cream cheese,
   softened
1 pkg. powdered sugar, sifted

½ stick margarine, softened
1 cup chopped pecans
1 tsp. vanilla

Cream shortening and sugar together. Add egg yolks. Dissolve soda in buttermilk; add mashed bananas. Mix with shortening and sugar. Add flour and vanilla. Mix well. Fold in nuts and beaten egg whites. Put in two 9-inch round cake pans. Bake at 350° for 25 to 30 minutes. Cool. To make icing, combine ingredients and spread over cooled cake.

—Fern Mears

7-UP POUND CAKE

3 cups sugar	1 tsp. coconut flavoring
3 sticks margarine	1 tsp. vanilla extract
5 eggs	½ tsp. salt
1 tsp. lemon extract	3 cups flour
1 tsp. butter flavoring	7 oz. 7-Up

Mix well and bake at 300° in well-greased and floured tube or bundt pan for 1½ hours or until done, starting in **cold** oven. Cool on wire rack before removing from pan.

— *Frances Folkes*

GRAHAM CRACKER CAKE

1½ cups sugar	1 tsp. baking soda
2½ Tbls. shortening	3½ cups graham cracker
2 eggs	crumbs
1½ cups sour milk	Dash of salt

TOPPING

1 cup sugar	1 cup hot water
1 cup dates, chopped	2 Tbls. flour

Blend all cake ingredients well and bake in moderate (350°) oven. While cake is baking, mix and cook together the topping ingredients. Spread date mixture on cake while it is still hot. Serve with whipped cream.

BEAVER CAKE

1 pkg. German chocolate cake	6 oz. chocolate chips
mix	1 bag caramels
1 stick butter, melted	½ cup nuts
⅔ cup Pet milk, divided use	

Mix together the cake mix, butter and half (⅓ cup) milk. Divide the dough and press half of it into a 13"x9" cake pan. Bake in 350° oven for 10 minutes. Sprinkle chocolate chips on top of the baked mixture. Melt the caramels with remaining one-third cup milk and spread over chocolate chips. Mix nuts into remaining half of the cake mix and sprinkle over caramels. Bake in 350° oven for 10 to 15 minutes. Very rich.

DESSERTS . . .

KATHLEEN'S IRISH APPLE PIE

2 cups all-purpose flour	3 large cooking apples
1½ sticks salted butter	½ cup sugar
⅓ cup buttermilk	1 tsp. cinnamon

Mix flour and butter, preferably in a processor, until mixture resembles cornmeal. Add enough buttermilk to moisten mixture. Form into a ball, dust with flour, and wrap in waxed paper. Chill for at least one hour. Roll half the dough into a 12" round and drape over 10" pie pan. Trim excess. Peel, core and thinly slice the apples. Combine sugar and cinnamon. Place apples in pie crust and sprinkle with sugar-cinnamon mixture. Roll remaining dough, and by moistening rim of both bottom and top crusts, press both parts firmly together on the edges and use a fork to form decorative design. Cut a vent hole in the middle. Bake in 350° oven, preheated, for about 50 minutes until golden brown. Let cool completely on a rack. This pie is also excellent with heavy or whipped cream.

K. C.'S HOT MILK CAKE

¼ lb. butter	2 cups sugar
1 cup milk	1 tsp. baking powder
4 eggs, beaten	¼ tsp. salt
2 cups flour	1 tsp. lemon or vanilla extract

Combine butter and milk and heat until butter melts (don't boil). Beat eggs until light. Add the flour, sugar, baking powder and salt. Add the butter and milk mixture and flavoring. Bake in 375° oven for 45 minutes to 1 hour.

—*Kathie Cirelli*

God knows YOU by name. . .
God never mistakes you in the crowd.
When a person fully realizes how much he or she matters to God — then
he doesn't have to go out and prove to the world how much he matters.

From *"Be Somebody"* by Mary Crowley

228

RUSSIAN DRESSING
(Serve on Angel Food Cake)

4 egg yolks
1 cup sugar
⅓ cup orange juice or one
    orange

2 tsp. orange rind, grated
½ pt. cream, whipped
½ cup walnuts, cut fine, added
    just before serving

Beat egg yolks until light and lemon colored. Blend in orange juice, sugar and grated rind. Cook in double boiler stirring constantly, until thick (about 20 minutes). Fold in stiffly beaten whipped cream. Fold in nuts just before serving.

—Stella Sterling

GRASSHOPPER ICING

1 envelope gelatin, unflavored
¼ cup water
½ cup creme de menthe

⅓ cup white creme de cacao
1 lg. container Cool whip

Soften gelatin in water. Heat creme de menthe with creme de cacao, add to softened gelatin and stir until dissolved. Let cool. Mix in Cool Whip and whip together. Keep refrigerated until served. Ice any chocolate cake with this light green icing.

—Carolyn Banning

Memory System

Forget each kindness that you do as soon as you have done it;
Forget the praise that falls to you as soon as you have found it;
Forget the slander that you hear before you can repeat it;
Forget each slight, each spite, each sneer, wherever you may meet it.

Remember every kindness done to you whatever its measure;
Remember praise by others won and pass it on with pleasure;
Remember every promise made and keep it to the letter;
Remember those who lend you aid and be a grateful debtor;
Remember good, remember truth, remember heaven's above you;
And you will find, through age and youth, that many hearts will love you.

DESSERTS...

ALL ABOUT CAKE PANS

Cakes may be baked in loaves, sheets, cupcakes, tubes or the ever popular layers. Many recipes cannot be interchanged, however. If the recipe specifies a tube pan, the cake must be baked in a tube pan for best results.

Cake pans may be made of aluminum, heavy tin or oven-proof glass. Use the pan size recommended in the recipe. Check the pan size by measuring it across the top.

Use bright shiny pans. Discolored pans cause uneven browning. Avoid warped pans, too. They will cause uneven baking. If glass pans are used, follow the manufacturer's directions. Glass usually requires a lower baking temperature.

MIXING MAGIC

There are two commonly used methods for making cakes — the *creaming* method and the *quick* method.

CREAMING METHOD: In this method the shortening, sugar, eggs and salt are creamed or blended together until light and smooth. Then the dry ingredients and liquid are added alternately and blended until smooth. Most of the old-time favorite cake recipes are made by this method.

QUICK METHOD: The shortening, dry ingredients and part of the liquid are mixed for two minutes, then the eggs and remaining liquid are added and mixed for two or more minutes. This is a modern method and takes advantage of today's improved products.

The special properties of a top quality vegetable shortening make it possible to bake excellent cakes by either method.

DESSERTS...

Honey was the only sweetner known in Biblical times, until the Queen of Sheba brought sugar cane to Solomon, seeking his wisdom in exchange for her many gifts. Nutritionally, honey is much better for you than the refined sugar of today, and sugar cannot duplicate its delicate sweetness which enhances the flavor of any fresh fruit.

> As the apple tree among the trees of the wood, so is my beloved among the sons. I sat down under his shadow with great delight, and his fruit was sweet to my taste.
>
> —Song of Solomon 2:3

HONEYED APPLES

4 cooking apples
1 cup water
1 cup honey

1 stick cinnamon
Sour cream
Nutmeg

Core and slice the apples into eighths. In a saucepan place the cinnamon stick, honey and water and bring to a boil. Lower the flame and add some of the apple slices a little at a time. Do not crowd too many in the pan or they willl not cook evenly. Cook slowly until they are tender, turning several times and transfer to individual dessert dishes. When all the slices have been cooked, bring the syrup in the pan to a boil again for a minute, then let it cool slightly. Remove the cinnamon stick and pour the syrup over the apple slices, some in each dish. This is delicious served while still warm, topped by a dollop of cold sour cream and dusted with a little fresh grated nutmeg. It is also a wonderful side dish served plain with pork.

Take time to think... it is the price of success.
Take time to read... It is the foundation of wisdom.
Take time to be friendly... it is the road to happiness.
Take time to laugh... it is the music of the soul.
Take time to give... it is too short a day to be selfish.
Take time to play... it is the secret to eternal youth.
Take time to love... and be loved... it is a God-given privilege.
Take time to pray... it is because of God that you are here.

FRUIT CREAM PIE

1 large pkg. instant pudding and pie filling	1 8-oz. package frozen berries (thawed and drained)
1 small tub Cool Whip	1 8" or 9" pre-cooked pie shell

Make up pudding as instructed on the box, except slight the liquid a little. Chill until partially set. Fold in Cool Whip and berries. Pour into pie shell and chill.

—Nancy Haldarman

PRIZE WINNING CUSTARD PIE

5 large eggs, or 6 small ones	2 Tbls. melted butter
1 cup sugar	1 tsp. vanilla
2 cups warm milk	Unbaked pie shell

Beat eggs until foamy, then add sugar and beat until foamy again. Add milk, butter, vanilla and salt. Pour into unbaked pie shell. Bake at 400° until foamy top starts to brown. Turn oven down to 350°. Let bake until about 1½ inches of outside of custard is firm. Take out before center is firm. May be baked as a custard (without crust) in pan with one inch water.

—Pollyanna Core

CORNMEAL PIE

1 cup brown sugar	2 eggs
2 Tbls. cornmeal	1 cup white sugar
½ Tbls. vanilla	2 Tbls. butter
1 Tbls. water	Unbaked pie shell

Mix all ingredients together, then pour into an unbaked pie shell. Bake in 400° oven for 45 minutes.

—Linda Stabler

The best place to spend your vacation this summer is somewhere near your budget.

DESSERTS...

PUMPKIN CHIFFON PIE

2 envelopes gelatin, unflavored
¼ cup cold water
2 eggs, separated
1½ cups pumpkin pie filling
1 cup milk

¾ cup brown sugar, divided use
2 tsp. pumpkin pie spice
½ tsp. salt
1 8-oz. container Cool Whip
Graham cracker crust

Combine gelatin with water to soften. Beat egg yolks together and add pumpkin, milk, ½ cup only of brown sugar, spices and salt. Cook over low heat until thick, stirring constantly. Pour in gelatin water mixture and put in refrigerator to cool. Now beat egg whites to peaks and add remaining brown sugar until stiff. Fold in cooled mixture and Cool Whip. Pour into graham cracker crust. This pie will keep in refrigerator for two weeks.

—Lynn Gordon

DAIQUIRI PIE

1 pkg. lemon pie filling
   (4-oz. size)
1 3-oz. pkg. lime Jello
⅓ cup sugar
2½ cups water

2 eggs, slightly beaten
½ cup Bacardi light rum
2 cups non-dairy whipped
   cream, thawed
1 9" crumb crust

Mix pudding, Jello and sugar in saucepan. Stir in ½ cup water and eggs; blend well. Add remaining water. Stir over medium heat until mixture comes to full boil. Remove from heat and stir in rum. Chill about 1½ hours. To hasten chilling, place bowl of filling mixture in larger bowl of ice water; stir until mixture is cold. Blend topping into chilled mixture. Spoon into crust. Chill until firm. Garnish with additional whipped cream or graham cracker crumbs.

—Sherrie Kautz

Any woman, no matter how large her family, can always get some time alone by doing the dishes.

MILLION DOLLAR PIE

2 graham cracker crusts
1 can Eagle Brand milk
¼ cup lemon juice
1 sm. can angel flake coconut

1 13-oz. can crushed
  pineapple, drained
1 cup pecans, chipped
1 13-oz. container Cool Whip

Cream milk and lemon juice with beater. Add coconut, pineapple and pecans. Fold in Cool Whip. Put into crusts. Makes 2 pies.

—Esther Graham

HERSHEY BAR PIE

1 cooked pie crust, or 1 graham
  cracker pie crust, or 1 butter
  cookie pie crust

8 oz. Hershey bars, melted
8 oz. Cool Whip
Shaved chocolate

Fold room temperature melted chocolate into Cool Whip. Fill pie shell. Garnish with additional Cool Whip and shaved chocolate. Best when refrigerated overnight.

—Suzanne Terrell

EASY BUT RICH CHOCOLATE PIE

1 1-lb. Hershey chocolate bar,
  with or without almonds

1 pie crust, ready to eat
1 8-oz. container Cool Whip

Use your favorite pie crust, pastry, graham cracker, whatever. Melt the chocolate bar to a blending consistency. Blend melted chocolate with Cool Whip, reserving a few tablespoons for decorating the top of pie. Pour chocolate mixture in pie crust and refrigerate for about 2 hours and enjoy!

—Lynn Knapik

What you are is God's gift to you . . .
what you make of yourself . . . that's your gift to God.

CHERRY CHEESECAKE PIE

2 cups graham cracker crumbs
   (about 14 double crackers)
½ cup (1 stick) butter, melted
1 cup (½ pint) whipping
   cream
½ cup fresh lemon juice
1 8-oz. pkg. cream cheese

1 can Eagle Brand milk
1 envelope gelatin, unflavored
¼ cup cold water
1 tsp. pure vanilla extract
1 can cherry pie filling (ready
   for use)

Combine graham cracker crumbs and butter. Line 9" deep dish pie plate with graham cracker mixture. Stir lemon juice into cream, let stand 10 minutes. Mash cream cheese thoroughly. Gradually beat in Eagle Brand milk. Mixture should be smooth. Add gelatin to water; let stand 5 minutes, then dissolve over hot water. Whip lemon-cream mixture just until it begins to stiffen. Pour in cream cheese mixture and continue beating until well blended. Stir in gelatin and vanilla. Pour into pie crust; chill until firm, about 1½ hours. Top with cherry pie filling and chill a while longer. 8-10 servings.

—Debbie Scott

CHERRY-TOPPED CHEESE PIE

1 8-oz. pkg. cream cheese
½ cup sugar
2 cups Cool Whip

1 9" graham cracker crust
1 cup cherry pie filling

Beat softened cream cheese and sugar together until creamy. Blend in thawed Cool Whip. Pour into unbaked pie crust. Top with cherry filling. Chill at least 3 hours before serving.

—Pat Steinberg

When God measures men, He puts the tape around the heart
— not around the head.

DESSERTS...

STRAWBERRY GLACÉ PIE

1 pie crust shell, or 1 graham
   cracker shell
1 qt. fresh strawberries, cut up
1 cup sugar
3 Tbls. cornstarch

1 cup water
1 cup whipping cream,
   whipped and sweetened
Red food coloring

Mix 1 cup sugar and cornstarch in 2-quart saucepan. Stir in water gradually until smooth. Add half of cut-up berries. Cook and stir over medium heat until thick and clear. Stir in a few drops red food coloring. Cool. Stir in remaining berries, saving ¼ cup for garnish. Pour into pie shell. Chill until firm, about 3 hours. Top with whipped cream, and garnish with berries. Serves 6.

FABULOUS STRAWBERRY PIE (Makes 2 Pies)

2 graham cracker crusts
1 8-oz. pkg. cream cheese
1 cup sugar
1 cup Cool Whip

1 lg. box strawberry Jello
2 cups hot water
2 10-oz. pkgs. frozen
   strawberries

Mix cream cheese, sugar and Cool Whip well and put in pie crust; refrigerate. Combine Jello and water and then add strawberries. Pour on top of cream cheese mixture and refrigerate.

—Patty Karl

STRAWBERRY PIE

1 baked pie shell
1 qt. halved strawberries
⅔ cup water
1 cup sugar

3 Tbls. cornstarch
⅓ cup water
Whipped cream

Mix 1 cup of halved strawberries and ⅔ cup water, simmer on stove. Blend in sugar, cornstarch and ⅓ cup water. Cook until thick and clear. Let cool. Fill baked pie shell with remaining halved strawberries. Cover with cooled glazed mixture and add whipped cream on top. Garnish with strawberries on top. Chill 2 to 3 hours before serving.

—Judi Houdek

236

IMPOSSIBLE PIE

1 stick margarine	4 eggs
2 cups milk	½ cup flour
2 tsp. vanilla extract	¼ tsp. salt
1 cup sugar	1 cup coconut, shredded

Place all ingredients in a blender and combine thoroughly. Grease and flour a 10" pie pan. Pour mixture into pan and bake in a preheated oven at 350° for 30 to 40 minutes or until set. "Pie" will make its own crust as it cooks. Serve at room temperature.

—Rosa Garner

IMPOSSIBLE COCONUT PIE

4 eggs	1 can coconut
3 Tbls. butter	2 cups milk
½ cup sugar	1 tsp. vanilla
½ cup Bisquick	

Put all ingredients into blender and blend on mix for 15 seconds. Bake in well greased 9" pan for 40 minutes at 350°.

—Bee Fraley

PINK LEMONADE PIE

1 sm. can frozen pink lemonade	1 8-oz. pkg. Cool Whip
1 can Eagle Brand milk	Food coloring as desired
	Graham cracker pie crust

Mix all ingredients together and pour into a graham cracker crust and freeze. Thaw 10 minutes before serving. This is a beautiful and easy-to-make dessert.

—Anita Davidson

Duty makes us do things well. . . but love makes us do them beautifully.
—Phillips Brooks

APPLE-BERRY PIE

5-7 medium tart apples	2 Tbls. flour
1 can blueberry pie filling	1½ tsp. cinnamon
(cherry or blackberry, if	¼ tsp. nutmeg, optional
desired)	3 Tbls. butter or margarine
¾-1 cup sugar	Dash of salt

Pare apples and slice thin; in a large bowl put in apples, sugar, flour, cinnamon, nutmeg and salt. Mix well. Line a 9" pie plate with pastry pie crust and fill with ½ the apple mixture, ½ the blueberry filling, and remaining apples, then blueberry. Dot with butter and add top pie crust. Seal sides. Make three small cuts in top then sprinkle with sugar. Bake in a hot oven at 400° for 50 minutes or until crust is done.

CRUST RECIPE

3 cups sifted flour (1 lb.)	2 eggs
2 sticks margarine, softened	¼ cup sugar

To make crust, take flour and margarine and crumble together, then make a well in the center. Mix eggs and sugar together then add to flour mixture. Mix well. Should feel like cookie dough. Take half the mixture and roll out for your pie plate.

—Jan M. Klarner

RAW APPLE CAKE

1 cup granulated sugar	1 tsp. cloves
1 cup brown sugar	2 tsp. cinnamon
1 cup margarine	1 Tbls. cocoa
1 tsp. vanilla	1 cup water
3 eggs	1½ cups dates, chopped
3 cups flour, sifted	4 cups raw apples, cubed
2 tsp. baking soda	1 cup nuts, chopped
1 tsp. salt	

Cream sugars, margarine, vanilla and eggs. Then add flour, baking soda, salt, cloves, cinnamon, cocoa and water. Mix well. Fold in the dates, apples and nuts. Bake for 1 hour in 350° oven. Makes one large 9"x13"or two 8"x8" cakes. Better the next day.

—Evelyn Redle

WALNUT PIE

22 Ritz crackers, crushed
1 cup sugar
1 cup walnuts, chopped

1 tsp. baking powder
3 egg whites
Cool Whip (reserve for serving)

Beat egg whites until stiff, then gently mix in the rest of the ingredients. Generously butter a 9" pie pan and pour mixture into it. Bake 30 minutes at 350°. Cool completely and serve topped with Cool Whip.

—Liz Vasquez

DELUXE PECAN PIE

3 eggs
¾ cup Karo dark syrup
1 cup sugar
4 Tbls. margarine (or ½ stick
    butter), melted

1 tsp. vanilla
1 cup pecans
1 unbaked 9" pastry shell

Melt butter over low heat. Remove from heat and mix in sugar and corn syrup. Blend in eggs and vanilla extract. Add pecans and pour into pie shell. Bake in 350° oven for 35 to 40 minutes or until well done.

—Patricia R. Lormand

PECAN PIE

3 egg whites
1 cup sugar
20 Ritz crackers

1 cup pecans, chopped
1½ tsp. vanilla
Whipped cream for topping

Beat egg whites until stiff. Add sugar, fold in crushed crackers and pecans. Add vanilla. Pour into greased 8" or 9" pie pan. Bake at 350° for 25 minutes. If using glass pan, 325° oven. Serve with whipped cream topping. Let cool before adding topping.

—Jeanette Ferguson

PUMPKIN PECAN PIE

3 eggs, slightly beaten
1½ cups pumpkin, canned or
    fresh pumpkin that has
    been cooked and mashed
½ cup granulated sugar
½ cup brown sugar
½ cup light corn syrup
½ cup milk

2 tsp. flour
1 tsp. vanilla
1 tsp. pumpkin pie spice
¼ tsp. salt
1 unbaked 9" pie shell
1 cup pecans, chopped
Whipped cream for topping

In a small mixing bowl, combine eggs, pumpkin, sugars, syrup, milk, flour, vanilla, spice and salt. Mix well. Pour into unbaked pastry shell. Top with chopped pecans. Bake in moderate oven, 350° for 40 minutes or until knife inserted half way between center and edge comes out clean. Chill. Serve with whipped cream. Makes one 9" pie.

—Pauline Mitchell

PECAN PIE

⅔-1 cup sugar
1 cup dark corn syrup
3 eggs
¼ tsp. salt

1 cup pecans, chopped
1 tsp. vanilla
4 Tbls. margarine, melted

Mix all together and pour into 9-inch pie shell. Bake 350° for 45 minutes to 1 hour.

PIE CRUST

1½ cup flour, plain
½ tsp. salt
¼ tsp. baking powder

½ cup Crisco shortening
¼ cup cold water

Sift dry ingredients together. Cut Crisco into this mixture for several minutes. Add cold water; mix well. Put dough onto floured surface and roll out to form a 9-inch pie round.

—Anita Taylor

BREAD PUDDING

2 cans Carnation evaporated milk	½ stick butter
1 cup sugar	1 loaf bread
4 eggs (beat whites separately)	1 tsp. vanilla
	1 small box raisins

Boil milk; add sugar, eggs, and butter and pour over softened bread wet with water, add vanilla and raisins. Bake in preheated oven at 350° for 40-45 minutes.

—*Patricia Lormand*

HOMEMADE BANANA PUDDING

1 cup sugar	1 tsp. vanilla
2 Tbls. flour	½ stick butter
3 eggs	1 box vanilla wafers
1 sm. can Pet evaporated milk	3 medium bananas
1 cup water	Pinch of salt

Mix sugar, flour, eggs, evaporated milk, water, vanilla, butter and salt in a double boiler and cook over medium heat; bring to a boil stirring often. Continue cooking until mixture thickens like pudding. Lay vanilla wafers in bottom of medium casserole dish, crumble two or three handfuls of wafers and add to pudding mixture after removing from heat. Slice bananas and arrange them on top of wafers in the bowl. Pour pudding on top of wafers and bananas. Chill until thick, or eat while warm.

Note: This basic pudding recipe can be used as the base for any of these pies:

> Coconut — add coconut
> Cocoa — add cocoa
> Pumpkin — add pumpkin

—*Cynthia Shumway*

Always be enthusiastic. . . imperfections are lost in the glory of enthusiasm.

CORNSTARCH PUDDING

¼ cup cornstarch	2¾ cups milk
⅓ cup sugar	2 Tbls. margarine
⅛ tsp. salt	1 tsp. vanilla

Mix cornstarch, sugar, and salt in small saucepan. Stir in milk slowly, keeping mixture smooth. Cook over medium heat, stirring until it comes to a boil. Boil gently for 1 minute, take off heat. Stir margarine and vanilla into hot pudding. Pour into serving dishes. Cool and chill. Makes eight ½ cup servings. For chocolate pudding, add 3 tablespoons cocoa, and increase sugar to ⅔ cup. Mix extra ingredients with cornstarch as directed above.

RICE PUDDING

1 qt. milk	½ cup raw rice
½ cup sugar	½ tsp. salt
½ tsp. nutmeg	½ cup raisins

Combine all ingredients and pour into buttered pan (cake pan is good). Bake at 350° for 2 hours, stirring occasionally in the first hour.

—Mildred Yahn

PEACH COBBLER

1 lg. can peaches, sliced	1 cup walnuts
1 butter brickle cake mix	¼ lb. butter
1 cup coconut	Cool Whip or ice cream

Pour peaches with juice into cake pan. Sprinkle cake mix over peaches. Sprinkle coconut over cake mix, then sprinkle walnuts over coconut. Melt butter and pour over entire mixture. Bake at 350° for 40 minutes. Can be turned upside down. Serve with Cool Whip or ice cream.

—Karen Olson

RHUBARB COBBLER
BASE

1 cup sugar

⅓ cup pancake mix

9 cups rhubarb, cut in ½"
pieces

TOPPING

¾ cup pancake mix

⅔ cup sugar

1 egg, beaten

¼ cup butter or margarine,
melted

To make base, combine sugar, pancake mix and add rhubarb. Toss lightly. Place in 13"x9"x2" pan.

To make topping, combine pancake mix and sugar. Stir in egg until mixture resembles coarse crumbs. Sprinkle evenly over rhubarb base. Drizzle with melted butter or margarine. Bake at 375° for 35 to 40 minutes.

—JoAnn Weber

NO-FAIL PIE CRUST

2 cups flour

1 cup Crisco shortening

½ cup cold water

2 Tbls. sugar

Pinch of salt

In medium Tupperware mixing bowl, place flour, salt, sugar and shortening. Put seal on and shake very briskly. Then add water, replace seal, and shake again. Dough will need very little if any handling.

—Janice McCalip

Nothing in the world can take the place of patience.
Talent will not; nothing is more common than unsuccessful men with talent.
Genius will not; unrewarded genius is almost a proverb.
Education alone will not; the world is full of educated derelicts.
Persistance and Determination are omnipotent.

LOW CALORIE CHEESECAKE

2 envelopes gelatin, unflavored
1 cup reconstituted nonfat dry
   milk
4 eggs, separated
Artificial sweetener equivalent
   to 1¼ cups sugar
¼ tsp. salt
1 tsp. lemon rind, grated
1 tsp. orange rind, grated

1 Tbls. lemon juice
1½ tsp. vanilla
½ tsp. almond extract
3 cups creamed cottage
   cheese
½ tsp. cream of tartar
⅓ cup graham cracker crumbs
⅛ tsp. cinnamon
⅛ tsp. nutmeg

Sprinkle gelatin over milk in top of double boiler; add egg yolks and stir until completely blended. Place over hot water and stir constantly for about 5 minutes until gelatin dissolves and mixture thickens slightly. Remove from heat, stir in sweetener, salt, rinds, lemon juice, vanilla and almond extract. Sieve or beat cottage cheese on high speed of mixer for 3 or 4 minutes or until smooth. Stir into gelatin mixture. Chill, stirring occasionally until mixture mounds slightly when dropped from spoon. Beat egg whites and cream of tartar until very stiff. Fold into gelatin mixture. Combine cracker crumbs, cinnamon and nutmeg. Sprinkle about half of the crumb mixture over the bottom of an 8" or 9" springform pan. Pour gelatin mixture into pan, sprinkle with remaining crumb mixture. Chill until firm. Loosen from side of pan with sharp knife, release springform. Yields 12 servings.

—Ruby M. Jameson

MAGIC FRENCH FUDGE

3 6-oz. pkgs. semi-sweet
   chocolate chips
1 can Eagle Brand sweetened
   condensed milk

1½ tsp. vanilla
½ cup nuts, chopped
   (optional)
Pinch of salt

In top of double boiler, melt chocolate and milk over low heat until chocolate is melted and mix is smooth. Add vanilla, salt and nuts. Stir until smooth. Turn into waxed paper lined 8" square pan. Chill. Store in airtight container. Makes 2 pounds.

—Joyce Moss

LILLIE'S BABAS

1 pkg. yellow cake mix	3 Tbls. orange peel, cut into thin
¾ cup sugar	slivers (white part removed)
¾ cup water	Whipped cream
¾ cup orange juice	

Prepare the batter for cake mix according to package directions. Place well-greased paper hot-drink cups on a baking sheet and spoon in the batter, filling the cups about half full. Bake in moderate oven (375°) for 25 minutes or until done. Meanwhile, make syrup. Combine sugar, water, orange juice and orange peel. Cook mixture for 5 minutes. When cakes are done, cool a minute or two, then turn out of cups onto serving plate. Drizzle immediately with the hot orange syrup, soaking the cakes well. Chill. Serve cold with whipped cream. Makes 9 or 10.

—Lillie Wheeler

O'HENRY BARS

⅔ cup margarine	½ cup dark or light syrup
4 cups dry oatmeal	1 cup semi-sweet chocolate
(quick-cooking)	chips
1 cup brown sugar	⅔ cup Skippy super chunk
2 tsp. vanilla	peanut butter

Melt margarine. Add oatmeal, brown sugar, vanilla and syrup. Spread in greased 9"x13" pan. Bake in 350° oven for 12 minutes or until mixture is bubbly. Remove from oven and cool for 10 minutes.

Melt chocolate chips and peanut butter in double boiler. Spread this over first mixture. This may be put in the refrigerator to set.

—Ann Dee Hermann

It is a thousand times better to have common sense without education than to have education without common sense.

GOAT'S MILK FUDGE (White Fudge)

2¼ cups white sugar
½ cup sour cream
¼ cup milk
2 Tbls. butter
1 Tbls. light corn syrup

¼ tsp. salt
1 Tbls. vanilla
⅓ cup candied cherry halves
(optional)

In saucepan combine sugar, sour cream, milk, butter, corn syrup and salt and stir over medium heat until sugar is dissolved and mixture reaches a boil. Boil for 10 minutes, remove from heat and let set for 1 hour until lukewarm. Add vanilla and beat with mixer until mixture holds shape. Add cherries. Put in buttered 9"x9" pan immediately. Makes 1½ pounds.

—Kim DeRosa

CHOCOLATE CHEESE FUDGE

2 3-oz. pkgs. cream cheese,
softened
2 Tbls. milk
1 tsp. vanilla extract
⅛ tsp. salt

4 cups confectioner's sugar,
sifted
4 oz. unsweetened chocolate,
melted
1 cup walnuts, chopped

Mix cheese, milk, vanilla extract and salt. Add sugar gradually and mix well. Add warm chocolate and mix thoroughly. Add nuts and mix. Press into a buttered 8" square pan. Chill until firm enough to cut (about 15 minutes). Yields approximately 2 pounds.

—Pat Motyka

FUDGE

4 cups sugar
1 tall can Pet milk
1 7-oz. jar Kraft marshmallow
cream

3 6-oz. pkgs. chocolate chips
2 sticks margarine
3 cups nuts (or more)
2 tsp. vanilla

Combine sugar and milk and cook together. After mixture comes to a boil, boil 9 minutes (no longer), stirring constantly. Turn heat off and add the remaining ingredients. Mix well and pour into a large (18"x11") pan. Cool and cut into squares.

246

—Ethel Serpa

CARAMEL TURTLES

CARAMEL

1 cup margarine	Dash of salt
1 can Eagle Brand milk	1 cup light corn syrup
1 lb. brown sugar	1 tsp. vanilla

TURTLES

1 12-oz. pkg. milk chocolate chips	1/3 bar paraffin
1 pkg. Baker's German sweet chocolate	Pecans

In heavy pan, melt margarine, add milk, brown sugar and salt. Stir in syrup gradually. Cook to 245° or almost hard ball. (I cook to 250°.) Remove from heat, stir in vanilla and pour in buttered 9"x13" pan. Will cover 20 medium apples or make 8"x8" pan.

To make turtles, press pecans into each square of caramel. Melt chocolate chips, German chocolate and paraffin together and pour over caramel pecan patties.

—Irene Myers

CARAMELS

2 cups sugar	1 2/3 cup evaporated milk
1 cup butter	4 tsp. vanilla
1 3/4 cup light corn syrup	1 cup nuts, chopped (optional)

Combine sugar, butter, corn syrup and milk in large saucepan. Cook over high heat, stirring frequently to 210° (about 5 minutes). Reduce heat to medium. Cook, stirring constantly to hard ball stage. Remove from heat immediately. Add vanilla and nuts, stirring quickly to blend. Pour mixture into a well-buttered 9" square pan. Cool thoroughly. Turn candy out onto a wooden cutting board. Cut into small squares with a sharp knife. Wrap each piece in heavy waxed paper. (May use a cookie sheet with edges for thinner caramels, if desired.) Yield: 3 pounds of caramels.

—Linda Hollinshead

DELICIOUS INEXPENSIVE CARAMELS

2 cups sugar
½ cup white corn syrup
½ cup milk
1 tsp. vanilla

4 Tbls. butter
1 cup cream (canned milk
    works wonderfully)

Cook ingredients except vanilla to stiff ball stage or 246°. Remove from stove and add vanilla. Pour into buttered pan. When cool, cut into squares and wrap in waxed paper.

—Kathy Martinez

TOFFEE

1 cup almonds, chopped
¾ cup brown sugar
½ cup butter or margarine

1 bar (4½-oz.) milk chocolate,
    broken into pieces

Butter 9"x9"x2" pan. Spread almonds in pan. Heat sugar and butter to boiling, stirring constantly. Boil 7 minutes over medium heat, stirring constantly. Immediately spread mixture over nuts in pan. Sprinkle chocolate pieces over hot mixture, place baking sheet over pan so contained heat will melt chocolate. Spread melted chocolate over candy. While hot, cut into 1½" squares. Chill until firm. This recipe burns easily on electric stoves, so be careful.

—Nance Randall

HOLIDAY BONBONS

½ lb. walnuts, shelled
½ lb. dates, pitted
1 egg white

2 Tbls. sugar
Food coloring, if desired

Grind nuts and dates fine. Knead and shape into date shaped bonbons. Chill overnight. Beat egg white slightly, add sugar and food coloring if desired. Dip bonbons into mixture. Place on greased baking sheet. Bake in 300° oven until crisp.

—Mary Morgret

EASY TOFFEE BARS

Graham cracker sections
½ cup butter
½ cup margarine

1 cup brown sugar
½ cup pecans, chopped

Line bottom of broiler pan or similar type pan with graham cracker sections. Cover top of broiler pan (rack) with foil and wax paper and set aside. Melt butter, margarine, brown sugar and boil gently until syrupy and no longer grainy looking. Pour over graham crackers and top with pecans. Bake in preheated 350° oven for 8 to 10 minutes. Let cool several minutes; remove each piece separately and place on wax paper to cool completely.

—Betty Jensen

CHOCOLATE NUT CRUMB

1 pkg. graham crackers
1 cup ground nuts
½ cup oleo, melted
½ gal. ice cream
½ cup oleo

3 squares baking chocolate
2 cups powdered sugar
1 tsp. vanilla
6 eggs, separated

Mix first three ingredients together. Line pan with half and bake at 400° for 5 minutes. Cream oleo and sugar, add egg yolks, then melted chocolate and vanilla. Fold in beaten egg whites. Spread half of mixture on baked crumbs, and refrigerate 1 hour, then spread ½ gallon ice cream over mixture, and repeat. Top with remaining crumbs.

—Betty Dufer

*Let me be a little kinder, let me be a little blinder
To the faults of those about me; let me praise a little more;
Let me be, when I am weary, just a little bit more cheery;
Let me serve a little better than those that I am striving for;
Let me be a little braver, when tempations bid me waver;
Let me strive a little harder to be all that I should be;
Let me be a little meeker with the brother that is weaker;
Let me think more of my neighbor and a little less of me.*

PLUM CAKE

2 cups self-rising flour
1 cup cooking oil
2 small jars strained plum
   baby food
3 eggs

2 cups sugar
1 tsp. cinnamon
1 tsp. cloves
1 cup nuts, chopped

Sprinkle nuts in bottom of well-greased bundt pan. Combine all ingredients and pour into pan. Bake at 350° for 55 minutes.

—Debra Woods

MAKE YESTERDAY DESSERT

Pie crust, your choice to cover
   bottom of 9"x13" pan,
   baked as necessary
1 8-oz. pkg. cream cheese
1 container Cool Whip

1 cup powdered sugar
2 pkgs. chocolate pudding,
   prepared according to
   directions
½ cup nuts, chopped

Stir cream cheese, half the Cool Whip and powdered sugar together and spread over the pie crust. Over that, spread chocolate pudding. Cover with remaining Cool Whip. Sprinkle with nuts. Chill and cut into 12 squares.

—Bonnie and Sheila Dunn

ICE CREAM DESSERT

½ cup butter
2 squares chocolate
2 cups powdered sugar
2 eggs yolks, beaten
3 egg whites

1 tsp. vanilla
1 packet graham crackers,
   crushed
½ gal. vanilla ice cream

Melt together butter and chocolate; cool. Add powdered sugar and egg yolks. Beat the egg whites, then add vanilla and the first mixture; add graham crackers, crushed. Spread in 9"x15" pan, reserve ½ cup for topping. Use ½ gal. vanilla ice cream over crumb mixture, then top with remaining crumbs.

—Marvis Johnson

ICE CREAM DESSERT

24 Oreo cookies, crushed
1/3 cup butter, melted
1/2 gal. vanilla ice cream,
    softened
1 tsp. instant coffee
3 squares semi-sweet
    chocolate (or 1 sm. bag
    Nestle's semi-sweet
    chocolate chips)

1 cup sugar
2 sm. cans evaporated milk
2 Tbls. margarine
1 9-oz. carton Cool Whip
Nuts

This dessert is made in layers, freezing after each layer is added.
Layer One: Combine cookies and butter; mix and freeze.
Layer Two: Combine ice cream and coffee; put on top of first layer and freeze.
Layer Three: Combine chocolate, sugar, evaporated milk and margarine. Mix and cook 10 to 20 minutes until thick. Cool completely. Mixture will thicken as it cools. Pour over ice cream and freeze.
Layer Four: Spread with Cool Whip, sprinkle with nuts and freeze again.

—Joyce Bright

ICE CREAM PIE

1/2 gal. vanilla ice cream,
    softened
2 cups chocolate chips

1 7-oz. pkg. miniature
    marshmallows
1 tall can evaporated milk
2 graham cracker crusts

Mix chocolate chips, marshmallows and milk in a double boiler. Cook until melted. Cool thoroughly (1 hour in refrigerator). In graham cracker crust layer 1/4 ice cream, 1/4 sauce, 1/4 ice cream, 1/4 sauce. Repeat for second pie. Freeze overnight.

—Nancy Frizzell

Sight is a faculty; seeing is an art.
—George Perkins Marsh

251

FRUIT PIZZA

Prepared dough for 3 dozen
   sugar cookies
1 8-oz. pkg. Philadelphia
   cream cheese
½ cup sugar
1 tsp. vanilla
Strawbery glaze

Fresh fruit — Suggestions:
   strawberries, peaches,
   cherries, bananas or
   pineapple
Nuts, optional
Whipped cream, optional

Roll cookie dough out on a cookie sheet. Bake, then let cool. Top with mixture of cream cheese, sugar and vanilla. Top with strawberry glaze and any kind of fresh fruit. Then top with nuts and whipped cream, if desired.

—Janet David

LEMON DELIGHT

1½ cups flour
1½ sticks margarine
½ cup nuts, chopped
1 8-oz. pkg. Philadelphia
   cream cheese
1 cup powdered sugar

1 9-oz. carton Cool Whip
2 pkgs. lemon instant pudding
   (chocolate or butterscotch
   may be used)
3 cups milk
Chopped nuts for garnish

Blend flour, margarine and nuts and press into 9"x13" pan. Bake at 350° for 20 minutes. Cool. Mix cream cheese, sugar and half of the Cool Whip. Spread over baked crust. Mix pudding mix with milk and pour over cream cheese mixture. Spread the rest of the Cool Whip over top and sprinkle with chopped nuts.

—Kathy Moore

PARTY DIET DELIGHT

2 lg. pkgs. strawberry Jello
2 lg. pkgs. lime Jello
2 lg. cans fruit cocktail

1 lg. container Cool Whip
1 sm. bottle cherries

Prepare Jello early and have ready to serve. Just before party, in clear glasses or goblets, layer Jello, starting with strawberry, fruit cocktail, and Cool Whip. Top with cherries. Yields 15 servings.

—Dorothy Gonzales

FROZEN STRAWBERRY DESSERT

CRUST

1 cup flour
¼ cup brown sugar

½ cup butter or margarine, melted
½ cup walnuts, chopped

Spread in 13"x9" pan. Bake 20 minutes at 350°, stirring often to crumble. Cool. Remove some to sprinkle on top of dessert.

FILLING

2 egg whites
¾ cup sugar
1 10-oz. pkg. frozen strawberries, partially thawed

2 Tbls. lemon juice
1 cup whipped cream or Cool Whip

Combine egg whites, sugar, berries and lemon juice and beat at low speed for 2 minutes, then on high speed for 10 to 12 minutes until really firm. Fold in whipped cream or Cool Whip. Spoon over crust, and sprinkle with reserved crust mixture. Freeze 6 hours or overnight.

—Sandy Sears

RASPBERRY DESSERT

1 cup water
½ cup sugar
2 tsp. lemon juice
2 10-oz. pkgs. frozen raspberries in syrup
4 Tbls. cornstarch
¼ cup cold water

50 lg. marshmallows
1 cup milk
2 cups cream, whipped
1¼ cups graham cracker crumbs
¼ cup nuts, chopped
¼ cup butter, melted

Heat raspberries with 1 cup water, sugar and lemon juice. Dissolve cornstarch in ¼ cup cold water. Stir into raspberries and cook until thickened and clear. Cool. Melt marshmallows in milk in double boiler and cool. Whip cream and fold into marshmallow mixture. Mix graham crackers, nuts and butter in a 13"x9"x2" pan. Press firmly into bottom of pan. Spread marshmallow cream mixture over crumbs. Spread raspberry mixture over top. Refrigerate until firm.

—Sylvia Osterbauer

RASPBERRY DESSERT

1¼ cups graham cracker
crumbs
¾ cup pecans, finely chopped
5 Tbls. margarine, melted
1 pkg. lemon Jello
1 cup boiling water
4 Tbls. lemon juice
1 cup sugar
1 tsp. vanilla

1 8-oz. pkg. Philadelphia
cream cheese
2 cups cream, whipped
1 pkg. Danish dessert
(raspberry)
2 pkgs. frozen raspberries,
drained and thawed
(reserve juice)
Whipped cream, reserved for
topping

Combine cracker crumbs, pecans and margarine and press in 9"x12" pan. Bake 10 minutes at 300°. Combine Jello, boiling water and lemon juice and set aside after dissolving to cool. When Jello starts to set, beat until fluffy. In another bowl, beat sugar, vanilla and cream cheese. Beat into thickened Jello. Fold in whipped cream. Pour on crust and chill until set. Add enough water to reserved raspberry juice to make 2 cups. Add to Danish dessert. Mix and bring to a boil, stirring constantly. Boil 1 minute and cool. Add whole raspberries and pour over Jello layer. Chill. Top with whipped cream.

—Sue Dilts

PUDDING DESSERT

1 cup soda crackers
2 cups graham crackers
1 stick margarine, melted
1 box instant butterscotch
pudding
1 box instant vanilla pudding

2 cups milk
4 cups vanilla ice cream
1 9-oz. carton Cool Whip
topping
1 Butterfinger candy bar,
crushed

Crush crackers together, mix in margarine and put ¾ of crumbs in bottom of a 9"x13" pan. Mix puddings and milk and add ice cream. Put in pan and add a layer of Cool Whip. Cover with remaining crumbs and crushed Butterfinger. Keep in refrigerator.

—Janese Gengenbach

OREO ICE CREAM CAKE

24-30 Oreo cookies, crushed
½ cup melted butter
½ gal. vanilla ice cream
1 can Hershey's chocolate
  syrup

1 can Eagle Brand condensed
  milk
½ cup butter
1 tsp. vanilla
8 oz. Cool Whip

Combine cookies and butter. Press into 9"x13" pan. Freeze 30 minutes. Top cookie layer with softened ice cream. Freeze 30 minutes. Combine condensed milk, syrup and butter in saucepan. Bring to boil; simmer 5 minutes. Cool thoroughly. Add vanilla. Put over layer of ice cream. Frost with Cool Whip. Serves 12 or more. 100,000 calories per serving, but worth it! Easy — can be done ahead.

—Fern Mears

WATERGATE DESSERT

FILLING

1 pkg. pistachio pudding mix,
  instant
1 9-oz. pkg. non-dairy whipped
  topping

1 20-oz. can crushed pineapple
  (do not drain)
½ cup miniature marshmallows
½ cup chopped nuts

Mix all ingredients and chill. Do not prepare pudding, just use the powder as it comes from the box.

CRUST

1 cup flour
¼ cup brown sugar

½ cup butter
¾ cup nuts, chopped

Press into bottom of 9"x13" pan. Bake at 350° for 15 minutes. Cool before pouring in above dessert mixture.

—Jill Roen

The mother's heart is the child's schoolroom.
—Henry Ward Beecher

DREAM WHIP TORTE

6 egg whites
¾ tsp. cream of tarter
2 cups sugar
2 tsp. vanilla
2 cups unsalted cracker
   crumbs (broken, not
   rolled)

1 cup walnuts, chopped
1-2 cans cherry or blueberry
   pie filling
2 pkgs. Dream Whip

Beat eggs with cream of tarter until the mixture forms soft peaks. Add sugar slowly, and beat until glossy. Add vanilla. Mix crumbs and nuts, add to egg mixture carefully, folding gently. Pour into greased 9"x13" pan and bake at 350° until golden brown, approximately 15 to 20 minutes. Remove and cool before removing from pan. Spread Dream Whip on cool torte. Spread pie filling over Dream Whip. Chill and serve.

—Terri Cota

FROZEN LEMON DESSERT

6 eggs
1 cup sugar
3 Tbls. lemon juice

1 pt. whipping cream
1½ cups graham cracker
   crumbs

Separate egg yolks from whites. Mix yolks with sugar and juice. Cook until thick (do not boil). Remove and cool. Beat egg whites. Whip cream until stiff. Gently stir lemon mixture into whites. Pour this gently into cream. Sprinkle half the crumbs on bottom of pan, then pour in dessert. Top with remainder of crumbs. Freeze for several hours before serving.

—Linda George

Those who bring sunshine into the lives of others cannot keep it from themselves.

—Sir James Barrie

256

DESBERTS...

REFRIGERATOR DESSERT

1 angel food cake
2 Tbls. sugar
2 pkgs. chocolate chips

3 eggs, separated
1 pt. whipping cream

Melt sugar and chocolate chips in a double boiler. Cool for 5 minutes and add beaten egg yolks. Beat whipping cream. Beat egg whites. Add whipped cream mixture to chocolate mixture, then add egg whites. Pour over bite sizes pieces of angel food cake. Make in two layer pans. Chill overnight.

—Lynn Richards

4-LAYER DESSERT

1 cup flour
½ cup margarine, melted
½ cup nuts, chopped fine
1 8-oz. pkg. cream cheese
1 cup powdered sugar
1 lg. size container Cool Whip

2 pkgs. instant butterscotch
  pudding mix*
3 cups milk (only)
1 tsp. vanilla
1 tsp. burnt sugar flavoring
  (essential)

Mix flour, margarine and nuts and pat into 9"x13" pan. Bake 15 minutes in 350° oven. Cool. Combine cream cheese, powdered sugar and 1 cup of the Cool Whip. Mix and spread on crust. Chill 2 hours. Mix pudding with mixer according to the package directions and pour over filling. Chill. Cover with remaining Cool Whip and sprinkle with chopped nuts. Chill several hours or overnight before serving. Serves 12 to 18.

* Instant chocolate pudding may be used, omitting burnt sugar flavoring. Coconut cream pudding is delicious with toasted coconut sprinkled on top.

—Margaret Hamler

The sky is the daily bread of the eyes.
—Emerson

4-LAYER DELIGHT DESSERT

1 cup flour
½ cup butter
½ cup nuts, chopped
1 8-oz. pkg. cream cheese
1 cup powdered sugar

1 9-oz. carton Cool Whip
2 3-oz. pkgs. chocolate
pudding mix (or favorite
flavor)
3 cups cold milk

First Layer: Mix flour, butter and nuts as for pie crust. Pat into 9"x13" pan. Bake 15 minutes in 350° oven. Cool.
Second Layer: Combine softened cream cheese, powdered sugar and 1 cup Cool Whip. Spread on crust.
Third Layer: Combine pudding and milk as for pie. When slightly thickened, add on top.
Fourth Layer: Top with remaining Cool Whip. Refrigerate.

—Audrey Kavajecz

PUMPKIN DESSERT

44 graham crackers, crushed
⅓ cup sugar
1 stick margarine, melted
2 eggs, beaten
¾ cup sugar
1 8-oz. pkg. cream cheese
2 cups pumpkin
½ cup sugar
½ cup milk
½ tsp. salt

1 Tbls. cinnamon
3 egg yolks
1 envelope Knox gelatin
¼ cup cold water
3 egg whites, beaten
¼ cup sugar
Dash cream of tartar
Cool Whip
Pecans

Combine graham crackers, ⅓ cup sugar and margarine and press into 9"x13" pan. Combine 2 eggs, ¾ cup sugar and the cream cheese. Beat and pour over crust. Bake 20 minutes in 350° oven. Mix together the pumpkin, ½ cup sugar, milk, salt, cinnamon and egg yolks. Cook until thick and remove from heat. Dissolve the gelatin in ¼ cup cold water, then add to pumpkin mixture. Cool. Beat the egg whites and add ¼ cup sugar and a dash of cream of tartar. Fold into the cooled pumpkin mixture. Pour egg mixture and pumpkin mixture over cream cheese mixture. Spread Cool Whip over top and sprinkle with pecans.

—Glorene Horder

BUTTERSCOTCH DESSERT

CRUST

1 cup flour
½ cup butter

½ cup nuts, chopped

Mix ingredients together and press into a 9"x13" pan. Bake 15 minutes in 350° oven. Cool.

FILLING

1 8-oz. pkg. cream cheese
1 cup powdered sugar
1 pkg. butterscotch pudding
   mix

1 pkg. coconut cream pudding
   mix
3 cups milk
Cool Whip

Cream the cream cheese with powdered sugar. Fold in 1 cup Cool Whip and spread over cooled crust. Cook together the pudding mixes and 3 cups milk and allow to cool. When cooled, pour pudding mixture over cheese layer and frost with Cool Whip.

—Shelly Larson

BUTTERFINGER DESSERT

2 cups crushed graham
   cracker crumbs
1 cup soda cracker crumbs
1 stick butter, melted
2 pkgs. instant vanilla pudding

2 cups milk
1 qt. vanilla ice cream
10 oz. whipped topping
4 frozen Butterfingers

Combine crumbs and butter. Press two-thirds of the mixture into bottom of a 9"x13" pan. Prepare pudding according to the package directions using only 2 cups of milk. Blend in the ice cream until smooth. Freeze until partly firm. Remove and cover with whipped topping. Crush candy and add to the remaining crumb mixture. Sprinkle on top of the dessert. Refrigerate (do not freeze) several hours.

—Vicki Livingston

DESSERTS...

BUTTER BRICKEL DESSERT

1 1-lb. can peach slices   ¼ lb. butter
1 butter brickel cake mix

Preheat oven to 350°. In 9"x13" pan, put peach slices and juice in the bottom of the pan. Sprinkle dry cake mix over the top of peach slices. Melt butter and drizzle it over the top of cake mix. Bake 35-40 minutes at 350°. Cool and serve with ice cream or other topping.

—Annis Fredrickson

LORNA DOONE DESSERT

1 pkg. Lorna Doone cookies   1 qt. butter pecan or
1 stick butter   chocolate ice cream
2 small pkgs. instant vanilla   2 or 3 Heath Bars, crushed
   or chocolate pudding   2 cups Cool Whip
2 cups milk

Melt butter in small saucepan and mix with crushed cookies. Pat into 13"x9" pan like crust. Mix the pudding with the milk and beat until thick. Add the ice cream to this mixture and pour over crust. Refrigerate until firm. Put Cool Whip on top. Crush the Heath Bars and sprinkle over the Cool Whip. Keep refrigerated.

—Pat Ward

LOVE transforms... Ambition into aspiration,
Greed into gratitude,
Selfishness into service,
Getting into giving,
Demands into dedication.

From "Be Somebody" by Mary Crowley

260

DESSERTS...

SHERBET DESSERT

½ gal. sherbet ice cream,
   flavor optional
2½ cups Rice Chex, crushed
1 cup brown sugar

1 cup coconut
⅔ cup butter, melted
15 Oreo cookies

Mix together Rice Chex, brown sugar, coconut, and melted butter. Place 1" to 1½" of this mixture into bottom of a styrofoam cup. Soften ice cream sherbet just enough to work with easily and press into cup, close to full. Crush Oreos and sprinkle on top of sherbet ½" to 1" to top of cup. Garnish with permanent blossom. This easy and clever desert resembles your favorite potted plant.

—*Marce Kollars*

YUMMY DELIGHT

1 stick margarine or butter
1 cup flour
½ cup pecans, chopped
1 8-oz. pkg. cream cheese
1 cup Cool Whip (out of 9-oz.
   size)
1 cup powdered sugar

Coconut
2 pkgs. instant French vanilla
   pudding mix
3 cups milk
Cool Whip
Coconut
Pecans, toasted and chopped

First Layer: Cream margarine or butter with flour. Add pecans and pat out in 9"x12" pan. Bake in 350° oven for 20 minutes.

Second Layer: Combine cream cheese, Cool Whip, and powdered sugar and spread over first layer. Sprinkle with coconut.

Third Layer: Combine pudding mix and milk and spread over second layer.

Fourth Layer: Use the remainder of Cool Whip and spread over third layer, then sprinkle with coconut and pecans. Refrigerate.

—*Marcia Liverman*

COCONUT DELIGHT

1 cup flour
½ cup butter
½ cup pecans, chopped
1 8-oz. pkg. cream cheese, softened
1 cup powdered sugar

1 9-oz. carton whipped topping
2-3 ¾-oz. pkgs. instant coconut pudding
2 cups milk
⅓ cup coconut, toasted

Combine flour, butter and pecans. Pat into 9"x13" pan. Bake 15 minutes in 350° oven. Cool. Beat cream cheese and sugar until smooth. Combine instant pudding and milk and beat 2 minutes. Add cream cheese mixture and one cup of the whipped topping to pudding and pour over crust. Spread remaining topping and sprinkle with toasted coconut. Chill until firm. Cut into squares to serve. Freezes well. Serves 16 to 24.

—Sheila Huffman

PUDDING TORTE

1 cup flour
½ cup margarine
½ cup nuts, chopped
1 cup Cool Whip (or more for thicker layer) from large size container
1 cup powdered sugar

1 8-oz. pkg. cream cheese
2 3⅝-oz. pkgs. chocolate pudding mix
3 cups milk
Cool Whip (remainder)
Chopped nuts

Crust: Mix flour, margarine and ½ cup nuts together as pie dough and press in oblong pan. Bake in 350° oven for 15 minutes. Cool.

First Layer: Mix 1 cup Cool Whip, powdered sugar, and cream cheese together and spread on crust.

Second Layer: Combine pudding mix and milk and cook. Cool and spread over first layer.

Third Layer: Use the remainder of the Cool Whip and spread over second layer. Sprinkle with chopped nuts.

—Augie Knor

DESSERTS...

FELOZES (Portuguese Doughnuts)

4 cups flour
4 large eggs
⅛ tsp. cinnamon
⅛ tsp. nutmeg
2 Tbls. sugar
1 tsp. salt

1 cup milk
1 Tbls. butter
2 pkgs. dry yeast
¼ cup warm water (to dissolve yeast)

COATING

¼ cup cinnamon   1½ cups sugar

Beat eggs with sugar, salt, nutmeg and cinnamon. Heat milk and butter to "warm" and add to egg mixture . Dissolve yeast in warm water and add to mixture. Then add flour and beat. Cover and let rise 1 hour. Beat down with spoon. Let rise until its size has doubled and then beat down again. Now dip hands in water or milk and pinch off small ball of dough (about ⅛ cup) and stretch into size of small pancakes. Deep fry until golden brown; drain well and then dip both sides in the coating mixture of sugar and cinnamon. Makes 4 dozen. (Leftovers can be wrapped in foil to freeze and then be reheated in oven before serving. Can also be made ahead for holidays.)

— Mary Raddingan

PLAIN DOUGHNUTS

1 cup sugar
¼ tsp. salt
2 eggs
1 Tbls. shortening
1 cup sour milk (or 1 cup milk, ½ tsp. vinegar)

⅓ tsp. ginger
1¼ tsp. nutmeg
1 tsp. baking soda
1 tsp. baking powder
3⅔ cups flour
½ tsp. vanilla

Combine all ingredients to make dough. Roll out. Cut and fry in deep fat 420° until brown, then turn over.

— Helen Bronn

DESSERTS...

DOUGHNUTS

1 cup sugar
1 cup cooked potatoes,
    mashed
1 egg
½ cup milk

1 Tbls. butter, melted
3 cups (plus a little more)
    flour
2½ tsp. baking powder
Powdered sugar

Combine all ingredients except powdered sugar and mix well. Drop into hot cooking oil and fry until brown and crispy. Cool on brown paper bag. Roll in powdered sugar.

—Shirley Young

PUMPKIN ROLL

3 eggs
1 cup sugar
⅔ cup pumpkin
¾ cup flour
1 tsp. baking powder
2 tsp. cinnamon
1 tsp. ginger

½ tsp. nutmeg
½ tsp. salt
1 cup powdered sugar
2 3-oz. pkgs. cream cheese
4 Tbls. butter
½ tsp. vanilla

Beat eggs for 5 minutes at high speed. Add sugar and pumpkin and mix. Add flour, baking powder, spices and salt and mix. Bake on greased and floured cookie sheet in 375° oven for 15 minutes. Turn onto towel that has been dusted with flour and powdered sugar. Roll while hot. Cool. Blend together the powdered sugar, cream cheese, butter and vanilla. Fold onto roll and chill.

—Pam Pollock

In the affairs of life or business, it is not intellect that tells so much as character — not brains so much as heart — not genius so much as self-control, patience, and discipline, regulated by judgement.

—Samuel Miles

CHOCOLATE CINNAMON ROLLS

¾ cup warm water
1 pkg. yeast
¼ cup shortening
1 tsp. salt
¼ cup sugar
1 egg

⅓ cup cocoa
2½ cups flour
1 Tbls. butter, softened
1½ tsp. cinnamon
3 Tbls. sugar
Nuts, optional

In mixer bowl dissolve yeast in warm water. Add shortening, salt, ¼ cup sugar, egg, cocoa and 1 cup flour. Beat 2 minutes at medium speed. Stir in remaining flour. Blend well. Cover and let rise until double in bulk (about one hour). Roll on floured board. Combine butter, cinnamon, 3 tablespoons sugar and nuts (if desired). Spread on dough. Bake in 350° oven for 20 minutes.

—Marge Kautz

CINNAMON ROLLS

1 pkg. cake mix, white or
   yellow
1 pkg. yeast
2½ cups warm water

5½-6 cups flour
Brown sugar
Cinnamon
Butter

GLAZE

½ cup powdered sugar
2 tsp. butter, melted

1 tsp. water

Dissolve yeast in warm water. Add cake mix and flour. Then knead dough. Let rise twice. Roll about ¼" slices. Put brown sugar, cinnamon, and butter in bottom of pan; then place rolls on top. Let rise. Bake in 350° oven for 15 to 20 minutes. While warm, put on powdered sugar glaze.

—Linda Hollinshead

Kindness is the golden chain by which society is bound together.

BAKED PINEAPPLE

1 cup white sugar
3 eggs
2 Tbls. cornstarch
½ cup water

2 Tbls. butter, melted
1 large can pineapple, crushed
or chunk

Combine first five ingredients and blend in blender. Pour into large, buttered casserole dish. Add pineapple and fold into mixture. Bake at 350° for 90 minutes. Stir at 15-minute intervals.

—Sharon Pierce

PINEAPPLE SOUFFLE

6 slices white bread, cubed
1½ sticks butter or margarine
2 eggs

¾ cups sugar, or less
2 #2 cans pineapple tidbits
2 Tbls. flour

Melt butter, pour over cubed bread and toss. Beat eggs, add sugar, flour, and pineapple, including the juice. In a greased casserole dish, layer bread and pineapple mixture, ending with bread. Bake at 350° about 45 minutes. Makes eight generous portions.

—Barbara Rice

MUFFIN CHEESECAKES

2 8-oz. pkgs. Philadelphia
cream cheese, softened
¾ cup sugar
2 eggs

1 Tbls. lemon juice
Cherry pie filling
Vanilla wafers (optional)

Mix together cream cheese, sugar, eggs, and lemon juice. Fill 18 muffin cups. Bake 15 minutes at 375°. Spoon pie filling into them after they are filled and baked. You can also put vanilla wafers in the bottom of muffin cups before you bake.

—Irene Noblin

BLACK BOSTON CUPCAKES

1 8-oz. pkg. cream cheese,
    room temperature
1/3 cup sugar
1/8 tsp. salt
1 egg, unbeaten
1 6-oz. pkg. chocolate chips,
    optional
1½ cups flour, sifted
¼ cup cocoa

1 cup sugar
1 tsp. soda
½ tsp. salt
1 cup water
1/3 cup cooking oil
1 Tbls. vinegar
1 Tbls. vanilla
Sugar
Nuts

Combine cream cheese, sugar, salt and add egg and chocolate chips. Set aside. Sift next 5 ingredients together. Mix water, oil, vinegar, vanilla together and add to the dry ingredients. Beat until smooth. Fill paper cups 1/3 full of batter. Top each with a heaping tsp. of cream cheese mixture. Sprinkle top with sugar and nuts. Bake at 350° for 30-35 minutes.

—Iris Salmen

CHOCOLATE CHIP CUPCAKES

1 8-oz. pkg. cream cheese,
    softened
Pinch of salt
1 egg
½ cup white sugar
1 cup real chocolate chips
1½ cups flour
1 cup white sugar

1 tsp. soda
½ tsp. salt
¼ cup cocoa
1 cup water
½ cup vegetable oil
1 tsp. vinegar
1 tsp. vanilla

Make filling first; beat cream cheese, salt, egg and sugar. Stir in chips. Set aside. Combine flour, sugar, soda, salt, cocoa. Stir or beat in water, oil, vinegar and vanilla until smooth. Fill paper cups in tins half full. Add heaping teaspoon of filling into center of each cup. Bake at 350° for 25-30 minutes. Makes 20-24 cupcakes. NOTE: These are best with no frosting.

—Donna Johnson

PEANUT BUTTER CUPS

1½ cups 100% granola cereal
1 cup dry instant milk

1 cup chunky peanut butter
1 cup honey

Place paper liners in 8 to 12 muffin pan cups. Combine all ingredients in a medium-sized bowl. Divide mixture evenly among the muffin cups depending upon the size desired. These are easy, nutritious, and delicious for those who carry sack lunches.

—Reina McCarthy

PECAN TASSIES

1 3-oz. pkg. cream cheese
½ cup butter or margarine
1 cup flour, sifted
1 egg
¾ cup brown sugar

1 Tbls. butter or margarine
Vanilla
Dash of salt
⅔ cup broken pecans

Let cream cheese and ½ cup butter soften to room temperature, chill about 1 hour after combining them with flour. Put small amounts in ungreased muffin pans. Press dough evenly against bottom and sides. Beat egg, sugar, butter, vanilla, and salt just until smooth. Divide half the pecans among pastry line pans; add egg mixture and top with remaining pecans. Bake in slow oven, 325° 25-30 minutes. Cool completely before removing from pans. Makes two dozen.

—Sandy Bliss

BUCKEYES

2 lbs. chunky peanut butter
1 lb. margarine
3 lbs. powdered sugar

1 Tbls. vanilla
1 12-oz. pkg. chocolate chips
2 slices paraffin

Mix peanut butter, margarine, sugar and vanilla and roll into small balls. In double boiler combine the chocolate chips and paraffin. Use toothpick and dip balls into chocolate mixture, then let set. When ready, yummy!

—Linda Hollinshead

ORANGE SHERBET SALAD

1 pkg. orange Jello
1 pt. orange sherbet
1 small can Mandarin oranges,
   drained
1 small can pineapple, drained
   but save juice
1 cup boiling water
2 rounded Tbls. flour

1 egg, beaten
½ cup sugar
1 cup pineapple juice
2 Tbls. butter
1 small pkg. cream cheese,
   frozen
1 cup whipped cream

Add water to package Jello. While still hot, add sherbet. Mix well. Then add oranges and pineapple. Mix and let set until firm. Cook flour, egg, sugar, pineapple juice, and butter until thick. Be careful — scorches easily. Cool. Then add whipped cream or prepared dessert topping. Spread on salad. Garnish with frozen grated Philadelphia cream cheese.

—Malinda Clinton

SKILLET COFFEE CAKE

¾ cup butter or oleo
1½ cups sugar
2 eggs
1½ cups self-rising flour

1 tsp. vanilla
½ cup raisins
Cinnamon

Line large iron skillet with aluminum foil. Melt butter and add to sugar in mixing bowl. Beat in eggs, one at a time. Add about one-third of flour at a time, mixing well after each. Add vanilla. Pour into skillet lined with foil. Take some cinnamon and the raisins and sprinkle over mix and swirl in lightly with a knife. Put in 350° oven and cook about 30 minutes or until it looks slightly brown. Take about ⅛ cup of sugar and ½ teaspoon cinnamon and sprinkle over cake. Return to oven and cook about 10 minutes more. Remove from skillet with foil and when cool, cover with another piece of foil. Cool thoroughly before removing foil from cake.

—Denise Gore

FROZEN KRANZ
(Delicious Filled German Coffee Cake)

4 cups flour, sifted
1 tsp. salt
1 cup butter
1 cup milk
1 Tbls. sugar
1 cake compressed yeast
4 egg yolks

1 cup brown sugar, firmly
   packed
¼ cup maraschino cherries,
   drained and quartered
1 cup pecans, chopped
Melted butter

Blend flour, salt and 1 cup butter together with pastry blender for pie crust. Scald milk; cool to lukewarm. Add sugar and crumbled yeast and stir until dissolved. Add to flour mixture and beat. Add egg yolks, one at a time, beating well after each addition. Cover and place in refrigerator overnight. Divide dough into three parts. Roll each into oblong 8"x12". Spread generously with melted butter. Combine brown sugar, cherries and nuts. Sprinkle over dough. Roll like a jelly roll, making sure edges are sealed. Place seam side down on greased baking sheets. Form into crescent shape. Cover and let rise 2 hours. Bake in preheated oven (375°) for 30 minutes. Remove onto cooling racks. When cool, frost with confectioner's sugar frosting and decorate with pecan halves and candied cherries. Yields 3 crescents of Kranz.

—Jackie Taylor

CHEESE POCKETS

2 pkgs. crescent rolls
2 8-oz. pkgs. Philadelphia
   cream cheese
1 large egg

¾ cup sugar
1 tsp. vanilla
Powdered sugar

Line 9"x13" greased pan with crescent rolls — up sides and ends. Beat remaining ingredients until fluffy. Pour filling into pan and roll edges of dough down. Bake at 350° for 30 minutes. Sprinkle with powdered sugar. Enjoy!

—Nancy Clemmer

MEMO'S MAJESTIC

1 angel food cake
1 lg. box strawberry Jello
1 lg. box banana pudding

1 lg. container frozen
strawberries

Tear cake into small pieces and put into oblong dish. Prepare Jello according to directions on package. While Jello is still hot, pour over cake, being sure that all of the Jello is absorbed. Set in refrigerator until set, approximately 1½ hours. Prepare pudding according to directions on package. Wait 10 minutes, then pour pudding over cake and Jello (after Jello has set). Garnish with strawberries that have been thawed. Bananas may be substituted or added to strawberries.

—Vivian Reichert

BANANA NUT BREAD

1 cup butter
3 cups sugar
4 eggs, beaten
2 tsp. vanilla

4 cups plain flour
2 tsp. baking soda
8 ripe bananas
2 cups nuts

Cream butter, sugar and eggs together. Add vanilla, flour and baking soda. Mash bananas with fork and fold into batter. Add the nuts. Grease and lightly flour loaf pan or for round loaves use #303 tin cans. Fill cans only ½ full. Bake in 375° oven for 20 minutes. Bread freezes well. Nice served with cream cheese also.

PUMPKIN PECAN PIE

4 slightly beaten eggs
2 cups canned or mashed
    cooked pumpkin
1 cup sugar
½ cup dark corn syrup

1 tsp. vanilla
½ tsp. cinnamon
¼ tsp. salt
1 unbaked 9-inch pie shell
1 cup chopped pecans

Combine ingredients except pecans. Pour into pie shell — top with pecans. Bake at 350° degrees for 40 minutes, or until set.

—Nancy Reagan

RAISIN BARS

1 cup raisins	1 tsp. cinnamon
2 cups water	½ tsp. nutmeg
1 cup sugar	½ tsp. salt
1 tsp. baking soda	1⅓ cups flour
½ cup shortening	

Boil raisins in water for 10 minutes. Add sugar, baking soda, shortening, cinnamon, nutmeg and salt. When this mixture is very cool, add the flour. Bake in 10"x15" pan at 350° for 20 minutes. Cool and top with your favorite icing.

—Linda Hollinshead

SOUR CREAM RAISIN BARS

2 cups raisins	1 tsp. baking soda
1½ cups water	3 egg yolks
1 cup brown sugar	1 cup sugar
1 cup margarine	1½ cups sour cream
1¾ cup flour	2½ Tbls. cornstarch
1¾ cup quick oatmeal	1 tsp. vanilla

Cook raisins and water over medium heat for 10 minutes. Drain and cool. Mix brown sugar, margarine, flour, oatmeal and soda together. Pat one half into bottom of 9"x13" pan and bake for 7 minutes at 350°. Mix and boil yolks, sugar, sour cream and corn-starch until thick, stirring constantly. Add raisins and vanilla. Pour over bottom crust and sprinkle remainder of oatmeal mixture over top. Bake at 350° for 30 minutes. Cool and keep in refrigerator.

—Marien Baker

Greatness does not depend on the size of your command, but on the way you exercise it.
—Marshal Foch

SPICY PEACH-CRANBERRY RING

1 29-oz. can peach halves,
   undrained
1 tsp. whole cloves
1 3" stick cinnamon
¼ cup sugar

1 Tbls. vinegar
1 3-oz. pkg. lemon-flavored
   gelatin
¼ cup brandy

Drain peaches, reserving juice. Set peaches aside. Add enough water to juice to make 1½ cups. Add cloves, cinnamon, sugar and vinegar to juice mixture. Simmer, uncovered, about 10 minutes. Add peaches and simmer 5 minutes. Remove peaches. Arrange cut side up in a lightly oiled 3 quart ring mold. Strain juice mixture; add boiling water to make 1½ cups. Add gelatin, stirring until dissolved. Stir in brandy and allow to cool. Pour over peaches and chill. Spoon cranberry relish on top of peach layer. Chill until firm. Unmold and serve with lemon-cream mayonnaise. Yields 10 to 12 servings.

CRANBERRY RELISH

1 cup fresh cranberries
½ orange, unpeeled
⅓ cup sugar

1¾ cups boiling water
1 3-oz pkg. cherry flavored
   gelatin

To make the relish, wash cranberries; drain. Cut orange half into quarters. Position knife blade in food processor bowl; add cranberries and orange. Process 30 to 45 seconds on high. Stir in sugar. Add boiling water to gelatin, stirring until gelatin dissolves. Cool. Stir in cranberry-orange mixture. Yields about 3 cups.

LEMON-CREAM MAYONNAISE

1 cup whipping cream
½ cup mayonnaise
3 Tbls. lemon juice

3 Tbls. powdered sugar
⅛ tsp. salt

To make the lemon-cream mayonnaise, whip cream and combine with remaining ingredients. Chill.

—Gene Ingram

ICE BOX COOKIES

Graham crackers
2 sticks margarine
1 cup sugar
½ cup milk
1 egg

1 cup pecans, chopped
1 cup coconut
1 tsp. vanilla
1 cup graham cracker crumbs

TOPPING

1 stick margarine, melted
1 box powdered sugar
1-3 Tbls. milk

1 tsp. vanilla
2-3 drops green food coloring

Line 12"x15" pan with graham crackers. Melt margarine. Combine sugar, milk and egg; add to the margarine and bring to a boil. Add pecans, coconut, vanilla and cracker crumbs. Mix the above and pour over crackers. Top with another layer of graham crackers. Mix topping ingredients together and spread over top layer of graham crackers and let set in refrigerator overnight.

—Anita Taylor

DIET PEANUT BUTTER COOKIES

1¼ cups flour
½ cup peanut butter
¼ cup cooking oil
¼ cup water

½ cup Sprinklesweet or honey
1½ tsp. baking powder
1 tsp. vanilla
1 egg

In large mixing bowl, combine all ingredients. Mix well. Shape into 1" balls, using about 1 teaspoon of dough for each. Place 2" apart on ungreased cookie sheet. Flatten with fork. Bake at 375° for 12 to 15 minutes or until lightly browned.

—Cathy Gilmer

Life by the yard is hard — but by the inch it's a cinch.
From *"Be Somebody"* by Mary Crowley

DESSERTS...

ICE CREAM DESSERT

16 graham crackers
16 soda crackers
½ cup (1 stick) butter or
   margarine, melted
2 pkgs. vanilla instant pudding
1 cup milk

1 qt. vanilla ice cream,
   softened
9 oz. Cool Whip (or 8 oz.
   cream, whipped)
2 Butterfinger candy bars,
   crushed

Crush crackers. Mix with melted butter. Press into 9"x13" pan or two 10" round cake pans. Mix instant vanilla pudding with the milk and combine with ice cream. Spread over crumb crust. Top with Cool Whip and sprinkle with crushed candy bars. Refrigerate 12 to 24 hours. Freezes well.

—Shirley Birkeland

PISTACHIO DESSERT

1 cup flour
2 tsp. sugar
½ cup butter
¼ cup chopped nuts
1 8-oz. pkg. cream cheese
⅔ cup powdered sugar

1 9-oz. Cool Whip
2 pkgs. Royal pistachio instant
   pudding
3 cups milk
Chopped nuts for garnish
   (optional)

Mix flour, sugar, butter and nuts and press into a greased 9"x13" pan. Bake at 375° for 15 to 18 minutes. Cool. Soften cream cheese and beat in powdered sugar. Use half of the Cool Whip in cream cheese mixture. Save the rest for top layer. Spread cream cheese/Cool Whip mixture over crust. Prepare pudding with 3 cups milk, and spread over cream cheese/Cool Whip mixture. Let stand for 30 minutes in refrigerator. Spread remaining Cool Whip on top of pudding. Garnish with chopped nuts if desired.

—Ruth Ann Hockins

STRAWBERRY ICE CREAM MOLD

This is a SPECIAL GOODY for showers or large dinner parties. I use a 12" round fluted mold 3" high.

BOTTOM LAYER

18 fresh strawberries with green stems attached
3 3-oz. pkgs. strawberry Jello

3 cups hot water
3¾ cups cold water

TOP LAYER

2 3-oz. pkgs. strawberry Jello
2 cups hot water

2 pts. vanilla ice cream

Mix ingredients for bottom layer (except strawberries). Pour in mold and let set partially. Push fresh strawberries through bottom of mold, arranging in circular pattern and ending with one in center.

Combine ingredients for the top layer and stir until ice cream melts. Pour over set layer. Refrigerate overnight. Unmold on 15" platter.

—Doris True

THREE GATES

If you are tempted to reveal
A tale someone to you has told
About another, make it pass
Before you speak, three gates of gold,
Three narrow gates: "First, is it true?"
Then, "Is it needful?" In your mind
Give truthful answer, and the next
Is last and narrowest, "Is it kind?"
And if to reach your lips at last
It passes through these gateways three,
Then you may tell, nor ever fear
What the result of speech may be.

Good to know: A decorative ice ring can be made to float beautifully on your punch. Boil water (so ring won't be cloudy). Pour into ring jello mold. Add maraschino cherries, or lemon, lime or orange slices for decoration.

CALIFORNIA PARTY PUNCH

1 large can pineapple juice
2 large cans frozen orange
   juice
2 large cans frozen lemonade

1 pt. orange sherbet
½ gallon vanilla ice cream
1 large can ginger ale

Mix frozen juices with water as directed on cans. Cut ice cream and sherbet in two inch squares and add to fruit juices. Chill. Add ginger ale just before serving.

—*Maida Godwin*

FROZEN FRUIT PUNCH

2 lemons, juiced
2 oz. citric acid, powdered
   (from drug store)
3 cans frozen orange juice,
   diluted
1 qt. bottle Tropicana orange
   juice

1 46-oz. can pineapple juice,
   sweetened to taste
1 #3 can crushed pineapple
7 cups sugar
2 large bottles cherries with
   juice
Green or red cake coloring

Pour 2 quarts boiling water over acid and sugar. Add 4 quarts cold water, then other ingredients. Freeze in plastic cartons. Can be kept frozen 3-4 weeks without change of taste. To thaw: let melt about 3¼ hours in punch bowl; not necessary to add ice. Serves 100.

—*Irene Noblin*

SPICED TEA MIX

1 cup instant tea mix with
    lemon
2 cups orange Tang

3 cups sugar
1 tsp. cinnamon
½ tsp. cloves, ground

Combine all ingredients. Mix well and keep in tight container. Use 2 teaspoons per cup hot water.

—Sandi Marcum

ALMOND PUNCH

1 12-oz. can frozen orange
    juice
1 12-oz. can frozen lemonade

1 cup sugar
1 tsp. vanilla extract
1 tsp. almond extract

Combine all ingredients and add water to make one gallon. Garnish with orange or lemon slices.

—Donna Gardner

LIME PUNCH

4 28-oz. bottles Bubble-Up
½ gal. lime sherbet
1 sm. can frozen lemon or
    lime juice, undiluted

Red maraschino cherries
Green maraschino cherries

Ice mold is made from lemonade, lemon slices, and maraschino cherries. Use both red and green cherries to add color.

—Chela Cortez

PUNCH

1 cup sugar
2 pkgs. Kool-Aid, any flavor
2 qts. cold ginger ale

1 lg. can pineapple juice,
    sweetened

Mix sugar and Kool-Aid with small amount of water. Add pineapple juice, finish filling gallon jug almost full with water. Add ginger ale.

—Barbara McDonald

To God be the glory, great things He hath done!
  So loved He the world that He gave us
        His Son
Who yielded His life an atonement for sin
  And opened the Lifegate that all may go in.

Praise the Lord, praise the Lord, let the earth
        hear His voice!
  Praise the Lord, praise the Lord, let the
        people rejoice!
Oh come to the Father through Jesus, the Son,
  And give Him the glory, great things He
        hath done!

—Fanny Crosby

Mary's Rightside-Up Cake!

Mix together equal
parts of Diligence
and Perseverance;

pour in a cup running
over with Joy...

...melted with the
warmth of Love;

toss lightly with Laughter;

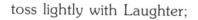

280

top with a sense of Humor
layered with a sense of Wonder;

garnish with Hope;
bake Patiently,
glaze with Prayer;

serve with Anticipation!

MARY'S MOUNTAIN RECIPES

283

CHICKEN BREAST AND
SHERRY SOUR CREAM SAUCE

Chicken breasts
2 tsp. onion
2 tsp. butter
1 lg. carton sour cream

2 cans mushroom soup
1 sm. can mushrooms
1/3 cup cooking sherry
Salt and pepper to taste*

Place chicken breasts in 9"x13" pan. Sauté onion in butter. Add remaining ingredients. Cover chicken with mixture and bake at 325° for one hour.

* May use Vege-sal, an all purpose seasoning salt. Now vegetized. Put out by Modern Products, Inc., Milwaukee, Wisconsin.

HAWAIIAN CHICKEN

2 fryers, cut up (brown ahead
   of time, or you can use
   Kentucky Fried Chicken)
1 lg. can pineapple chunks,
   drained, reserve juice

1 green bell pepper, sliced
1/2 tsp. ginger
1 bunch green onions,
   chopped

Arrange chicken in a baking dish and top with pineapple and bell pepper. Sprinkle with ginger.

SAUCE

1 cup pineapple juice, drained
   from chunks
1/2 cup wine vinegar
1/2 cup brown sugar

2 Tbls. cornstarch
2 Tbls. soy sauce
Pinch of salt

To make the sauce, combine ingredients and bring to a boil. Cook, stirring continually, until thickened and clear. Pour over chicken and bake in 350° oven for one hour. Top with green onions.

Have you had a kindness shown? Pass it on.
'Twas not given for you alone. Pass it on.
Let it travel down the years,
Let it wipe another's tears,
'Til in heaven the deed appears. Pass it on.

SOUR CREAM DELIGHT

2 cups sour cream
¾ cup sugar
1 tsp. salt
1 lg. can crushed pineapple
   and juice

6 bananas, mashed or cut finely
1 Tbls. lemon juice
2 sm. (or 1 lg.) pkg. frozen
   strawberries, thawed
¾ cup pecans

Mix sour cream, sugar and salt together. Add remaining ingredients, mix and freeze. Serve slightly thawed.

—Mary C. Crowley

SOUR CREAM AND RICE

Rice
Butter
Chicken bouillon
Salt and seasoned salt

Monterrey Jack cheese
Jalapeño peppers
Sour Cream

Cook rice by instructions on box. When cooking, add chicken bouillon to water with butter and salt. When rice is ready, pour a layer into a buttered casserole dish. Sprinkle seasoned salt on top. Put several pats of butter on top of rice. Put a layer of Monterrey Jack cheese, then a layer of jalapeño peppers, then another layer of rice. Top with cheese. Bake in 350° oven until cheese is melted. Take from oven.

Just before serving, spread sour cream on top and serve. (Use jalapeño peppers according to taste. If you like lots of peppers, then use them; if not, use a few thin strips.)

—Connie Sapien

We thank Him for His kindness, We thank Him for His love,
We've been in heavenly places, Had blessing from above,
We've shared in all the good things the Family could afford.
Let's just turn our praise toward heaven and praise the Lord...

From "Let's Just Praise the Lord" by Gaither

"WILLY'S WINNER" SALAD

1 can French style green
  beans, drained
1 can small early June peas,
  drained

1 lg. tomato, chopped
1 med. onion, chopped
1 med. green pepper, chopped
2 Tbls. mayonnaise

Mix all the ingredients together. Add mayonnaise, mix well and serve. Makes 4 to 6 servings.

—*Willean Claybrook*

MARY'S VEGETABLE SUPREME CASSEROLE

2 pkgs. frozen baby lima
  beans
2 pkgs. frozen mixed
  vegetables

2 pkgs. frozen baby peas
Vege-Sal*
Celery salt

TOPPING

2 cups whipped cream
1 cup mayonnaise

½ cup cheddar cheese, grated
½ cup Parmesan cheese

Thaw and drain vegetables and layer in buttered casserole dish. Add Vege-Sal and celery salt.

Make the topping, folding the cheeses and mayonnaise into whipped cream. Spread on top of vegetables. Bake in 350° oven for one hour, until golden brown.

* An all purpose seasoning salt, now vegetized. Put out by Modern Products, Inc., Milwaukee, Wisconsin.

SUPER SALAD

1 bunch fresh broccoli
1 bunch green onions
1 lb. fresh mushrooms

1 reg. size Wishbone Italian
  dressing
Cherry tomatoes

Slice the broccoli, green onions and mushrooms. Cut cherry tomatoes in half and add to broccoli, onions and mushrooms. Pour dressing over all and marinate 8 hours.

—*Barbara Hammond*

BAKED SQUASH

Hubbard squash
¾ cup water
Brown sugar, approx. 1 tsp.
   per slice

Nutmeg, or cinnamon if
   preferred

Wash squash and cut in serving size. Hollow out, removing seeds. Place on flat pan with water in bottom of pan. Cover tightly with foil. Bake until tender (1 hour mountain time, less time elsewhere). Remove foil and sprinkle with brown sugar. Dot with butter and sprinkle with nutmeg (or cinnamon). Return to 400° oven for about 15 minutes to simmer and brown.

—Grace Shakes

MEXICAN CASSEROLE

3 lbs. ground chuck (I use
   ground lean meat)
2 onions, chopped
2 cans Ranch Style beans
2 cans Rotel tomatoes
   (or Ortega tomatoes and
   chilies)
2 cans cream of chicken soup

1 lg. pkg. soft tortillas (I use
   corn tortillas)
2 lbs. sharp Old English
   cheese
Lowery's salt
Pepper
Garlic powder
Paprika

Brown meat and onions and pour off any excess grease. Add beans, tomatoes and soup. Layer in a large casserole dish the soft tortillas, then meat mixture, then grated cheese. Do another 3 layers, ending with a lot of cheese. Sprinkle with paprika. Bake in 350° oven until bubbly, about 35 minutes. Feeds approximately 20 people.

—Margaret Broyles

And he said unto me, My grace is sufficient for thee: for my strength is made perfect in weakness. Most gladly therefore will I rather glory in my infirmities, that the power of Christ may rest upon me.

II Corinthians 12:9

TACO SALAD

1 lg. bag Fritos, crushed
1 lb. ground meat, browned
1 cup green onions, chopped
1 green pepper, chopped
3 gloves garlic, or 1 Tbls.
   garlic salt

1 Tbls. cumin
½ tsp. chili powder
1 lb. Velveeta cheese
1 lg. head lettuce, shredded
2-3 tomatoes, chopped
1 can Rotel tomato sauce

Combine cheese, tomato sauce, garlic, chili powder and cumin and set aside. In a large bowl, combine lettuce and chopped tomatoes. Add Fritos, ground meat, onions and green pepper. Pour cheese sauce over the lettuce and meat mixture just before serving and toss.

—Joan Horner

BUENO SNACKS

1 lg. can whole green chilies
6 eggs
1-2 Tbls. dry minced or
   chopped onions

½ lb. or more longhorn
   cheese, grated
Salt

Spread chilies in a buttered 9" pan. Beat eggs, add salt and onions, and pour over chilies in pan. Top with cheese. Bake in 325° oven for 20 to 30 minutes or until cheese is melted and golden. Slice into squares and serve.

—Karen Baker

MAGIC FRUIT COBBLER

¼ lb. butter or margarine
1 lg. can (or 2 med.) cans fruit
   with juice
¾ cup milk

1 cup sugar
1 cup flour
1½ tsp. baking powder

Melt butter in bottom of baking dish. Mix milk, sugar, flour and baking powder and pour **over** butter. Do **not** stir. Pour fruit over batter. Do **not** stir. Sprinkle sugar over top. Bake 1 hour at 350° to 375°. Fruit will sink and batter will rise. Add a little cinnamon to peaches or apples and almond flavor to cherries. Use your imagination. Never fails!

MARY'S GLORIFIED BREAD PUDDING

2 cups brown sugar
8 slices Orowheat "Old Raisin
    Bread" (or any kind), but-
    tered lavishly and cubed

6 eggs, slightly beaten
4 cups milk
2 tsp. vanilla
Coconut

Put brown sugar in large double boiler. Place bread cubes over sugar. Combine eggs, milk and vanilla. Mix and pour over bread cubes. *Do not stir.* Sprinkle coconut on top. Place lid on and boil for 1½ hours, not stirring. Chill in pot and serve with lemon sauce or whipped cream. When dipping up to serve, be sure you dip up some caramel syrup from the bottom. This is a wonderful way to use stale bread deliciously.

GOLDEN TASSIES

BASIC CRUST RECIPE

1 cup margarine
2 3-oz. pkgs. cream cheese

2 cups sifted flour

Let margarine and cream cheese soften. Then work with a wooden spoon until smooth and creamy. Add flour and blend. Using fingers, press dough into very small muffin tins (1¾" in diameter).

Use ½ the basic recipe with the filling below. Makes 2 dozen.

PECAN FILLING

1 egg, slightly beaten
¾ cup brown sugar, firmly
    packed
1 Tbls. margarine, melted

¾ cup pecans, chopped
Vanilla
Dash of salt

Beat egg only enough to mix yolk and white. Add remaining ingredients. Bake at 350° for 15 to 18 minutes. Reduce heat to 250° and bake 10 minutes longer. Cool.

—*Margaret Broyles*

MILKY WAY CAKE

8 Milky Way candy bars
  (1⅞-oz. size)
1 cup butter or margarine,
  divided use
2 cups sugar
4 eggs

1 tsp. vanilla extract
1¼ cup buttermilk
½ tsp. baking soda
3 cups all-purpose flour
1 cup pecans, coarsely
  chopped

MILK CHOCOLATE FROSTING

2½ cups sugar
1 cup evaporated milk,
  undiluted
½ cup butter or margarine,
  melted

1 6-oz. pkg. semi-sweet
  chocolate pieces
1 cup marshmallow cream

Melt one-half cup butter or margarine in saucepan. Combine with candy bars. Place over low heat until candy bars are melted, stirring constantly. Cool. Cream sugar and the remaining one-half cup butter or margarine (softened) until light and fluffy. Add eggs, one at a time, beating well after each addition. Stir in vanilla extract. Combine buttermilk and soda. Add to creamed mixture, alternately with flour, beating well after each addition. Stir in candy bar mixture with pecans. Pour into greased and floured 10" tube pan. Bake at 325° for 1 hour and 20 minutes or until done. Let cool in pan 1 hour. Remove from pan and complete cooling on wire rack.

To make the frosting, combine sugar, milk and butter in heavy saucepan. Cook over medium heat until small amount dropped in cold water forms a soft ball. Remove from heat. Add chocolate pieces and marshmallow cream, stirring until melted. If necessary, add a small amount of milk to make spreading consistency.

—Southern Living

MARY'S GRAPE AND BANANA SALAD

Thompson seedless grapes   Miniature marshmallows
Bananas   Nuts, optional

SPECIAL FRUIT DRESSING

1 can Eagle Brand milk   ½ pt. whipping cream
½ cup lemon juice

Wash grapes and cut in half. Peel and slice bananas. Mix grapes, bananas, marshmallows, and nuts, and add special fruit dressing.

To make the dressing, combine Eagle Brand milk with lemon juice. (I use the Minute-Maid lemon juice. It's 100% pure lemon juice that is frozen fresh. Available in frozen foods department. Put in refrigerator and it will thaw and keep well.) Whip cream. Add Eagle Brand milk mixture and whip lightly. Pour over fruit mixture and toss lightly. Makes a fabulous, delicious dressing. Serve to *happy people!*

YUMMY ORANGE BALLS

1 stick butter or margarine,   1 cup pecans or walnuts,
   melted   finely chopped
1 12-oz. pkg. vanilla wafers,   1 6-oz. can frozen orange
   crushed   juice, thawed
1 lb. powdered sugar   Finely grated coconut

Put vanilla wafers in a zip-lock bag and crush by rolling a glass over them. Mix crushed wafers, powdered sugar and nuts. Add melted butter or margarine. (I cook with "love and butter", you know!) Add thawed orange juice and mix well. Roll into small balls. Roll the balls in *finely grated* coconut. Store in refrigerator overnight. They freeze well — if you have any left.

STRAWBERRY SHERBET

9 12-oz. cans strawberry drink   3 10-oz. cartons frozen sliced
3 cans Eagle Brand milk   strawberries

Mix together and freeze in 6-quart freezer. Super delicious and sooooo EASY to make!!

—Linda Carter

VANILLA ICE CREAM

6 eggs
1 qt. real cream
1½ cups sugar
3 Tbls. vanilla

½ tsp. salt
3 cans Eagle Brand condensed
milk
Sweet milk

Whip eggs in mixer. Add cream to eggs and whip. Add sugar slowly to egg and cream mixture and whip so all sugar is dissolved. Add 1 can of Eagle Brand milk, vanilla and salt and blend thoroughly. Then add 2 more cans Eagle Brand milk and put all in freezer can and fill with regular sweet milk until you reach the "fill line" on can. Stir well and freeze. Use a 6-quart freezer.

FRUIT SLUSH

3 cups water
1½ cups sugar
1 lg. can frozen orange juice
concentrate
1 lg. can crushed pineapple
with juice

2 lg. pkgs. strawberries,
thawed
6 bananas, sliced

Combine water and sugar and bring to a boil. Boil about 3 minutes, then add the remaining ingredients. Mix and freeze. Serve slightly thawed.

—Peggy DeVerter

CHOCOLATE SYRUP

1 cup sugar
¼ cup cocoa
¼ cup butter or margarine

¼ cup milk
1 tsp. vanilla

Combine all ingredients and bring to a boil. Boil 2 minutes at least. Test in ice water for chewyness. Add vanilla; cool. Delicious on ice cream.

MARY'S ITALIAN CREAM CAKE

1 cup buttermilk	½ cup shortening
1 tsp. soda	2 cups flour, sifted
5 eggs, separated	1 tsp. vanilla
2 cups sugar	1 sm. can coconut
1 stick butter or margarine	

Preheat oven to 325°. Combine buttermilk and soda. Cream sugar, butter and shortening. Add egg yolks one at a time, beating well after each. Add buttermilk mixture, alternating with flour, to cream mixture and stir in vanilla. Beat egg whites until stiff. Fold into batter gently. Fold in coconut. Bake in three pans 25 minutes.

CREAM CHEESE ICING

1 8-oz. pkg. cream cheese	1 tsp. vanilla
1 stick butter or margarine	4 mashed bananas or
1 1-lb. box confectioner's	strawberries*
sugar	1 cup pecans, chopped

Mix cream cheese, butter and vanilla. Beat in sugar a little at a time until spreading consistency. Stir in ¾ cup pecans. Add mashed bananas or strawberries. Sprinkle remaining ¼ cup pecans on top of cake after frosting.

* If using strawberries, garnish top with luscious fresh strawberries.

CHOCOLATE CHIP CAKE

1 pkg. yellow cake mix	1½ cups water
1 sm. pkg. vanilla instant	½ cup cooking oil
pudding	4 eggs
1 sm. pkg. chocolate instant	1 sm. pkg. chocolate chips
pudding	

Mix cake mix and both puddings with water and oil; beat 2 minutes. Add eggs all at once, mix another minute. Add chips. Bake in greased and floured bundt pan for 1 hour at 350°.

—Hannah Till

KENTUCKY JAM CAKE

1¾ cup flour
1½ cup sugar
1 cup salad oil
1 cup buttermilk
1 cup blackberry jam
1 tsp. soda
1 tsp. baking powder
1 tsp. cinnamon

1 tsp. nutmeg
1 tsp. allspice
1 tsp. vanilla
½ tsp. ground cloves
½ tsp. salt
3 eggs
1 cup pecans, finely chopped

Measure all ingredients, except pecans, into mixer bowl. Use low speed until mixed, then high speed, beating about 8 minutes until sugar is completely dissolved. Fold in pecans and pour into pan. Bake 40 minutes at 350° or until cake pulls away from pan. Cool on rack 20 minutes. Bake in two 9"x9" or three 9" round pans.

BUTTERMILK ICING

3 cups sugar
1 cup butter
1 cup buttermilk

2 Tbls. light corn syrup
1 tsp. baking soda
1 cup pecans, for topping

To make icing, combine all ingredients except pecans in 4-quart saucepan over medium heat, bring to boil, stirring constantly. Set candy thermometer in place and continue cooking, stirring occasionally until 238° (soft ball stage). Pour in mixer at high speed. Beat 7 minutes until spreading consistency. Fold in pecans. Ice cake.

—Joe Yoakley

HEAVENLY DIP

2 eggs
2 Tbls. sugar
2 Tbls. vinegar
Lowery's salt

2 3-oz. pkgs. cream cheese
½ green pepper, chopped
1 onion, chopped

Beat first four ingredients together and cook until thickened. Stir often. Then add to softened cream cheese. Beat until well blended and smooth. Add pepper and onion. If using fresh onions, toss in green tops and all.

BAKED CHEESE GOODIES

2 cups sharp cheddar cheese, shredded, about an 8-oz. pkg.

1¼ cups regular flour
½ cup butter, melted

With your hands work the cheese and flour together until crumbly. Add butter and mix well with a fork. If the dough seems dry, work it again.

SUGGESTED FILLERS

Small pimento-stuffed olives
Dates stuffed with sliced almonds

1-inch long pieces of cooked sausage (I use the small smoked links)

Mold 1 teaspoon of dough around the filler you choose and shape into a ball. Place 2 inches apart on an ungreased baking sheet. Chill for 1 hour or longer. Then bake 15-20 minutes at 400°. (These freeze very well, before or after baking.)

—Joan Horner

The Lord is my Shepherd — Perfect Salvation.
I shall not want — Perfect Satisfaction.
He maketh me to lie in green pastures — Perfect Refreshment.
He restoreth my soul — Perfect Restoration.
He leadeth me in the path of righteousness — Perfect Guidance.
I will fear no evil — Perfect Protection.
Thou art with me — Perfect Company.
Thy rod and Thy staff — Perfect Comfort.
Thou preparest a table — Perfect Provision.
Thou anointest my head — Perfect Consecration.
My cup runneth over — Perfect Joy.
Surely, surely — Perfect Confidence.
Goodness and mercy shall follow me — Perfect Care.
I will dwell in the House of the Lord forever — Perfect Destiny.

MARY CROWLEY'S YUMMY CAKE

1¼ cups boiling water
1 cup oatmeal
1 stick (¼ lb.) butter or
   margarine
1 cup brown sugar
1 cup white sugar

1⅓ cups flour, sifted
1 tsp. baking soda
1 tsp. cinnamon
½ tsp. salt
½ tsp. nutmeg

ICING

¾ stick butter or margarine
½ cup brown sugar
½ cup white sugar
¼ cup canned milk

1 tsp. vanilla
1 cup shredded coconut and
   nut meats, mixed
(I use pecans)

Pour boiling water over oatmeal and butter. Let stand 10 to 20 minutes. Add remaining cake ingredients and stir gently. Do not use mixer. Pour into buttered pan and bake 35 minutes in 350° oven.

Mix icing ingredients together and pour on cake after cake has baked. Place under broiler and let brown — about 10 minutes. Leave in pan and serve — Cut in squares.

**WARNING: Absolutely delicious!
FAMILY WILL RAID!**

These days lots of emphasis is put on nutrition, and many of these recipes contain lots of nutrition. But remember — whatever you cook — always cook with LOVE.

Michael
    Grandparents
619 - 475 - 8273 - 7

INDEX

299

INDEX . . .

INDEX...

301

INDEX...

303

INDEX...

INDEX...

My Favorite Recipes

My Favorite Recipes

❧ My Favorite Recipes ❧

My Favorite Recipes

❧ My Favorite Recipes ❧

My Favorite Recipes

My Favorite Recipes

My Favorite Recipes

My Favorite Recipes

My Favorite Recipes

My Favorite Recipes

Our Code of Ethics

We believe in the dignity and importance of women...

We believe that everything woman touches should be ennobled by that touch...

We believe that the home is the greatest influence on the character of mankind...

We believe that the home should be a haven...

> A place of refuge,
> a place of peace,
> a place of harmony,
> a place of beauty...

No home in America ever need be dull and unattractive.

We are dedicated to doing our part to make every home have

ATTRACTION POWER!